THE PROTESTANT ESTABLISHMENT REVISITED

E. DIGBY BALTZELL CIRCA 1964

THE PROTESTANT ESTABLISHMENT REVISITED

E. Digby Baltzell

Edited and with an introduction by
Howard G. Schneiderman

Transaction Publishers
New Brunswick (U.S.A.) and London (U.K.)

First paperback printing 2001

This book is printed on acid-free paper that meets the American National Standard for Permanence of Paper for Printed Library Materials.

Library of Congress Catalog Number: 90-24034
ISBN: 0-88738-419-6 (cloth); 0-7658-0664-9 (paper)
Printed in the United States of America

Library of Congress Cataloging-in-Publication Data

Baltzell, E. Digby (Edward Digby), 1915-
The Protestant establishment revisited : the collected papers of E. Digby Baltzell / edited by Howard G. Schneiderman.
p. cm.
Includes index.
ISBN 0-7658-0664-9 (paper : alk. paper)
1. Social classes—United States. 2. Upper classes—United States 3. Elite (Social sciences)—United States. 4. WASPs (People)—United States. I. Schneiderman, Howard G. II. Title.

HN90. S6B353 1991
305.5' 0973—dc20 90-24034
CIP

To
my wife and son,
Nancy and Benjamin,
and
My friend, teacher, and colleague,
E. Digby Baltzell

E. DIGBY BALTZELL CIRCA 1988

Contents

Introduction

Howard G. Schneiderman

> *The French nobility, after having lost its ancient political rights, and having ceased more than in any other country of feudal Europe to govern and guide the nation, had, nevertheless, not only preserved, but considerably enlarged its pecuniary immunities, and the advantages which the members of this body personally possessed; while it had become a subordinate class it still remained a privileged and closed body, less an aristocracy . . . but more and more a caste.*
>
> —Alexis de Tocqueville

The American upper class, in the latter half of the twentieth century, has, like the French nobility of the eighteenth century, become less an aristocracy, and more and more a caste. As it was for Tocqueville, this decline in upper-class authority has been the focus of the works of E. Digby Baltzell. A member of the upper class himself, Baltzell's criticism of the WASP upper class's decreasing contribution to national leadership has earned him the epithet "WASP with a sting" from the *Wall Street Journal.* In 1964 Baltzell published his best-known book, *The Protestant Establishment*, setting forth a much-cited but often misunderstood theory of the structure and function of the establishment. Twenty-six years have passed and it remains the only theory of its kind. Unlike cynical conceptions of the establishment, which view power and authority as evils, even if necessary ones, Baltzell sees an open and authoritative establishment as not only necessary, but also as a desirable part of the process of securing responsible leaders in a democratic society.

While this viewpoint may seem out of place in our increasingly egalitarian age, Baltzell is an honored figure in contemporary sociology whose work is much respected. Who is E. Digby Baltzell? What is his theory of the establishment? And why is it important? While some of these questions will be answered in this introduction, Baltzell's essays, collected here, speak for themselves. They are illustrative of the scope of his thinking about class and authority, and of his career as a sociologist and social critic.

Baltzell came from an upper-class family, which would today best be characterized as "WASP," a term that he himself made fashionable. Descended from an old stock English family, Baltzell's father, Edward Digby Baltzell, Sr., was born on a family estate called Digby, in the northeast part of Philadelphia, and was named after his grandfather and his birthplace. Baltzell's mother, Caroline Duhring, came from a family of German descent, which had come to Philadelphia in the 1840s. Her grandfather was a physician, and her father an Episcopal clergyman who was head of the City Mission. Baltzell himself was born in a house at 1915 Rittenhouse Street, right off Rittenhouse Square, one of Philadelphia's most fashionable addresses, but grew up in Chestnut Hill, one of the city's richest, old-family neighborhoods.

Privilege, however, is no insulator against hardship, or marginality. Baltzell, the eldest of three sons, was born dead, and his infant's heart started beating only after the doctor grabbed him by the feet and whirled him around in the air to revive him. Thus, although he was born to high status, his life, from the start, was not entirely easy. Although his family was an old one, they were somewhat down in the world—"impecuniously genteel," as Baltzell has described it. He was raised by a determined and domineering mother who, among other oddities, was fascinated with all sorts of fortune-tellers, and a father who was an alcoholic. But they managed to send him to Chestnut Hill Academy, a private day school, and then to St. Paul's, an exclusive boarding school in New Hampshire. During Baltzell's last year at St. Paul's, his father lost his job in an insurance company as a result of his drinking, and soon after died of a heart attack. After graduating from St. Paul's, Baltzell enrolled in the University of Pennsylvania, where he obtained a half-tuition scholarship and paid the rest with the proceeds of a summer job running a tennis club in Maine, and by working at all sorts of odd jobs supported by the New Deal's National Youth Administration (NYA).

The connection between Baltzell's childhood experiences and his eventual turn toward the academic life is worth noting. Although raised in the elite Chestnut Hill neighborhood, Baltzell himself has said that he and his young friends were as isolated, in their own way, from the rest of the city as were poor immigrants in their much less "golden" ghettos. The rest of society remained uncharted for him, and within his own relatively sheltered upper-class world, the combination of difficult parents and impecuniousness compared to his rich friends made Baltzell something of an outsider. His mother's belief in ouija boards and fortune-tellers became well known locally, and rumors spread among neighborhood children that she herself was a witch and that the Baltzell house was haunted. But it was his father's alcoholism that, more than anything, made Baltzell's early life difficult. He once said, "I was always on the outside looking in." In college, although he belonged to a rather heavy-drinking fraternity, he himself never drank until several years after graduating; in fact his half scholarship stipulated that the recipient be a good "Protestant boy who did not drink alcoholic beverages." Baltzell has often compared his own life to that of the novelist J.P. Marquand, whose family was much like his own, proud but poor—of, but not in, society. As a marginal upper-class insider, Baltzell, like Marquand, could see through a great many things his class took for granted. "The guys who have it," he says, "don't know whether they love it or not, do they?"

Even his attending the University of Pennsylvania was indicative of Baltzell's position at the edge of the upper class. Penn was not one of the preferred upper-class schools; all but two or three of his graduating class at St. Paul's went on to Harvard, Yale, or Princeton, but hard financial circumstances following his father's death dictated he stay closer to home and attend the local school. Although he started out in the School of Architecture, he was forced to drop out after his first year because he was out of money, and he worked as a salesman at Wanamaker's department store. Fortunately, he was rescued by a friend who lent him the money to pay one term's tuition ($200), allowing him to return to Penn, where he abandoned his dream of becoming an architect and instead majored in insurance at the Wharton School. As he said later, "I was worried to death about getting a good job." Odd as it might seem for someone born to privilege, Baltzell worked as a parking-lot attendant, a chauffeur, and a ticket-taker and usher at football games at Franklin Field to pay his expenses while at Penn.

Graduating with a B.S. in economics in 1939, he took a job with an insurance company as an underwriter. Within a year, however, he left for a job at twice the salary and with Saturdays off, at the market research department of Smith, Kline, and French Laboratories, a pharmaceutical company in Philadelphia. In this new position Baltzell eventually learned the techniques of social research firsthand, as he helped conduct attitude surveys in many cities.

Baltzell's career in business ended with the Japanese bombing of Pearl Harbor. Like many other patriotic Americans, Baltzell volunteered for the armed forces, joining the navy in 1942. While earning his wings as a navy pilot, he made friends with young men from far different backgrounds than his own; among them were "Meathead" from Brooklyn, a group of "Flying Hawkeyes" from the University of Iowa, and a truck driver from Minneapolis. And during his service in the South Pacific, as pilot and Air Combat Intelligence Officer, his circle of acquaintances expanded yet further.

For Baltzell, as for countless others, war was a great equalizer, breaking down peacetime class barriers. Baltzell's experiences in the navy galvanized to his natural intelligence a curiosity about the nature of society. For the first time in his life he was outside the precincts of his own privileged circle of family, friends, and business associates; and he began to question the class biases he had grown up with. This, of course, might never have occurred without the war.

As he became increasingly self-reflective, Baltzell also became a voracious reader. While stationed for several months in Hawaii, for instance, he wandered one day into the public library in Honolulu, where he browsed through several issues of the *American Journal of Sociology*, which he subsequently subscribed to. This odd and fortuitous event, along with the discovery in the same library of a book on race relations by the famous sociologist E.B. Reuther, helped Baltzell to decide to leave the business world, and to take advantage of the GI Bill to begin graduate studies in sociology.

As he noted in "Upper Class and Elites," in this volume, "The Bomb was dropped on Hiroshima in August 1945. As I had enough points to get out of the navy almost immediately, I was able to enroll in the Ph.D. program in sociology at Columbia University, in September." The war had changed him, and as Baltzell has said, "I decided I didn't want to work in business. I wanted to write and teach." In the flux of a world at war, a conventional business career ended and an intellectual career had been born.

Entirely unknown to Baltzell at the time, the sociology department at Columbia in 1945 was becoming the best in America. Baltzell was entering a department made up of Robert K. Merton, Paul Lazarsfeld, Robert Lynd, C. Wright Mills, and Robert MacIver, among others. It must have seemed a very long way from Chestnut Hill to Morningside Heights. Baltzell and his wife, the artist Jane Piper, settled into their apartment at 152nd Street and Broadway in Harlem, and he began his education as a sociologist at Columbia. Having never heard of Max Weber, to say nothing of Karl Marx, Baltzell recalls having to take stomach-settling medicine every Friday after listening to Gardner Murphy lecture in class. "I watched him over a cup of tea," Baltzell remembers of Murphy, "jot down three lines on a scrap of paper before class and then proceed to talk for two hours without stopping. It was all new to me, and extremely exhausting."

Exhausting, maybe, but Columbia provided a heady intellectual atmosphere. If Gardner Murphy was taxing, what must MacIver,

Mills, Lynd, Lazarsfeld, and Merton have been like? At any rate, it used to be said that Lynd was the "heart" and Merton the "mind" of the department, and Baltzell later wrote in the preface to *Philadelphia Gentlemen*, that "above all, I should like to thank Robert S. Lynd, without whose constant faith and encouragement at critical periods in my early academic career, this book would never have been completed." He also thanked Merton, and wrote, in the same preface, that "all who have studied under Professor Merton will appreciate my large debt to him."

His first year at Columbia, Baltzell read Lynd's two "Middletown" studies, co-authored with Helen Lynd, along with W. Lloyd Warner's "Yankee City" studies, with great care and attention; these helped him begin to formulate his ideas about the upper class and the elite. Among the best-known community studies ever done, the Lynds' Middletown and Warner's Yankee City studies presented two very different points of view about social class in America. *Middletown* was about the distribution of power and economic position in a new and changing society in the Middle West. In contrast to the Lynds' work, Warner's Yankee City series is concerned with the distribution of life-styles and social status in an old traditional community in New England. Impressed with these extremes—Warner's concentration on the *subjective* (status) elements of social class, and the Lynds' emphasis on the *objective* economic aspects of class—Baltzell felt that both approaches were important and saw the need for a synthesis of the two. He also saw that both the Lynds and Warner were influenced by studies of tribal cultures in their choice of small towns to study. He felt the need for urban studies, which led eventually to his *Philadelphia Gentlemen*. By the way, Baltzell also studied with Ruth Benedict; and her *Patterns of Culture* are central to his vision of Puritan Boston (Kwakiutl) and Quaker Philadelphia (Zuñi).

In a course with C. Wright Mills, Baltzell's ideas about social class were further clarified when he read a brilliant article-length review of Warner's first Yankee City volume, *The Social Life of a Modern Community*, written by Mills in 1942 for the *American Sociological Review*. He was particularly struck by the following passage:

> Are the intermarriage chances, the flow of prestige, influenced by what happens in banks? What is the distribution of legal skill, by family, by firm? Are there overlaps between the boards of banks, the elders of churches, and the prestige of ministers? Are "social circles" and the religious affiliations subtly interwoven with financial interests? How do "clubs" mark one's financial arrival? Are the chances to arrive financially enhanced by affiliation with clubs? . . . "it is to be regretted that such mechanics of interaction between the economic, social, and religious affiliations (not to mention "political" spheres) as may exist were not systematically examined in the case of Yankee City."

What Mills, a student of Weber, was saying is that one needs to divide the "sponge word 'class'" into "status"—or social class, and "class"—what Marxists would call economic class. Comparing Warner's study to that of the Lynds, Mills came down on the side of the latter, whom he said had "presented a far superior picture of the composition and mechanics of a modern community." The Middletown and Yankee City studies, as well as Mills's critique of them, absorbed Baltzell's attention; and his concepts of upper class and elite have from the start been used to address the kinds of questions posed by Mills.

Unlike his warm memories of the personally helpful Lynd, Baltzell's memories of Mills are somewhat cooler. "Mills was a prophet in life-styles as well as in Sociology, as he roared up to Fayerweather Hall on a motorcycle," wrote Baltzell, who later saw Mills as "very much in the anti-institutional and egalitarian tradition of the 17th century sectarians." Although they were contemporaries, both having been born in 1915, Mills, a tough, self-made intellectual and sociologist (of the iconoclastic type), hardly attracted Baltzell's admiration. As Baltzell remembers, this was especially so after Mills included parts of one of his long papers in *White Collar* without attributing any credit whatsoever to Baltzell.

Like Mills, nevertheless, Baltzell thought the Lynds' studies far superior to Warner's. He came to see that while the eponymous Middletown of the first study was dominated by elite businessmen at the top of the functional class hierarchy, the families of these individuals eventually formed an upper class at the top of the social class hierarchy by the time the Lynds came back to write *Middletown in Transition*. "Around the X clan," the Lynds wrote, "with their model farms, fine houses, riding clubs, and airplanes, has developed a younger set that is somewhat more coherent, exclusive, and self-consciously upper class." Lynd's course was an important, and serendipitous, component of Baltzell's early development as a theoretician of status and power.

While Lynd and Mills stimulated Baltzell's thinking about class, status, and power, Robert K. Merton, a native Philadelphian like himself, impressed Baltzell more than any other professor at Columbia. Born in a South Philadelphia slum in 1910, and raised there by his first-generation immigrant parents, according to a profile in the *New Yorker*, Merton was an academic prodigy throughout his student years. After graduating from Temple University and graduate study at Harvard, Merton spent a few years being bitten by southern charm while teaching at Tulane in New Orleans. He came to Columbia as an assistant professor in 1941. While Merton helped sharpen Baltzell's analytical abilities, it is interesting that the two Philadelphians from such opposite ends of the social structure should have had, contrary to the Marxist canon, such an affinity in ideas and values. "I learned everything from Bob Merton," Baltzell has said, "and while I have never looked back at my notes from his classes, I have never lectured about anything, nor written anything, that wasn't related to those notes."

Although Merton provided Baltzell with a point of view about sociology, and an enthusiasm for it, the subject that most fascinated him—social class and leadership—was deeply personal and had much to do with his family's marginal financial position. Moreover, as an athlete rather than an intellectual in his youth, Baltzell, like his friends, valued personal ability far more than background. In fact, as he has written, talk of social class was considered "effeminate," in his circle of friends. When he came to Columbia, however, he found that sociologists were obsessed by stratification. This was somewhat tough to take, and the relationship of social class and social status was both deeply distressing and deeply attractive to Baltzell. His very ambivalence toward thinking about social stratification, combined with his insider's heart and outsider's mind, made Baltzell uniquely qualified to study American elites and upper classes.

If Baltzell seemed destined to study elites and upper classes, it was sheer good luck for him that two of the works most influential to his career were published during his first year of graduate studies. Although Tocqueville's name was mentioned only once in his courses at Columbia, while browsing in the Columbia book store Baltzell found and bought a boxed copy of the newly published two-volume set of *Democracy in America* in December 1945, and read it eagerly. During the next summer he bought and read a copy of Gerth and Mill's just-published edition of *From Max Weber: Essays in Sociology*, containing, among others, the famous essay "Class, Status, and Party," which had the most profound and lasting effect upon his thinking.

The one mention of Tocqueville's name in a class at Columbia came in the fall of 1947 in a guest lecture by Albert Salomon, a sociologist from the New School for Social Research, who said that "the greatest book in the social sciences is Tocqueville's *Ancient Regime.*" This was, of course, before paperbacks of Tocqueville's books were readily available, and before many people were reading Tocqueville, and certainly before everyone was quoting Tocqueville without reading him. Unable to find a copy in New York, Baltzell spent over a year tracking one down, and eventually bought his copy from Blackwell's in Oxford. Together, the works of Tocqueville and Weber, along with the writings and teaching of Merton, formed the central core of his thinking for the next forty years; and the *Ancient Regime* was the direct model for Baltzell's analysis of the rise and fall of the Protestant establishment in America.

Just as Tocqueville concentrated on analyzing the fate of his aristocratic class before and after the French Revolution, so Baltzell has devoted himself to analyzing the more or less similar fate of his class in the years before and after World War II. While at Columbia, Baltzell found that Weber and Tocqueville provided him with a conceptual framework that he used to think about the relationship of upper classes and elites. He was now on his way to becoming a unique American intellectual—a social historian and sociologist—who would construct a theory of the establishment that tied social status to responsibility.

During his last year at Columbia, Baltzell visited Merton to discuss his idea for a dissertation about the relationship of elite economic position and social status in Philadelphia. After listening to Baltzell give a keynote lecture at the Eastern Sociological Society meetings in Philadelphia in March 1988, Merton recounted that interview and suggested that, to his mind, in doing his dissertation Baltzell "for the first time in the history of social thought, undertook to ask the question, and then proceeded to try to answer the question: how would one in truth, try to investigate empirically the 'circulation of the elite' in systematic fashion?" In a sense, Merton summed up the essence of Baltzell's career. No one has been more innovative than Baltzell in studying how elites circulate. He left Columbia in 1947, having started work on his doctoral thesis, and began his teaching career at the University of Pennsylvania, as an instructor of sociology. He completed his thesis and was awarded the Ph.D. in 1952. Although many opportunities to leave Penn presented themselves to Baltzell, he loyally taught there until his retirement in 1986—fifty years after starting there as a student. In his thirty-nine years on the Penn faculty Baltzell taught over 20,000 undergraduate students, as well as having had a major impact on the thinking of dozens of graduate students. He still teaches his legendary social stratification course once a year, during the spring term.

Baltzell has written three contemporary classics of social analysis: *Philadelphia Gentlemen*, *The Protestant Establishment*, and *Puritan Boston and Quaker Philadelphia*, along with numerous essays and articles, many of which are collected here.

Philadelphia Gentlemen: The Making of a National Upper Class, published in 1958, evolved from Baltzell's doctoral dissertation. Philadelphia's social structure was used as an example of how a national upper class was formed in American cities in the latter part of the nineteenth century. In a detailed analysis, Baltzell demonstrated how successful moneymakers—businessmen, bankers, lawyers, and physicians—many of whom came from lower-social-class backgrounds, founded families whose individual members through marriage, private school and college education, and club membership associated themselves with old-money families, generation after generation, thus constituting an upper class, with a distinctive set of traditional values. *Philadelphia Gentlemen* also provided, in Baltzell's words, "an excellent example of a business aristocracy which has too often placed the desire for material comfort and security above the duties of political and intellectual leadership." Nevertheless, as Baltzell showed, up to the Second World War upper class Philadelphia families dominated the business and cultural life of the city, his main point being that the organic upper class, almost an extended family with a sense of gemeinschaft-like solidarity, stabilized the elite of leaders in the city in those pre-World War II years. This class domination of the elite is what Baltzell conceptualized as an "establishment," which he further analyzed in later works.

Baltzell ended *Philadelphia Gentlemen* by asking, "What is the future function of a predominantly Anglo-Saxon and Protestant upper class in an ethnically and religiously heterogeneous democracy?" He noted that throughout this book he had showed that "the American upper class has been from the beginning open to new men of talent and power and their families." But by the time he was writing, at midcentury, a caste situation had developed, and upper-class status appeared to be limited to old and new families of Anglo-Saxon, Protestant origin only. He addressed this issue in his next book.

The Protestant Establishment: Aristocracy and Caste in America, published in 1964, examined the problems of privilege and authority. Introducing the acronym "WASP," Baltzell showed that the white, Anglo-Saxon, and Protestant upper class had become, by and large, a privileged caste rather than a ruling and authoritative class. As he wrote, "This book has been an attempt to analyze the decline of authority in America." Here Baltzell followed Tocqueville, who, in his *Ancient Regime*, showed that when new men of talent, wealth, and power were refused membership in the French aristocracy by noblemen who drew a caste line, class authority failed and set the stage for the French Revolution. A similar crisis of leadership in America had developed because the WASP upper class was becoming increasingly castelike. It excluded talented individuals and their families who were from ethnic or minority backgrounds, especially Jews, who had already become vital members of the elite of Philadelphia and other cities after World War II.

Baltzell's third book, *Puritan Boston and Quaker Philadelphia: Two Protestant Ethics and the Spirit of Class Authority and Leadership*, published in 1979, showed how the upper class in Puritan Boston, from the beginning, exercised authority over the elite, while the Quaker-turned-Episcopal elite in Philadelphia had never produced an authoritative leadership in the state or nation. Boston, in other words, was a deference, Philadelphia a defiant, democracy. Baltzell has often said that he was less interested in Boston and Philadelphia in a concrete sense than as lessons about America—which was more like Boston up until World War II and very much like Philadelphia since (see, for example, his essay "Cultural Pluralism in Modern America"). For this book Baltzell was presented the prestigious Sorokin Award of the American Sociological Association.

In all his work on leadership, Baltzell has emphasized the interrelationship of five concepts: upper class, elite, establishment, authority, and community. All societies are led by elite individuals (political leaders, economic leaders, and leaders in art, law, medicine, religion, and other professions). Elites are made up of successful, but morally neutral, men and women. Over the generations, any stable society will produce families descended from past elite members. These families—buttressed by upper-class institutions, such as schools, colleges, and clubs—form a real gemeinschaft-like community, which inevitably develops moral and social norms of its own. *Lady* and *gentleman* are class terms; *lawyer*, *doctor*, and *governor* are elite terms.

As Baltzell has shown, traditional authority is class authority as Weber uses the term. Classless elites, on the other hand, are given cohesion by charismatic or bureaucratic manipulators of authority. Finally, then, Baltzell sees that class and authority lie at the very core of community. Contrary to contemporary wisdom, egalitarian individualism will always run counter to community. "The idea of equality," Baltzell wrote in *The Protestant*

Establishment, "lies at the very heart of the American Dream and has become the basis of the various secular faiths of our time. While the socialist faiths, on the one hand, have centered on the vision of equality of condition in a classless society, our own best traditions have stressed equality of opportunity in a hierarchical and open-class, as opposed to a classless, society. Karl Marx well understood the strengths of the Anglo-Saxon version of democracy when he wrote in *Das Kapital*, that 'the more a ruling class is able to assimilate the most prominent men of the dominated classes, the more stable and dangerous its rule.' I have written this book because I believe that our traditions of mobility and equal opportunity, so dangerous to the Marxian dreams of revolution, are infinitely superior to the leveling ideals of socialism."

Here something should be said about the difference between Baltzell's ideas and those of his one-time professor, C. Wright Mills. Mills was obsessed with the "higher *immorality*" of the power elite. Baltzell has spent his time trying to show how an *amoral* power elite is to be transformed into an authoritative establishment.

Besides popular recognition for introducing the acronym WASP into everyday usage, Baltzell's really important intellectual contribution is his theory of the establishment. The establishment concept as Baltzell uses it implies an elite influenced and dominated by upper-class members and their values and norms. Those few members of any upper class who form an establishment stand in contrast to the majority who are satisfied to have high status but little or no authority, in other words, with those who form a caste. As Baltzell has said repeatedly, the aristocratic ethos of an establishment emphasizes the duty to lead, while the snobbish ethos of caste emphasizes only the right to privilege.

A moral force within the putatively amoral world of politics and power elites, an establishment of leaders drawn from upper-class families, is the final protector of freedom in modern democratic societies. Such an establishment of political, business, cultural, religious, and educational leaders succeeds in its moral function when it sets, follows, and enforces rules of fair play in contests of power and opinion.

In one of his most penetrating insights into the sociological functions of an establishment, Tocqueville wrote that "a powerful aristocracy does not merely shape the course of public affairs, it also guides opinion, sets the tone for writers, and lends authority to new ideas." In other words, it has hegemony over society. Whereas Marxists see hegemony as a social evil, Baltzell, following Tocqueville, sees it as necessary to the well-being of society. Hegemonic establishments give coherence to the social spheres of greatest contest. They don't eliminate conflict, but prevent it from ripping society apart.

Although Baltzell did not coin the term *establishment*, he is the first American sociologist to use it conceptually, and he is the only one who has articulated an actual *theory* of the establishment. While many have used *establishment* as a concept, no one else has clarified its relationship to other concepts (i.e., status, class, authority, power, legitimacy, elite, and caste), thus theorizing about it rather than merely defining it.

The modern use of the term *establishment* dates back to 1955 when a well-known British journalist, Henry Fairlie, used it in the *Spectator*. As it was first used, establishment meant something akin to elite, but with a sour twist of antidemocratic lemon added. For instance, Hugh Thomas, editor of *The Establishment*, a symposium published in 1959, wrote that "the word 'Establishment' simply indicates the assumption of the attributes of a state church by certain powerful institutions and people; in general these may be supposed to be effectively beyond democratic control."

It was not until 1961 that the term *establishment* was used seriously in America, again by a journalist. Richard Rovere, a much-published political essayist, wrote an article, "Notes on the Establishment in America," which appeared in the *American Scholar*. He defined an establishment as "a more or less closed and self-sustaining institution that holds a preponderance of power in our more or less open society." It is interesting that when he republished the article a year later in a collection of his essays, Rovere deemed it necessary to add the following note: "Many readers professed to be puzzled by my approach. Some even asked if I intended my work to be taken seriously. I found their questions disheartening and, I might as well add, more than a bit offensive. They cast doubt not only on my own integrity but on that of the distinguished journal which had the courage to publish my findings."

It is ironic that Rovere felt compelled to write that note, for a few years later what he suggested about the establishment would be taken for granted. Anyone old enough to have lived through the late 1960s might well remember that the term *establishment* had a cynical connotation. During that time terms like *the Eastern establishment*, *the liberal-intellectual establishment*, and *the educational establishment* came to signify concentrations of power and authority. In the leveling atmosphere of the day, these were seen as menaces to the ideals of social equality and justice.

Post-1960s, post-Watergate academic cynicism about power and authority continues unabated. Academic criticism of the vertical dimensions of social life, especially those that are authoritative, reflects a lack of confidence in American elites and institutions, and a tendency to look for and find conspiracy in them, which itself attacks their legitimacy. Such criticism is itself a significant sociological datum about the intellectual temper of our times.

When legitimacy begins to crumble, conspiracy theories of history and society come to the fore, rendering our truths into half-truths; and a culture of half-truths fosters the growth of cynicism. Thus in *Cultural Literacy*, a book that has been savagely criticized as elitist by the leveling deconstruction companies of the academic left, E.D. Hirsch lists "the establishment" as one of the ideas literate Americans should know. But for all the charges of elitism against him, Hirsch defines "the establishment" in a cynical manner his critics would applaud. In *The Dictionary of Cultural Literacy*, Hirsch describes the establishment as follows: "Individuals and institutions that exercise social, economic, and political authority over a society. The term has a pejorative connotation because it suggests that political and economic power is in the hands of the few." Perhaps all sociologists would agree with the first part of this description, but a few, and foremost among them Digby Baltzell, would disagree about the pejorative connotation attached to the term.

A deceptive myth in liberal democracies like America is that civil liberties and freedom of expression are valued by all members of the polity, and most certainly by those at the bottom and middle of the social structure. But as Samuel Stouffer amply demonstrated in his classic study, *Communism, Conformity, and Civil Liberties*, this is not the case. Such freedoms are always most highly valued and protected by the few. The last bulwark of freedom may well be, as Baltzell has suggested, "a unified establishment from within which the leaders of at least two parties are chosen, who, in turn, compete for the people's votes of confidence, from differing points of view and differing standards of judgement, yet both assuming the absolute necessity of using fair means in accusing their legitimate opponents of fallibility rather than treason." The sociological alternatives to rule by establishments have been, historically, rule by functionaries and bureaucrats or rule by demagogues, neither of which has proven satisfactory in protecting freedoms.

Baltzell's theory of the establishment, as well as his other contributions to sociology, respond to a basic paradox of democracy in America, namely that social classes as well as power and authority violate the egalitarian values at the core of American culture while at the same time being indispensable to democracy's survival. Baltzell's recognition of this paradox has led him to write: "Every civilized society in history has been faced with the twin problems of creating and preserving communal order on the one hand and answering legitimate demands for social justice on the other. As the social forces for order, hierarchy, and authority tend to be antithetical to those for equality and social justice, all societies are actually only relatively orderly and always unjust." Such Whiggish insight into one of the great paradoxes of modern society has allowed Baltzell to chart a theoretical course between the ideological Scylla of Marxism and the equally perilous Charybdis of "right-wing" authoritarianism. While avoiding ideological temptations, Baltzell has been the foremost sociologist engaged in studying the relationship between upper classes and power.

Much read, well-thumbed, and heavily marked and annotated, Baltzell's copy of Tocqueville's *Ancient Regime* sits on an easily reached shelf in his study. Boldly marked in Tocqueville's forward are these words: "I hope that I have written the present book without prejudice, but I do not pretend to have written it without passion." Significantly, Baltzell quoted those very words in his own preface to *The Protestant Establishment*. Like Tocqueville, Baltzell has blended warm passion and enthusiasm with cold factual examples to produce masterpieces of social analysis. That his writing is marked by a highly personal point of view and by personal involvement is not to say, however, that he is not objective. Like any well-qualified sociologist and historian, Baltzell has used many of the means of objective analysis (especially the comparative method). But he has never fallen under the seductive sway of objectivism, ideologically confusing merely useful objective means for ends in themselves. Many sociologists, of course, are objectivists, which is perhaps explained by the allure of objectivist ideologies such as Marxism, which, wrote Michael Polanyi, "enables the modern mind, tortured by moral self-doubt, to indulge its moral passions in terms which also satisfy its passion for ruthless objectivity." None of Baltzell's writings shows the slightest hint of moral self-doubt, nor a passion for ruthless objectivity. Baltzell's books and essays demonstrate that understanding does not come from facts alone, but from an emotional involvement with them.

"A really definitive, and good accomplishment," wrote Max Weber of scholarship, "is today always a specialized accomplishment." Baltzell's work is a beautiful example of this. For over forty years he has thought and written about the same thing—the interrelations of class, status, and authority—but each time he has approached them from different angles. He has often been heard to say that his ideal has been to rewrite the same problem in an endless variety of ways, much as Cézanne painted and repainted the same mountain outside of Aix-en-Provence, over and over with seemingly endless variations. The essays collected here show that Baltzell's devotion to this task has indeed resulted in a "really definitive" accomplishment.

In one of his first articles, "Social Mobility and Fertility in an Elite Group," published in 1953, Baltzell painted a landscape depicting the relationship of social class and the elite. Using *Who's Who in America* and the *Social Register* as indexes of membership in the top groups in the functional and social class hierarchies in Philadelphia, he shows that elite parents with high ascribed status, who are therefore less socially mobile, have significantly more children than self-made and more socially mobile elite parents with high achieved status. Baltzell displays ingenuity and resourcefulness in finding indexes of social and functional class, and sociological acumen in understanding and framing the problem he wants to address. These qualities, characteristic of Baltzell's books, are also evident throughout his essays.

Nowhere is the rationale for using the *Social Register* and *Who's Who in America* as indices of high social status and functional class position stated more cogently than in "Elite and Upper Class Indexes in Metropolitan America," in which Baltzell explains their usefulness as well as their limitations. Thirty-five years later, in our article, "Social Class in the Oval Office," Baltzell and I showed how historians' ranking of performance in office of the U.S. presidents could be used as an index of achievement, and how a prominent historian's evaluation of the social class origins of the presidents could be used as an index of social ascription. They were juxtaposed to see the interrelationship of social status to achievement in office, and demonstrated a strong correlation between high social class background and greatness in office, and an equally strong correlation between lower-class background and failure in office. This suggests that Baltzell may have been correct in his assumptions about the need for a strong establishment in democratic societies.

It has not been his methodological ingenuity, however, but his theoretical perspective that has made Baltzell's work so valuable. For example, in "Reflections on Aristocracy," Baltzell offers a theoretical design that allows one to see, contrary to conventional wisdom, that aristocracy and representative democracy are not incompatible. He shows that this combination may be preferable, to those who value freedom, to regimes more democratically chosen but autocratically ruled. This, of course, is in line with Baltzell's theory of the establishment, most cogently presented in *The Protestant Establishment*. This same theoretical framework can be found in all the essays in this volume, but is most interestingly developed in "The American Aristocrat and Other-Direction," "Upper Class and Elites," and "The Protestant Establishment Revisited."

If there is one idea in Baltzell's work that evokes his emotional involvement more than any other it is that "Americans have been trained to succeed rather than to lead," the animus behind his theory of the establishment. Like William James, he despises the "Bitch-Goddess SUCCESS." Caste ideals, wherever they are found, emphasize success and the protection of privilege at the expense of authority and leadership. An establishment exists, however, only when an upper class emphasizes aristocratic ideals, favoring power and leadership over success and the protection of privilege. This powerful theme, which is woven into all three of his books, is examined anew in his tour de force essay, "The Protestant Establishment Revisited." In this article Baltzell reflects on "the national consequences of the fact that our society has no secure upper class which is able to dominate our leadership and see that it remains rooted in some kind of tradition or institutional continuity." It is one of the most interesting and historically rich analyses of the crisis of authority in the America of the 1960s.

Born in 1915, Baltzell has lived through a social revolution in leadership. Whereas the WASP upper class dominated America's political, economic, and intellectual elites up to the late 1940s, thus controlling the nation, today WASPs no longer have that control, and as Baltzell has said many times, "in a real sense, no one does—and that's the problem." Included in this volume is Baltzell's autobiographical essay, "The WASP's Last Gasp," his most personal statement about the changing patterns of leadership in his native city. The stinging point first made in *The Protestant Establishment*, and reiterated in this article, is that the alternative to an establishment in any society is an atomized elite. The difference is of some consequence, because an establishment is a real group, a gemeinschaft, subject to all the forces of social control, which at least potentially can instill and enforce moral standards in its members. An elite, however, is a gesellschaft, not a real group, but merely a convenient sociological category, neither subject to the forces of social control nor a moral entity. Baltzell uses these categories to analyze Philadelphia's elite today.

That Baltzell's work has been as well received as it has been over the years is interesting when one considers that his emphasis on the need for an authoritative and responsible establishment has always run counter to conventional wisdom, especially of social scientists. Despite the respect he has received, Baltzell has often been pigeonholed as an elitist. But while there may be some truth in this categorization, the same would have to be said about the two intellectual giants whose work has influenced him most, Weber and Tocqueville, who would probably have agreed with Baltzell that "while social justice definitely has improved in the last fifty years, social order has just as definitely declined," and that this has not necessarily been a good thing, at least not unqualifiedly so.

Respect for Baltzell's work has been well earned. Few have come close to his ability to find empirical indexes of membership in historical and contemporary American upper classes and elites, and to use these to test propositions and theories about power and authority, and the circulation of elites. Baltzell's is one of the most important syntheses of the classical sociological writings on the relationship of status to power we have. His work challenges those who disagree to find alternative explanations for his data, which suggest that responsible elite leaders are drawn disproportionately from the upper classes.

Baltzell's research on, and musings about, class, status, and power found in the essays collected in this volume show how he explored these themes in ways no other sociologists have done. His originality in dealing with a subject that has been otherwise ignored, or worse, dealt with with cynical disregard of real ethnographic or other factual evidence, has made Baltzell something of a maverick among sociologists. He was one of the first of an ever-expanding circle of colleagues who see the importance of authority, establishments, classes, and hierarchy to the preservation of freedom in modern societies. It is interesting to note that this circle is to be found in the midst of a discipline in which the vertical dimensions of society are regarded as evils to be eliminated, or at least controlled.

By and large, American sociologists have been enamored of the poor and the powerless, and more often than not unquestioningly take their side against the rich and the powerful. While there is a seemingly endless stream of data about the American working classes, lower classes, and underclasses, not to mention the enormous banks of survey data about the middle classes, there is next to none concerning the American upper class. What little sociological data we have about the upper class are usually made suspect by misleading and hardly useful definitions of this class strictly in economic terms, or worse yet, by the simple but fallacious equation of the upper class with political and economic elites.

One of the outstanding exceptions to this has been Baltzell's work. He has been one of the few contemporary sociologists of note who have argued, *contra* Marxists and other would-be class levelers, that upper classes are not inherently evil, and in fact, when acting responsibly are, along with established authority, necessary to the well-being of society. In this sense, Baltzell has been, in his own way, something of an American Tocqueville.

As a member of the American upper class himself, Baltzell must have felt a special intellectual closeness to Tocqueville. He lived through the decline of the WASP establishment just as Tocqueville had been a member of a declining French aristocracy. In "Upper Class and Elites," a simply put and rather charming reminiscence of his days as a graduate student at Columbia during the sociology department's golden age, Baltzell recounts how he first encountered Tocqueville's work and hungered for more. He has obviously taken Tocqueville more seriously than most sociologists, extending his ideas in new and original ways.

Like Tocqueville, Baltzell has provided uncommon insight into the relationship of social class and power; and like Tocqueville, who seems to speak across a century and a half to do so, Baltzell also provides unique insight into contemporary American moral and social problems that arise from the perhaps unresolvable conflict between the dual ideals of social order and social justice.

Many scholars have written about Tocqueville, and even more have been influenced by him, but none, I suspect, could have felt the special affinity that Baltzell has for him. Unlike Karl Marx, his younger contemporary, Tocqueville was an aristocrat. Also unlike Marx, who detested all class hierarchies, Tocqueville translated his lament for the passing of strong aristocracies in his homeland into a fully articulated political and historical sociology of freedom and power.

While most contemporary American sociologists have been drawn from middle-class backgrounds, and while many of the most vocal among them favor Marx's humanistic concern for social justice and equality of conditions, Baltzell was cast in a different mold. He is the only major sociologist alive today who is truly a member of the American upper class, and is one of a diminishing minority who can be said to care more for equality of opportunity with its inevitable consequence, namely an inequality of condition, than for social justice and its leveling and destructive effects on individual freedom and individual justice.

While many sociologists might argue for the abolition of "elitist" upper-class institutions in the name of social justice, Baltzell's virtue has been to show the need for such institutions as "vital prerequisites of a secure and organic leadership structure." In this he has been singular. But a lonely voice is not necessarily a wrong voice. As the essays collected here show, Baltzell has made a cogent argument for his point of view. Unusual as that point of view has been, Baltzell is recognized by almost all sociologists interested in stratification as the foremost authority on the American upper class. His point of view may not be popular, but it has been impossible to ignore.

At age seventy-five, Baltzell is still an active scholar. He is hard at work on another book, in which he is tracing the decline of upper-class authority through the game of tennis. In this book Baltzell will show that lawn tennis was by and large an upper-class and amateur game played under the rules of a gentleman's code, and that it has become a classless sport, played by professionals under a mass of increasingly bureaucratic rules. In tracing the decline of manners in tennis, Baltzell hopes to show a correlation with the decline of Western civilization, especially since the 1960s.

In addition to the book, Baltzell and I continue to work on a series of studies of the relationship of social background to performance in office in our national government. The first of these studies, "Social Class in the Oval Office," is reprinted in this volume, and demonstrates that high social class background was correlated with both getting to the presidency as well as to above-average performance in office. In our second study, "From Rags to Robes: The Horatio Alger Myth and the Supreme Court," we show that social class background has been less important to getting appointed to the Court than to election to the presidency, and that performance on the bench is less dependent on social class background than was presidential success. As this second study indicates, perhaps performance in the Oval Office depends to a greater extent on the subtleties of upper-class habits of authority, whereas professional competence and superior intelligence are more essential for Supreme Court performance.

Like many sociologists of his generation, Baltzell's thinking has been influenced by his reaction to the upheavals of the 1960s. "I think the '60s were a tragic disaster," he has said, "and we're still paying for it. It was a very great revolt against civilization. . . . People identified downward instead of upward. It was a very sad time." His essays and books written since the 1960s reflect this sense of tragedy and despair, which continues to animate his work. In spite of the conventional wisdom that has developed since then that elitism is an evil and that the equality of everything should prevail, Baltzell continues throughout his work to press the claim that what is needed in American society is *more* authority, not less. If we really are in the process of destroying Western civilization, Baltzell's books and essays need to be taken very seriously now, lest at some future time they are looked back on as merely brilliant analyses, which warned of the dangers of abolishing class distinctions and established authority but which went unheeded.

I met Digby Baltzell in September 1970. Having just entered the Ph.D. program at Penn, I enrolled in one of his courses, and later he was assigned to be my adviser. Since the completion of my doctoral dissertation under his supervision, we have become close friends, intellectual affineds, and co-authors. Much of the biographical information in this introduction is based on conversations with Baltzell over the course of our friendship. Since Baltzell has been interviewed extensively in national and local newspapers and magazines—the *New York Times*, the *Wall Street Journal*, the *Philadelphia Inquirer*, the *New Republic*, and *Philadelphia Magazine* among others—it was easy to use these as additional sources of information. A transcript of Baltzell's speech delivered as part of the Eastern Sociological Society's Distinguished Lecturer Series in Philadelphia in 1988 was also useful to me. I would like to thank Digby for his help in answering my questions about his life with patience and dignity.

Two of the essays are published here for the first time: "Cultural Pluralism in Modern America," written in 1982, and "Upper-Class Clubs and Associations" (1989). "Elite and Upper-Class Indexes" first appeared in 1953, in *Class, Status, and Power*, edited by Reinhard Bendix and Seymour M. Lipset. "Social Mobility and Fertility" also appeared in 1953, in the *Milbank Quarterly*. "The American Aristocrat and Other-Direction" was first published in 1961, in *Culture and Social Character*, edited by Seymour M. Lipset and Leo Lowenthal. Four of the articles were published in 1968: "Thorstein Veblen: Scientism and the Modern Mood" appeared in *ERA*; "W.E.B. Du Bois and *The Philadelphia Negro*" was Baltzell's introduction to a reprint of Du Bois's book; "Reflections on Aristocracy" appeared in *Social Research*; and "The Search for Community in Modern America" was Baltzell's introduction to a book by that name, which he had edited. In 1972 "To Be a Phoenix" was published in the *American Journal of Sociology*. "The Protestant Establishment Revisited" was first published in 1976, in the *American Scholar*. "The WASP's Last Gasp" first appeared in 1988, in *Philadelphia Magazine*. "Social Class in the Oval Office," which I co-authored with Baltzell, was also published in 1988, in *Society*. "Upper Class and Elites" was published in 1990, in *Society*.

1

Elite and Upper-Class Indexes in Metropolitan America

In the 1930s and 1940s, the sociological literature in America was enriched by a wealth of monographs in which social stratification was the central theme.[1] With staffs trained in interviewing techniques, the filling out of schedules, and the operation of "IBM" machines, sociologists made numerous painstaking, investigations of stratification in the small community. Such terms as "upper-upper," "lower-upper," and "lower-lower" were added to the language of social thought, and, even in America, aristocracy was found cohabiting with democracy.

Of the multitude of monographs describing the small community in America, the contrasting conceptual approaches of the Lynds on the one hand, and W. Lloyd Warner and his disciples on the other, represent the two divergent emphases in class analysis.[2] The Lynds, who begin both their *Middletown* volumes with a chapter on "Getting a Living," emphasize the dynamics of the economic class system and the differential distribution of power in a *changing* society. On the other hand, Warner, an anthropologist who had recently returned from a study of preliterate cultures in Australia when he began the "Yankee City" study, categorically rejects an economic interpretation of stratification and emphasizes the differences in ritual and style of life as between subcultural class levels in a comparatively *static* and traditional New England community.[3] Whereas Warner defines a class system in *subjective* terms as "two or more orders of people who are believed to be, and are accordingly ranked by members of the community, in socially superior and inferior positions," the Lynds employ an *objective* definition which differentiates between the "business" and "working" classes.[4] While the members of the "upper-upper" class in Yankee City, a majority of whom are *women*, are emulated and exercise a measure of social control because of their "lineage," their "good-breeding," and the fact that they "know how to act," in *Middletown*, in the 1930s, the "passage of first generation wealth into second generation power" had created a newly self-conscious upper class whose *male* members tended to dominate the business and financial life of the city.[5]

At the present stage in the development of American sociology, the conceptual approach of the "Warner School" represents the dominant trend in stratification analysis. As perhaps the current emphasis on the subjective aspects of class is an over-reaction on the part of American social scientists to the admittedly incomplete Marxian emphasis on the objective economic indexes of class position, a more balanced approach may be achieved by utilizing *both* the subjective and the objective class concepts as differentially related variables in various social situations.[6] It is not a question of whether the objective class concept is more, or less, "real" than the subjective class concept; rather, both concepts are abstractions from concrete reality, and the failure to treat them as such may lead to reification or a sterile circular reasoning. In other words, the behavior patterns, values, and attitudes of groups of people differentially situated in any class system are presumably conditioned both by their position in the productive process (occupational rank or income) and by their subjective class position (social access, family position, and so forth). Generals who are aristocrats may be expected to behave differently than generals who are not aristocrats.

Separating out the subjective and the objective aspects of class position for purposes of analysis, in this paper, the *elite* concept refers to those *individuals* who are the most successful and stand at the top of the functional (objective) class hierarchy. These individuals are leaders in their chosen occupations or professions;

they are the final-decision-makers in the political, economic, or military spheres as well as leaders in such professions as law, engineering, medicine, education, religion, and the arts. On the other hand, in any comparatively stable social structure, over the years, certain elite members and their families will tend to associate with one another in various primary group situations and gradually develop a consciousness of kind and a distinctive style of life. The *upper-class* concept, then, refers to a group of *families*, descendants of successful individuals (elite members) one, two, three, or more generations ago, who are at the top of the social (subjective) class hierarchy. As Dixon Wecter puts it:

> A group of families with a common background and racial origin becomes cohesive, and fortifies itself by the joint sharing of sports and social activities, by friendships and intermarriage. Rough and piratical grandfathers had seized their real estate, laid out their railroads, and provided for its trust funds. The second and third generation, relieved from the counting-house and shop, now begin to travel, buy books and pictures, learn about horses and wine and cultivate the art of charm.[7]

While the numerous sociological studies of small American communities have unquestionably contributed valuable knowledge about the ways of human behavior and the nature of social organization, it is perhaps fair to say that the large metropolitan area is more representative of American life in the middle twentieth century. In order to gain some insight into the nature of stratification in metropolitan America, *Who's Who in America*, a listing of individuals of high functional class position (achieved status), and the *Social Register*, a listing of families of high social class position (ascribed status), may be useful indexes of a metropolitan elite and upper class, respectively.[8] The limited task of this paper is to show how, in the last part of the nineteenth century, the *Social Register* became a metropolitan upper-class index, and how, in certain large cities in 1940, this upper class was related to the elite, those listed in *Who's Who in America*.

The Social Register

For those who see history as a record of man's creative efforts to choose between alternatives in an endless chain of historical situations and not only as a series of reactions to various abstract causes, geographic, climatic, racial, or economic, which more or less determine his destiny, human society is an historical process wherein each generation sifts to the top particular individual types, warriors, prophets, priests, merchants, bankers, or bureaucrats, whose talents are needed in any given period; these individuals, in turn, and within limits, make the decisions which shape the course of history. Thus Brooks Adams saw the history of England as partly reflected in the circulation of elites, wherein the feudal warrior, whose power lay in men and spears, was replaced during the Reformation by the large landowners who ruled England from the time of Henry VIII to 1688, when the rising merchant adventurer or bourgeois elites finally won their rights, only to be followed by the manufacturing men such as Watt and Boulton whose talents led them to power after the Industrial Revolution; and finally, from the time of the defeat of that symbol of martial power on the hill at Waterloo, the manufacturing and landowning elites were dominated by, and often in debt to, the money power of Lombard Street.[9] The English upper class, often called an aristocracy, centers in a group of families who are descendants of these successful individuals of the remote and recent past and of course alloyed with, and having an influence on, those with a talent for power in the modern bureaucratic period.

As in England, America has witnessed a procession of successful men who have risen to positions of wealth and power, and whose children and grandchildren have been brought up and lived in more or less socially isolated subcultural worlds. As the Beards say:

> On the eve of the Civil War there had been many "seasoned clans" on the Eastern seaboard, some of them dating their origins back a hundred years or more, and boasting of ancestors who had served as preachers, judges, warriors, and statesmen in colonial times, in the heroic epoch of the Revolution, and in the momentous age of the new Republic. Able to hold their own socially, if not politically, these select families had absorbed with facility the seepage of rising fortunes that gradually oozed into their ranks until the flood of the new plutocracy descended upon them.[10]

All families are equally old; "old families" are those whose ancestors rose to positions of affluence in an earlier period than the so-called new families.[11] As late as the 1870s or 1880s in America, "Society" in the older eastern seaboard cities was a rather well-defined, primary group of families who knew one another well and knew "who" belonged in "polite society." Even in the middle of the twentieth century in these cities, the "old families," the "Proper" Bostonians, Philadelphians, or New Yorkers, are those whose fortunes were made in the pre-Civil War period; late nineteenth century wealth is still considered new. As Cleveland Amory says of Boston:

> All through Boston history, when a family loses its financial stability, it has a way of beginning to disappear. After the Revolution, or better still, after the War of 1812 and lasting roughly through the Civil War, in the great Family-founding days of the nineteenth century, somewhere along the line there must be a merchant prince, the real Family-founder.[12]

As with so much else in American life, the 1880s mark a turning point in upper-class history; the local familistic-communal upper classes were absorbed in a new upper class which was increasingly extra-communal and associationally defined.[13] After the "Second American Revolution," in which the industrial North brought the planter aristocracy to its knees, new fortunes of undreamed-of proportions were created;[14] as transportation and communication improved, from all parts of the great American continent, barons (of dry goods, utilities, coal, oil, and railroads) moved their families to New York, built ostentatious Victorian piles, entertained, and, where possible, moved into "Society." By the 1880s, New York was the center of social life in the United States.[15]

There was the usual resistance at first, but "by one process or another amalgamation was affected and new varnish softened by the must of age. As the landed gentlemen of England had on various occasions saved their houses from decay by discreet jointures with mercantile families, so many of the established families in Boston, New York, Philadelphia, and Baltimore escaped the humiliation of poverty by judicious selections from the onrushing plutocracy."[16] Amidst this incredible "Gilded Age," in the year 1887, the *Social Register* was copyrighted by the Social Register Association and the first volume appeared for New York City in 1888. There were less than two thousand families listed in this "record of society, comprising an accurate and careful list of its members, with their addresses, many of the maiden names of the married women, the club addresses of the men, officers of the leading clubs and social organizations, opera box holders, and other useful social information."[17] As Dixon Wecter put it in his *Saga of American Society*:

> Here at last, unencumbered with advertisements of dress-makers and wine merchants, enhanced by large, clear type and a pleasant binding of orange and black—which if anything, suggested the colors of America's most elegant university—was a convenient listing of one's friends and potential friends. It was an immediate triumph.[18]

The New York *Social Register* was soon followed by volumes for Boston and Philadelphia in 1890, Baltimore in 1892, Chicago in 1893, Washington, D.C., in 1900, St. Louis and Buffalo in 1903, Pittsburgh in 1904, San Francisco in 1906, and Cleveland and Cincinnati-Dayton in 1910. Volumes for all these twelve cities have been issued yearly down to the present and in substantially the same form as the original New York *Social Register*. Other volumes were issued for Providence (1905–1926), Minneapolis-St. Paul (1907–1927), Seattle-Portland (1914–1921), Pasadena-Los Angeles (1914–1926), Detroit (1918–1927), and Richmond-Charleston-Savannah-Atlanta (1906–1927) but were discontinued because of lack of interest.[19]

It is interesting that the *Social Register* is privately owned and lists social status, as it were, for a profit. The register is issued yearly in November and is sent to all families who are listed within its pages. The yearly charge for a subscription ranges from five to ten dollars per city volume. Potential members must make application themselves and include written references from present members (see below); the only exceptions to this rule are to be found in Washington, D.C., where the president, the vice-president, the Supreme Court, the cabinet, various members of the diplomatic corps, and all United States senators (not representatives) are listed automatically.[20] This last point reflects the nature of stratification in a bureaucratic social structure where, like the military services, social-class position follows functional position, and the senator, like the naval officer, is automatically a "gentleman."[21]

What evidence is there which would indicate that the *Social Register* is an index of families who are descended more or less from elite members in the past? What is the relationship between the families listed in the contemporary *Social Registers* (1940) and the captains of industry and finance who came to power in the "Gilded Age"? In the first place, Frederick Lewis Allen takes ten "Lords of Creation" as ideal typical examples of the American financial elite at the turn of the century and shows how they—and their sons and grandsons—alloyed their gold with an American upper class.[22] Of interest here is the fact that, of these ten men—J. Pierpont Morgan, George Fales Baker, James Stillman, Edward H. Harriman, John D. Rockefeller, William Rockefeller, Henry Huddlestone Rogers, William K. Vanderbilt, James R. Keene, and Jacob H. Schiff—all but the last named were listed in the *Social Register* as of 1905;[23] Allen notes that the exclusion of Schiff was "presumably due to the fact that he was a Jew, and the Jews constituted a group somewhat apart; the fashionable clubs were almost exclusively gentile; and the 'Social Register' was virtually a gentile register."[24] As it illustrates the dynamics of upper-class formation in America, it is of interest to observe that Jacob Schiff's grandson, who married George Fales Baker's granddaughter, is listed in both the *Social Register* and *Who's Who* as of 1940.

Ferdinand Lundberg's *America's 60 Families* is a study of America's wealthiest families, the majority of whose fortunes were made between the Civil War and World War I.[25] Of these sixty consanguine family units, over three-fourths have traceable descendants (the same given and surnames as the family founder) who are listed in the 1940 *Social Register*; these descendants are intermarried one with another and with others of less spectacular wealth but of higher social standing.[26]

Finally, the rather ponderous *History of the Great American Fortunes* by Gustavus Myers is another useful volume for validating the *Social Register* as an American upper class index.[27] This well-known book is an exhaustive study of the men who have amassed the greatest fortunes in America from colonial times to the present (1936). The names of these wealthy family-founders (taken from the index of Myers' book) have been carefully checked against the names of the families listed in the twelve 1940 *Social Registers*. The family-founders whose descendants are listed in the 1940 *Social Registers* of these cities are shown in table 1.1.

The distinguished historian, Samuel Morison, once facetiously remarked that he attached great significance to the fact that the founding of the Brookline Country Club in 1882 coincided with the closing of the frontier in America. Certainly the closing of the frontier (1890), the Sherman Anti-Trust Act (1890), the formation of the United States Steel Company (1901), the founding of Groton School (1884), the opening of the new "millionaires' country club" at Tuxedo Park, New York (1885), the rule of Mrs. Astor and Ward McAlister (1880s and 1890s), the Bradley Martin ball (at the cost of $369,200 in 1897), and the first issue of the *Social Register* (1888) were important variables in a social situation which pointed to a centralized America in the middle twentieth century. As wealth centered in New York and the financial elite became dominant, the *Social Register* became an index of a new upper class in America. For the first time, subcultural socializing agencies other than the family operated on almost a national scale in the form of the New England boarding school and the fashionable eastern university. The elder Morgan and his contemporaries were on the boards of trustees and gave their money to these privately run institutions where they, in turn, sent their sons to be educated together. Groton School, for example, which opened its doors in 1884 with the elder Morgan as an original trustee, was founded by Endicott Peabody, a descendant of Joseph Peabody (see table 1.1) who "in the days when Salem was at its greatest, was the greatest merchant in Salem."[28] Of the 87 men listed in table 1.1, no less than 53 had one or more descendants who had attended either Groton or St. Paul's schools in the period between 1890 and 1940. In other words, these exclusive boarding schools, and universities like Harvard, Yale, and Princeton, serve to create and preserve an upper class, intercity solidarity. The school, or college club, "tie" or "hatband" are status symbols among this new upper class in *all* cities. The available evidence at least suggests that the *Social Register* is an index of this intercity upper class in 1940.

TABLE 1.1

Deceased Elite Individuals in American Economic Life with Descendants Who Are Listed in the 1940 Social Register; the Names Are Taken from the Index of History of the Great American Fortunes, by Gustavus Myers

Deceased elite individual	Period when wealth was acquired*	Occupation: or the way in which wealth was acquired†
(Elite individuals with descendants listed in the Philadelphia *Social Register* in 1940)		
Baer, George F.	Late 19th century	Railroads
Biddle, Nicholas	18th-19th century	Finance
Cassatt, A. J.	Late 19th century	Railroads
Cope, Thomas Pym	18th-19th century	Merchant
Dolan, Thomas	Late 19th century	Utilities
Drexel, Anthony	Late 19th century	Finance
Du Pont, Coleman	20th century	Chemistry
Elkins, William L.	Late 19th century	Utilities
Hopkins, Johns	Early 19th century	Railroads
Knox, Philander	Late 19th century	Law
Penrose, Boies	20th century	Politics
Ridgeway, Jacob	18th-19th century	Merchant
Scott, Thomas	Late 19th century	Railroads
Wanamaker, John	Late 19th century	Merchant
Widener, P. A. B.	Late 19th century	Utilities
(Elite individuals with descendants listed in the Boston *Social Register* in 1940)		
Adams, Charles F.	Late 19th century‡	Railroads
Aldrich, Nelson	Late 19th century	Finance
Ames, Oakes	Late 19th century	Railroads
Brooks, Peter C.	18th-19th century	Merchant
Cabot, George	18th-19th century	Merchant
Derby, Elias	18th-19th century	Merchant
Peabody, Joseph	18th-19th century	Merchant
Perkins, Thomas	18th-19th century	Merchant
Thorndike, Israel	18th-19th century	Merchant

TABLE 1.1
(Continued)

Deceased elite individual	Period when wealth was acquired*	Occupation: or the way in which wealth was acquired†
(Elite individuals with descendants listed in the New York *Social Register* in 1940)		
Astor, J. J.	Early 19th century	Furs, land
Baker, George F.	Late 19th century	Finance
Beekman, Henry	18th-19th century	Land
Belmont, August	Late 19th century	Finance, utilities
Blair, John I.	Late 19th century	Railroads
Brevoort, Henry	18th-19th century	Land
Brown, Alexander	Late 19th century	Finance
Carnegie, Andrew	Late 19th century	Manufacturing
Choate, Joseph	Late 19th century	Law
Clews, Henry	Late 19th century	Finance
Cravath, Paul	Late 19th century	Law
Cromwell, W. Nelson	Late 19th century	Law
Dodge, Cleveland	Late 19th century	Copper
Duke, James B.	20th century	Cigarettes
Flagler, H. M.	Late 19th century	Oil
Ford, Henry	20th century	Automobiles
Goelet, Peter	18th century	Land
Gould, Jay	Late 19th century	Railroads
Griswold family	18th-19th century	Merchants
Harriman, E. H.	Late 19th century	Railroads
Havemeyer, H. O.	Late 19th century	Sugar
Hill, J. J.	Late 19th century	Railroads
James, D. Willis	Late 19th century	Copper
Ledyard, L. Cass	Late 19th century	Law
Lee, Ivy	20th century	Public relations
Livingston, Robert	18th century	Land
Lorillard, Pierre	Early 19th century	Snuff, land
Morgan, J. P.	Late 19th century	Finance
Payne, O. H.	Late 19th century	Oil
Perkins, George	Late 19th century	Finance, insurance
Phelps, John T.	Late 19th century	Copper
Phillips, Adolphus	18th-19th century	Merchant
Rhinelander, William C.	18th-19th century	Land
Rockefeller, John D.	Late 19th century	Oil

TABLE 1.1
(Continued)

Deceased elite individual	Period when wealth was acquired*	Occupation: or the way in which wealth was acquired†
Rogers, H. H.	Late 19th century	Oil, finance
Roosevelt, James	18th-19th century	Land
Ryan, T. Fortune	Late 19th century	Utilities
Schermerhorn, Peter	18th century	Land
Schiff, Jacob	Late 19th century	Finance
Schley, Grant B.	Late 19th century	Finance
Schuyler, Peter	18th-19th century	Land
Stettinius, Edward R.	Late 19th century	Matches, finance
Stillman, James	Late 19th century	Finance
Stokes, Thomas	Late 19th century	Copper
Taylor, Moses	Early 19th century	Railroads
Vanderbilt, Cornelius	Early 19th century	Shipping, railroads
Van Rensselaer, K.	18th century	Land
Villard, Henry	Late 19th century	Railroads
Whitney, William C.	Late 19th century	Utilities
(Elite individuals with descendants listed in the Chicago *Social Register* in 1940)		
Armour, J. Ogden	Late 19th century	Manufacturing
Field, Marshall	Late 19th century	Merchant
Leiter, Levi	Late 19th century	Merchant
McCormick, Cyrus	Late 19th century	Manufacturing
Palmer, Potter	Late 19th century	Merchant
Patterson, Joseph M.	Late 19th century	Publisher
(Elite individuals with descendants listed in the Baltimore, Cincinnati, Pittsburgh, San Francisco, St. Louis, or Washington *Social Register* in 1940)		
Crocker, Charles	Early 19th century	Railroads
Elkins, Stephen B.	Late 19th century	Land
Frick, Henry Clay	Late 19th century	Manufacturing
Garrett, John W.	Early 19th century	Railroads
Longworth, Nicholas	18th-19th century	Land

TABLE 1.1
(Continued)

Deceased elite individual	Period when wealth was acquired*	Occupation: or the way in which wealth was acquired†
Mellon, Andrew	20th century	Finance, mfg.
Mills, D. O.	Early 19th century	Finance
Pulitzer, Joseph	Late 19th century	Publisher

*The Family-Founders in America can be conveniently divided into three periods. First, there were the romantic merchant capitalists of the late eighteenth and early nineteenth centuries. The descendants of these men are the "Proper" Philadelphians, Bostonians, Baltimorians, or New Yorkers of the present day. Second, there were the industrial, railroad, utility, and financial capitalists who made their money in the period between the Civil War and World War I. Finally, there are the twentieth century, manufacturing, Family-Founders.

†The occupations listed are of necessity limited to the principal field of endeavor. There is much overlapping. While "land" is listed for only a few individuals, almost all of the great fortunes in this country (and in England) have profited from the ownership of urban real estate. Finally, several lawyers and politicians are listed because these men were prominent in their day and were listed in the Index of Myers' book.

‡While Charles Francis Adams (Jr.) was a prominent railroad executive, he was a man of inherited wealth. When Charles Francis Adams I, the father of Henry, Charles, and Brooks, married the daughter of Peter Charndon Brooks, one of Boston's first millionaire merchants, the Adams family became wealthy for the first time.

Who's Who in America

As a group, an upper class is intimately connected with history as long as the family remains as the institution which introduces each generation into the culture. Thus the validity of the *Social Register* as an upper-class index depends on the relationship between its members and past elites. On the other hand, an elite has no group history—only the individual members have a past; elite members are making history and some of their heirs may become part of a future upper class.

Who's Who in America is a nationally recognized listing of brief biographies of the leading men and women in contemporary American life. As such, it is a perfectly democratic index of high functional class position and has wide prestige. In response to a standard form sent to all those persons chosen to be included in the current issue, each completed biography in *Who's Who* lists the following information: name, occupation, date and place of birth, full name of both parents, education and degrees received, marital status—including name of spouse, date of marriage, and the full names of any children—occupational career, military experience, directorships and trusteeships, honorary society and associational memberships, fraternal organizations, religious and political affiliations, club memberships, publications, and finally, home and business addresses.

The following aims of the publishers of *Who's Who*, are indicative of the nature of this elite index.

> The present edition contains down-to-date "Who's Who" biographies of 31,752 outstanding contemporary men and women.
>
> The names in *Who's Who in America* are selected not as the best but as an attempt to choose the best known men and women in the country in all lines of *reputable achievements*—names much in the public eye, not locally, but nationally.
>
> The standards of admission divide the eligibles into two classes: 1) those who are selected on account of special prominence in creditable lines of effort, making them the subject of extensive interest, inquiry, or discussion in this country; and 2) those who are arbitrarily included on account of official position—civil, military, naval, religious, or educational.[29]

No index is perfect, nor any sociological classification as homogeneous as might be desired. We are aware of the inadequacies of *Who's Who* as an index of an American elite. In the first place, it is too heavily weighted with educators and churchmen relative to the organizing elites of business, government, and labor. Secondly, in the distribution of power in any large community, especially urban America, one must always remain aware of the social power exercised by those persons, such as the political "boss," who are not strictly of the respectable world. *Who's Who* gives no clue to the extent of this power in America. Finally, we are well aware of the fact that certain persons are included in *Who's Who* more because of their prestige or prominence than because of any real achievement in a functional sense.

On the other hand, whatever its inadequacies, *Who's Who* is a universally recognized index of an American elite and as such, contains accurate information about a class of persons which the social scientist would be unable to secure on his own; people in this category, as a rule, do not have either the time or the inclination to supply such data solely for the purposes of sociological analysis. Finally, and of utmost importance, *Who's Who* is a useful elite index because it is felt that one must be able to make comparisons between social structures if one is to go beyond mere anecdotal description to generalization from a systematic analysis of empirical evidence; this index may be used to compare various types of communities as well as the same community at two different periods.

One of the important differences between *Who's Who* and the *Social Register*, and very indicative of the difference between an upper class and an elite, is the way in which new members are added from time to time. On the one hand, new families are added to the *Social Register* as a result of their making a formal application to the Social Register Association in New York. In other words, a family having personal and more or less intimate social relations (in business, church, school, club, or neighborhood activities) with the various members of certain families who are members of the upper class and listed in the *Social Register* reaches a point where inclusion within the Register seems expedient; someone listed in the *Social Register*, presumably a friend of the "new" family, obtains an application blank which in turn is filled out by the new family (usually by the wife) and returned to the Social Register Association in New York along with several endorsements by present upper class members as to the social acceptability of the new family; after payment of a nominal fee, the next issue of the *Social Register*, including all pertinent information on the new family, will arrive the following November. The new family might be listed in the Philadelphia *Social Register*, for example, somewhat as follows:[30]

Van Glick,	Mr. & Mrs. J. Furness III (Mary D. Bradford)	R,RC,ME,Y'15
	Miss Mary Bradford—at Vassar	
Juniors	Mr. John F. IV—at Yale	Phone 123
	Miss Sarah—at Foxcroft	"Boxwood"
	Mr. Bradford—at St. Paul's	Bryn Mawr, Pa.

In contrast to the *Social Register*, persons are listed in *Who's Who*, not on the basis of personal friendships or recommendations by present members, but rather on the objective basis of personal achievement or prominence; one does not apply for membership in this index nor is there even a nominal charge for being included; "not a single sketch in this book has been paid for—and none can be paid for."[31]

The Upper Class and the Elite in Metropolitan America

The history of Western civilization has been, in many ways, the story of the rise and fall of great metropolitan centers: Athens and Rome in the ancient world; Constantinople in the age of transition; Paris, along with Naples, Venice, and Milan in the Renaissance; London in the eighteenth and nineteenth centuries; and finally New York in the twentieth. Each in its day, marked the center of pomp and power in the Western world over a span of twenty-five centuries. And in each city, at the zenith of its power, an aristocracy of wealth or an upper class has emerged; thus the last years of the Republic in Rome where the Senate was an aristocracy of wealth, and the "Gilded Age" in America when the Senate was known as the "Millionaires' Club" may be similar sociological periods.

In the same vein, American history is partly reflected in the rise of different cities to position of affluence and power. Salem and Newport rose to prominence along with the merchant shipper of the eighteenth century. Atlanta, Charleston, Richmond, New Orleans, and Mobile were centers of affluence in the days when the planter aristocracy sent their leading men to the United States Senate, which they tended to dominate until just before the Civil War. Within the last few decades, Los Angeles and Detroit manifest a modern opulence as they supply the demands of a mass culture for movement and entertainment. Not the least indication of the trend of our times is the growth of the national capital as a result of the shift in power from Wall Street to the government bureaucracy.

In any complex civilization, social power tends to gravitate towards the large metropolitan areas and especially is this the case in modern bureaucratic society. Ultimately, the pattern of stratification in any social structure is reflected in the distribution of social power as between various functional and social class levels; thus, in terms of social power in America, any significant study of social stratification must inevitably be done in the large metropolis. An attempt has been made in the first part of this paper to show that if there is an upper class in America, the *Social Register* is a useful index of its membership in twelve large cities. How is this upper class related to the contemporary elites in these cities?

The twelve metropolitan areas in the United States which had *Social Registers* in 1940 are shown in table 1.2. In table 1.2, column 1 shows the number of conjugal family units listed in the *Social Register* in each city, and column 2 shows the proportion of these listed in *Who's Who* in each city who are also listed in the *Social Register*. The concentration of power and talent in these cities is indicated by the fact that, while they make up only approximately 20 percent of the total population of the United States, 40 percent of all those listed in *Who's Who* in the country reside in these twelve metropolitan areas. Furthermore, it is certainly plausible to assume that the elite members in these cities have a more pervasive influence on the American social structure as a whole than the 60 percent who are listed in *Who's Who* from the rest of the country.

In 1940 there were approximately 38,000 conjugal family units listed in the *Social Register* (table 1.2); in that year, the estimated number of families in the country as a whole was 34,948,666.[32] Thus about one-tenth of 1 percent of the families in the country were members of the upper class which, in turn, contributed no less than 9 percent of all those listed in *Who's Who* in that year (31,752 individuals listed in *Who's Who*, 2,879 of whom were also listed in the *Social Register*). More important, of the 12,530 residents of these twelve metropolitan areas who were listed in *Who's Who*, 2,879 or 23 percent were also listed in the *Social Register* (table 1.2).

Of the eighteen metropolitan areas in the United States which had populations of over half a million in 1940, the twelve listed

TABLE 1.2
The Number of Conjugal Family Units Listed in the Social Registers of Twelve Large Metropolitan Areas in America, and the Proportion of Those Listed in Who's Who in These Cities Who Are Also Listed in the Social Register

	CONJUGAL FAMILIES IN THE *SOCIAL REGISTER* IN 1940	INDIVIDUALS LISTED IN *WHO'S WHO* AND ARE			
		In the Social Register		*Not in the* Social Register	
Metropolitan Areas	*No.*	*No.*	%	*No.*	%
New York	13,200	1,040	20	4,085	80
Philadelphia	5,150*	226	29	544	71
Boston	3,675	240	28	608	72
Washington, D.C.	3,530	715	30	1,670	70
Chicago	2,130	151	11	1,194	89
Baltimore	1,935	87	26	243	74
St. Louis	1,925	77	24	239	76
San Francisco	1,775	87	23	297	77
Pittsburgh	1,635	76	22	277	78
Cincinnati	1,305†	61	29	151	71
Dayton		11	17	51	83
Buffalo	1,125	43	37	72	63
Cleveland	1,065	65	20	260	80
All cities	38,450	2,879	23	9,651	77

*Upper class families in Wilmington, Delaware, including forty-five Du Pont conjugal family units, are listed in the Philadelphia *Social Register.*
†One volume of the *Social Register* includes families from both Cincinnati and Dayton.

in table 1.2 are the oldest social structures (they were the twelve largest in the country as of the 1990 Census). Detroit and Los Angeles, on the other hand, have grown to their present size largely in the twentieth century. The automobile and motion picture elites being relatively "new," there is apparently no coherent upper class in these cities (Henry Ford II and his family are listed in the New York *Social Register*; see table 1.1). Presumably, the age and size of a social structure, together with the rate of social change, are important variables in determining the nature of the class system. For example, Chicago, a young and rapidly changing, middle western metropolis, has twice as many individuals listed in *Who's Who*, and less than half as many families listed in the *Social Register*, as Philadelphia, an old and conservative eastern seaboard city. The upper class in Chicago, in turn, has less influence on the elite than the upper class in Philadelphia (table 1.2 shows that in Chicago 11 percent and in Philadelphia 29 percent of the elite are also in the upper class).

Although a more detailed analysis of the relationship between the elite and the upper class in Philadelphia will be treated in a forthcoming monograph, it is of interest here to observe that, of the Philadelphians listed in *Who's Who* in 1940, the members of some occupational categories were more likely to be listed in the *Social Register* than those in other categories. One of the functions of upper-class solidarity is the retention, within a primary group of families, of the final-decision-making positions within the social structure. As of the first half of the twentieth century in America, the final-decisions affecting, the goals of the social structure have been made primarily by members of the financial and business community. Thus the contemporary upper class in Philadelphia is a business and financial aristocracy. In table 1.3, the bankers, lawyers, engineers, and businessmen—the business elite—are more likely to be drawn from the upper class than those persons in other occupational categories. While table 1.3 shows that 75 percent of the members of the banking elite in Philadelphia are upper-class members, the presidents, and over 80 percent of the directors, of the six largest banking establishments in the city are upper-class members. Moreover, of the 532 directorships in industrial and financial institutions reported by *all* the Philadelphians listed in *Who's Who*, no less than 60 percent are reported by individuals also listed in the *Social Register*. Finally, while 51 percent of the lawyers listed in table 1.3 are upper-class members, over 80 percent of the partners of the six leading law firms in the city are upper-class members.

While the final-decision-making positions within the functional class hierarchy may be passed on from generation to generation, this is not the case, to the same extent, where technical or intellectual skills is a primary requirement for elite status. A Ford II, for example, may inherit a functional class position where an Einstein II may not. Thus two large occupational categories within

TABLE 1.3
Philadelphians in Who's Who in 1940—Occupation as Related to Social Class

	SOCIAL CLASS						
	Social Register		*Non* Social Register		Who's Who *total*		*Per cent of each occupation in* Social Register
Occupation	*No.*	%	*No.*	%	*No.*	%	
Bankers	24	11	8	1	32	4	75
Lawyers	20	9	19	4	39	5	51
Engineers	10	4	12	2	22	3	45
Businessmen	53	24	72	13	125	16	42
Architects	10	4	14	3	24	3	42
Physicians	16	7	27	5	43	6	37
Museum officials	5	2	9	2	14	2	35
Authors	14	6	30	6	44	6	32
Graphic artists	8	4	31	6	39	5	21
Public officials	7	3	26	5	33	4	21
Educators	31	14	147	27	178	23	16
Opinion*	7	3	46	8	53	7	13
Musical artists	2	1	14	3	16	2	12
Church officials	8	4	72	13	80	10	10
Retired capitalists	3		0		3		
Philanthropists	1		2		3		
Social workers	2	4	2	2	4	4	39
Librarians	0		5		5		
Others	5		8		13		
Total	226	100	544	100	770	100	29

*Public relations, advertising, radio, editors.

the elite in Philadelphia, the educators and the church officials, draw relatively few members from the upper class. On the other hand, the upper class in the city has a long tradition of good physicians and architects among its membership. Among other things, this may be due to the fact that inherited wealth is undoubtedly helpful in meeting the costs of education, and, in addition, the paying clients in these professions have traditionally been upper-class members. Finally, it is characteristic of changing social structures that *new* or potentially powerful elites are under-represented in any contemporary upper class. The opinion and political (public officials) elites, *new* and as-yet subservient to the money power, do not draw many members from the upper class in Philadelphia. On the other hand, it is interesting to observe that, as these words are being written, Philadelphians, led by Joseph Sill Clark, Jr., and Richardson Dilworth, have elected their first Democratic mayor in the twentieth century. As both these men are upper-class Philadelphians, this may well be a clue to the changing power structure in America.

In metropolitan America in the last two decades of the nineteenth century, local aristocracies of birth and breeding (old money) merged with that new and more conspicuously colorful world known as "Society."[33] As millionaires multiplied and had to be accepted, as one lost track of "who" people were and had to recognize "what" they were worth, the *Social Register* became an index of a new upper class in metropolitan America. In an age which marked the centralization of economic power under the control of finance capitalism, the gentlemen bankers and lawyers on Wall Street, Walnut Street, State Street, and La Salle Street sent their sons to Groton, St. Paul's, or St. Mark's and afterwards to Harvard, Yale, or Princeton where they joined exclusive clubs such as Porcellian, Fence, or Ivy.[34] These young men from many cities, educated together, got to know one another's sisters at debutante parties and fashionable weddings in Old Westbury, Tuxedo, or Far Hills, on the Main Line or in Chestnut Hill, in Dedham, Milton, or Brookline, and in Lake Forest. After marriage, almost invariably within this select circle, they lived in these same suburbs and commuted to the city where they lunched with their peers and their fathers at the Union, Philadelphia, Somerset, or Chicago clubs. Several generations repeat the cycle, and a centralized business nobility thus becomes a reality in America.

First published in New York in 1888, the current *Social Register* lists families of high social prestige in New York, Chicago, Boston, Philadelphia, Baltimore, San Francisco, St. Louis, Buffalo, Pittsburgh, Cleveland, Cincinnati-Dayton, and Washington, D.C. In 1940, approximately one-fourth of the residents of these twelve metropolitan areas who were listed in *Who's Who* in that year were also listed in the *Social Register*. In 1940, the upper class in Philadelphia was a business and especially a financial aristocracy. While 29 percent of the Philadelphians listed in *Who's Who* were also listed in the *Social Register*, the upper class contributed more than its share of leaders within the business community.

Notes

1. For an excellent recent review of the literature, see Milton M. Gordon, "Social Class in American Sociology," *American Journal of Sociology* 55, no. 3 (November 1949): 262–68.

2. See Robert S. Lynd and Helen Merrell Lynd, *Middletown* (New York: Harcourt, Brace, 1929); Robert S. Lynd and Helen Merrell Lynd, *Middletown in Transition* (New York: Harcourt, Brace, 1937); and W. Lloyd Warner and Paul S. Lunt, *The Social Life of a Modern Community* (New Haven: Yale University Press, 1941).
3. Warner and Lunt, *Social Life*, 81.
4. See Warner and Lunt, *Social Life*, 82, and Lynd and Lynd, *Middletown*, 22. It has been observed that, "in general, the leading exponents of the subjective (distributive) theories of class are oriented towards an examination of the forces of tradition, while the leading exponents of the objective (production) theories of class are more concerned with social change," Seymour M. Lipset and Reinhard Bendix, "Social Status and Social Structure: A Re-examination of Data and Interpretation," *British Journal of Sociology* 11, no. 2 (June 1951): 150.
5. See Warner and Lunt, *Social Life*, 83; and Lynd and Lynd, *Middletown in Transition*, 100.
6. For example, while in "Yankee City," a small and traditional New England community, subjective social class position may have been the independent variable in the class situation, in rapidly changing "Middletown," on the other hand, position in the dynamic productive process may have been the independent variable. An analysis of the changing relationships between these two variables in different communities raises the mere descriptive study of stratification to the level of scientific analysis.
7. Dixon Wecter, *The Saga of American Society* (New York: Charles Scribner's Sons, 1937), 6.
8. *Who's Who in America*, vol. 21 (Chicago: A.N. Marquis, 1940). *Social Register* (New York: Social Register Association, 1940). Separate volumes for New York, Philadelphia, Boston, Baltimore, Chicago, St. Louis, Buffalo, Pittsburgh, San Francisco, Cleveland, Cincinnati-Dayton, and Washington, D.C., are issued yearly in November.
9. Brooks Adams, *The Law of Civilization and Decay* (New York: Macmillan, 1896), 186ff.
10. Charles A. Beard and Mary R. Beard, *The Rise of American Civilization*, vol. 2 (New York: Macmillan, 1937), 387.
11. One of the reasons why W. Lloyd Warner discards an economic interpretation of stratification in Yankee City was that "old family" or "lineage" placed people in the "upper-upper" category although they often were less wealthy than "lower-upper," or "new family" people. While this undoubtedly vitiates any *static* economic interpretation, historically the "old families" became so largely because some ancestor had made money. Presumably, the "Riverbrook" families were just as *old* as those on "Hill Street." See Warner and Lunt, *Social Life*, 81.

    The "old families" on the eastern seaboard are not Mayflower descendants but the descendants of late eighteenth and early nineteenth century merchants or manufacturers. Hence the large number of "Proper" Bostonians, and even some Philadelphians and New Yorkers, who trace their lines back to "Salem Shippers." See S.E. Morison, *Maritime History of Massachusetts, 1783–1860* (Boston: Houghton Mifflin, 1921).

12. Cleveland Amory, *The Proper Bostonians* (New York: E.P. Dutton, 1947), 39–40.
13. The novelist, Edith Wharton, interprets this transitional period in the history of the New York upper class in three novels—*The Age of Innocence, The House of Mirth*, and *The Custom of the Country*. The first novel opens "on a January evening in the early seventies," and portrays a small and formal "society" that is soon to disappear before the assault of the parvenu, which she describes in the other two novels.
14. "Statisticians could only roughly estimate the strength of the spreading plutocracy and the size of its share gathered from the golden flood, but, according to one guess, there were only three millionaires in the United States in 1861 and at least thirty-eight hundred at the lapse of thirty-six years." Beard and Beard, *Rise of American Civilization*, 388.
15. For a description of "Society" in this age of transition, see Frederick Townsend Martin, *The Passing of the Idle Rich* (New York: Doubleday, 1911).
16. Beard and Beard, *Rise of American Civilization*, 388.
17. Quoted from the first *Social Register*, 1888.
18. Wecter, *Saga of American Society*, 232.
19. This information was obtained by checking the volumes of the *Social Register* in the Library of Congress.
20. See Wecter, *Saga of American Society*, 232–36.
21. Herbert Spencer saw "progress" in terms of the movement of society from the militant to the industrial type of social structure. In the modern state where social and functional classes merge in one all-inclusive bureaucratic hierarchy, Spencer's ideal typical militant social structure may well be a cogent description of the "Brave New World." See Herbert Spencer, *The Principles of Sociology*, vol. 2 (New York: D. Appleton & Co., 1896), chap. 18.
22. Frederick Lewis Allen, *The Lords of Creation* (New York: Harper & Brothers, 1935), chap. 3.
23. Ibid., 98.
24. Ibid., 98–99.
25. Ferdinand Lundberg: *America's 60 Families* (New York: Vanguard, 1937).
26. At one time or another, for example, "old families" such as Biddle, Peabody, Roosevelt, and so forth, have absorbed, or been absorbed by Drexels, Du Ponts, Fields, and Dukes.
27. Gustavus Myers, *History of the Great American Fortunes* (New York: Modern Library, 1937).
28. Frank D. Ashburn, *Peabody of Groton* (New York: Coward McCann, 1944), 5.
29. *Who's Who in America*, 1–2.
30. Insight into the structure and values of the upper class in America may be obtained by a perusal of the family listings in any contemporary volume of the *Social Register*. The ideal typical Mr. Van Glick, for example, belongs to three clubs in Philadelphia, the Rittenhouse and Racquet clubs in the city, and the Merion Cricket club along the Main Line; he is a graduate of Yale University in the class of 1915; he is educating his children at very acceptable educational institutions, and lives in a very fashionable neighborhood along the Main Line. The familistic values of this upper class are

indicated by the frequent retention of family given names (J. Furness, Mary Bradford, or Bradford, the son) and the use of "III" and "IV" as symbols of family continuity. The maiden name of the wife is always given and serves a useful genealogical function. The patriarchal nature of this family is shown by the fact that the college attended, if any, by the wife is never listed. In other words, family, club membership, education, and neighborhood all perform the status-ascribing function within this upper class.

31. *Who's Who in America*, 2.
32. Statistical Abstract of the United States (Washington, D.C.: U.S. Government Printing Office, 1947), 47.
33. It was in the 1880s that New York "Society" with a capital *S* was dominated by Mrs. Astor and guided by Ward McAlister. The latter coined the term "Four Hundred" in this period and finally gave his official list to the *New York Times* "on the occasion of Mrs. Astor's great ball, February 1, 1892," Wecter, *Saga of American Society*, 216.
34. These clubs are the means of upper class exclusiveness at these universities. At Harvard, Porcellian and A.D., the most exclusive, are followed by Fly, Spee, Delphic, and Owl. The narrow top drawer at Yale includes Fence, Delta Kappa Epsilon, Zeta Psi, and St. Anthony, while at Princeton, the more socially circumspect clubs on Prospect Street include Ivy, Cap and Gown, and Colonial. It is of passing interest to observe that Harvard's newest final club, the Delphic, was founded by J.P. Morgan in 1889.

2

Upper Class and Elites

The Bomb was dropped on Hiroshima in August 1945. As I had enough points to get out of the navy almost immediately, I was able to enroll in the Ph.D. program in sociology at Columbia University in September. In that academic year, I read Max Weber and Alexis de Tocqueville for the first time. In December I bought Tocqueville's *Democracy in America* in a handsomely boxed, two-volume set that had just been published by Alfred A. Knopf. No book has ever influenced me more than the second volume of this classic. Although Marx was endlessly quoted and referred to, Tocqueville's name was never mentioned in class during my two years of graduate study, except once by a visiting lecturer from the New School for Social Research, who noted in the course of his lecture that Tocqueville's *Ancient Regime* was one of the finest books ever written in political science and sociology. This was before the paperback revolution, but, after more than a year's search, I found a copy at Blackwell's Bookstore in Oxford. In the early summer of 1946, I bought and read a just-published copy of *From Max Weber: Essays in Sociology*, translated, edited and with an introduction by H.H. Gerth and C. Wright Mills.

The great value of the writings of Tocqueville and Weber is that they abound with what Robert K. Merton has called theoretical insights of the middle range; and it is just such theoretical insights that stimulate and guide us in asking pertinent questions, and ordering relevant facts, about any social structure. It was Weber's famous essay, "Class, Status, Party," that first stimulated me to ask questions about class, status, and authority, which I have continued to do (in the style, I like to think, of Cézanne's endless paintings of his beloved mountain outside Aix-en-Provence) for more than four decades since that summer of 1946 when I began to write a dissertation that eventually became *Philadelphia Gentlemen*.

Stratification theory, as developed in Weber's famous essay, involved two logically distinct aspects: a hierarchy of class situations on the one hand, and a hierarchy of status situations on the other. Classes are not communities, but consist of individuals with similar life chances or economic positions in the market. In time, and especially over generations, hierarchies of classes tend to produce communities of families that often "stand in sharp opposition to pretensions of sheer property" or the market. The key to Weber's understanding of status groups is to be found in the following paragraphs:

> In contrast to classes, status groups are normally communities. They are . . . determined by specific, positive or negative, social estimations of honor. . . . Status honor need not necessarily be linked with class situation. On the contrary, it normally stands in sharp opposition to the pretensions of sheer property.
>
> Both propertied and propertyless people can belong to the same status group and frequently do with very tangible consequences. . . . The "equality" of status among American "gentlemen" for instance, is expressed by the fact that outside the subordination determined by different functions of "business" it would be considered strictly repugnant—if even the richest "chief" while playing billiards or cards in his club in the evening, would not treat his "clerk" as in every sense fully his equal in birthright. It would be repugnant if the American "chief" would bestow upon his "clerk" the condescending "benevolence" marking a distinction of "position" which the German "chief" can never dissever from his attitude.

I had been born and raised among a privileged class of families in Philadelphia which almost exactly epitomized Weber's description of a status group quoted above; my friends in the schoolroom, on the playing fields, at dancing classes, and summer resorts were the sons and daughters of both very rich and powerful, as well as less wealthy and powerless, bankers, businessmen, lawyers, and physicians; within the class or status group, however, there existed a very real democratic spirit where all were treated on their individual merits; in my circle of sports-loving friends, at least, it was considered effeminate to mention such things as the social position or lineage of one's friends or acquaintances; as a matter of fact, I learned the economic history of many of my friends' extended families for the first time while researching and writing *Philadelphia Gentlemen*. It was no wonder, then, that I was frankly shocked at the invidious comparisons and snobberies, articulated as social science, which I found in the Columbia classrooms, as well as in such studies as the Lynds' two Middletown books or Lloyd Warner's Yankee City series, both of which I read during that first year in Fayerweather Hall, at Columbia. There is some truth in the waggish view that snobs and racists are merely amateurs (without Ph.D.'s) who talk like professional sociologists.

Most writers on the upper class tend to stress the envied style of life of the leisure classes enjoying their leisure. On the other hand, my central focus in *Philadelphia Gentlemen* and other writings has always been on the relationship between the upper class and the leadership structure of any society; I am more interested in the careers of such "socialites" as Franklin Roosevelt, Averell Harriman, or Henry Stimson than in the essentially boring lives of the likes of Ward McAlister, Harry Lehr, or *the* Mrs. Astor. As Theodore Roosevelt put it, "Personally, the life of the Four Hundred, in its typical form, strikes me as being as flat as stale champagne. . . . I suppose young girls and even young men naturally like a year or two of such a life as the Four Hundred lead; and it has its pretty, attractive, and not unwholesome sides. But I do not think that anyone can permanently lead his or her life amid such surroundings save at the cost of degeneration in character." Roosevelt, as with a minority of similarly minded American gentlemen since his day, was interested in being part of a governing, rather than a merely privileged, class. The next-to-last chapter of *Philadelphia Gentlemen*, entitled "A Primary Group of Prestige and Power," for example, sums up the essence of my view of class authority, both in that book and all I have written since: It showed how a small group of secure aristocrats dominated the economic and cultural life in the city in 1940.

In that summer of 1946, I almost immediately saw that the

Social Register, a listing of some five thousand conjugal family units of similar social honor in the city of Philadelphia in 1940, would make an ideal index of what I came to call the city's upper class; these families formed a class community with a consciousness of kind, or sense of gemeinschaft solidarity, unlike any other status level in the city. In any large city, it is only at the upper-class level that this kind of solidarity holds: there are middle and lower classes, but only one upper class. Moreover, as the subtitle of *Philadelphia Gentlemen* (The Making of a National Upper Class) suggests, this class solidarity and consciousness of kind extended not only across many neighborhoods in and around Philadelphia, but also to similar neighborhoods in other metropolitan areas across the nation, especially along the eastern seaboard. As of 1940, a Philadelphia debutante had a far greater chance of marrying within *Social Register* circles in New York, Boston, and Baltimore (or even San Francisco) than she would of marrying someone outside her class in Philadelphia. Upper-class families in 1940 were very conscious of their being patriarchal and historical, consanguine units.

While the *Social Register* proved to be an excellent index of upper-class status in Philadelphia in 1940, I also needed an index of high functional achievement and leadership. Somehow or other I came up with the idea of using *Who's Who*, and I still possess a well-thumbed and beaten-up copy of *Who's Who in America*, Volume 21, 1940–1941, which I bought at Leary's, once the city's most famous second-hand bookstore, in the summer of 1946. *Who's Who* lists successful individuals in America regardless of race, creed, or social origins. Using the geographical index, I found there were 770 men and women listed from Philadelphia that year; matching that list with the 1940 *Social Register*, I found that 226, or 29 percent, of the elite (770) were drawn from the upper class. The dominant banking and business leaders in the city, moreover, were far more likely to be drawn from the upper class than were members of less powerful occupations such as artists, writers, or professors.

Theoretical advances in any science are made by redefining old concepts and using them in new ways. I use the concept "upper class" to stand for Weber's *communal* status group of high honor;

this class community of extended families stands at the top of what I call the "social class system." My "elite" concept, on the other hand, stands for a statistical, or conceptual, group of *individuals* similarly ranked at the top of the division of labor, or what I call the "functional class system" (Weber's "class" as against "status" hierarchy). Actually, there are many functional elites, such as the Forbes 400, top executives of the Fortune 500 corporations, or the leading members of the American Medical Association, the American Bar Association, or the American Sociological Association. There is, on the contrary, only *one* upper class, which would include, for example, the four senior partners of Ballard, Spahr, Andrews and Ingersoll, one of Philadelphia's leading law firms in 1940, as well as such members of Andrews's famous Harvard class of 1910 as Thomas Sterns Eliot of St. Louis, Hamilton Fish of New York, George Peabody Gardner of Boston, and John Silas Reed, a first-family Oregonian, who now lies buried in Lenin's tomb in Moscow.

It is not new concepts themselves which are important, but rather the relationship between them—in this case, the relationships between various elites and the upper class. In 1940 Philadelphia, in other words, *Philadelphia Gentlemen* has shown that the elite was open, yet still dominated by powerful members of the upper class. At the same time, the upper class was also relatively open.

Class authority was characteristic of American leadership in 1940, which was still largely composed of white Protestants. *Philadelphia Gentlemen* closed on the following note:

> One more question remains to be raised even if it cannot be answered: What is the future function of a predominantly Anglo-Saxon and Protestant upper class in an ethnically and religiously heterogenous democracy? In many ways, this is the most important question of all. As Joseph Patrick Kennedy, Boston millionaire and American Ambassador to the Court of St. James under Roosevelt, once put it: "How long does our family have to be here before we are called Americans rather than Irish-Americans? " . . . The American upper class has been from the beginning open to new men of talent and power, and their families. By the middle of the twentieth century, however, upper-class status appears to be limited primarily to families of colonial and northern European stock and Protestant affiliations. Glancing back to the turn of the century, when a flood of immigrants came to these shores from southern and eastern Europe, to say nothing of the Irish Catholics who came

> earlier, one wonders if this American democracy has not produced somewhat of a caste situation at the upper-class level. Or are the talented and powerful descendants of these newer immigrants going to be assimilated into some future upper-class of life and social organizations?

It was this question which led to my second study of class authority and leadership, *The Protestant Establishment: Aristocracy and Caste in America*, published in 1964. This study was inspired by Tocqueville's classic analysis of the Old Regime and the French Revolution, which showed how violent revolution came to France because the nobility degenerated into a caste when it refused to assimilate new men of power and affluence—the bourgeoisie. The British upper class, on the other hand, absorbed new businessmen, avoided revolution, and remained a ruling class, or aristocracy. In other words, the French nobility retained its privileges at the expense of power and authority, while the British shared its privileges precisely in order to rule.

"We in America," I wrote at the beginning of *The Protestant Establishment*, "have followed in the British rather than the French tradition. And we have remained a relatively free and stable society largely because we have maintained a balance between the liberal democratic and the authoritative aristocratic social processes. On the other hand, there is a crisis in American leadership in the last half of the twentieth century that is partly due, I think, to the declining authority of an establishment which is not based on an increasingly caste-like White-Anglo-Saxon-Protestant (WASP) upper class." *The Protestant Establishment* was a historical and sociological analysis of forces of caste and aristocracy in American leadership in the years between the presidencies of Theodore Roosevelt and John F. Kennedy.

"An aristocracy in all its vigour," wrote Tocqueville in his *Ancient Regime*, "not only carries on the affairs of a country, but directs public opinion, gives a tone to literature, and the stamp of authority to ideas." My third book, *Puritan Boston and Quaker Philadelphia: Two Protestant Ethics and the Spirit of Class Authority and Leadership*, sought to show how the Puritan patricians of Boston, for almost three centuries after the city's founding in 1630, fulfilled Tocqueville's definition of a "vigorous" aristocracy, while the Quaker-turned-Episcopal members of Philadelphia's upper class did not. Following Max Weber's classic, *The Protestant Ethic and the Spirit of Capitalism*, I tried to show how the differences between these two branches of the American upper class were to be found in the differences between the hierarchical and elitist Puritan-Congregational ethic and the egalitarian, anti-elitist ethic of Quakerism.

It must be emphasized here that all three of my studies of class authority in America have been informed by the spirit of Tocqueville, whose aristocratic family was deeply rooted in the Ancient Regime and the soil of Normandy. They have, on the other hand, little intellectual sympathy with the spirit of Marxism, founded by a deracinated German Jew, writing in the British Museum. Thus I wrote on the first page of *Philadelphia Gentlemen*:

> Leadership and some form of stratification are inherent in all human social organization. . . . Only in that delightful land of Oz are there more generals than privates and surely Alice might have found a "classless society," like unwet water, only in Wonderland.
>
> Although scientific realism is deified in our time, modern social theory, from Rousseau through Marx to the present betrays, nevertheless, a utopian tendency to measure the good society, often equated with democracy, in terms of such sociological monstrosities as "majority leadership" or the classless society.

In summary, while Tocqueville and I have tried to understand how modern Western democracies can be held together in our atomizing and secular age without succumbing to the totalitarian temptation, Marx and his followers (both manifest and latent) have focused their energies on analyzing (and encouraging) the social forces of revolution and societal disintegration. But as Tocqueville foresaw over a century and a half ago, totalitarians have usually followed revolutionaries. Thus Marx once wrote in *Das Kapital* that "the more a ruling class is able to *assimilate* the most prominent men of the dominated class, the more *stable* and *dangerous* its rule" (italics mine). Following Tocqueville, I would consider such a stable ruling class desirable rather than dangerous.

3

The WASP's Last Gasp

My father was born on a family place called Digby near Fox Chase, then a small village in the far northeastern part of Philadelphia; he was named Edward Digby Baltzell, after his grandfather and his birthplace. I was born in 1915—at 1915 Rittenhouse Street—and named after my father. I now live three and a half blocks from by birthplace, probably a record among my peripatetic peers in the sociology profession.

When I was growing up in the years between the two world wars, Philadelphia was still a city of some 100 ancient neighborhoods, such as Torresdale, Holmesburg, Wissinoming, Kensington, Grays Ferry, Kingsessing, Swampoodle, Nicetown, and Mount Airy, a transitional neighborhood between solid and Quaker Germantown and fashionable and Episcopalian Chestnut Hill. Though differing in ethnic makeup and income level, all these traditional neighborhoods were homogeneous, close-knit, and cohesive. They were real communities, dominated by religious and family values that were faithfully emphasized in the neighborhood schools, both public and private. Families were still patriarchal, and fathers and brothers were supposed to be the moral guardians of the virginity of their darling daughters and sisters. Compared with other major cities at the time, moreover, home ownership in Philadelphia was high and the divorce and suicide rates were low.

Although born just off Rittenhouse Square, I was raised in Chestnut Hill. In those days, the fashionable families in Chestnut Hill were homogeneously WASP and predominantly Episcopalian. The few fashionable families of German or Sephardic Jewish origin had married Episcopalians for several generations. All too many of us were anti-Semitic, anti-Irish, and anti-Catholic. Our Mother of Consolation, the large Roman Catholic church across Chestnut Hill Avenue from St. Paul's Church (the citadel of proper Episcopalianism) was supported, as the fashionable stereotype had it, primarily by Irish-Catholic servants—housemaids, butlers, cooks, gardeners, chauffeurs, and so forth. (Even we impecunious genteel employed at least one full-time, live-in servant.) The Episcopal clergymen, who still commanded considerable communal authority, frowned on divorce and all sexual relations outside marriage, including homosexuality. At Chestnut Hill Academy, we boys filed into chapel first thing each morning to communicate with our maker. At the top of the social pyramid, ancient religious and familistic traditions were reinforced by the policies of the managers of annual Assembly Balls, held in town each winter at the Bellevue; divorced members of even the best Rittenhouse Square, Main Line, or Chestnut Hill families were denied invitations. Perhaps most important of all, communal order and class authority in those pre-World War II days were bolstered by a common moral vocabulary shared by the vast majority of families in the city, whether they lived in Chestnut Hill, Kensington, or South Philadelphia.

Chestnut Hill, like so many other neighborhoods throughout the city, is far less homogeneous today than it was fifty years ago when I was commuting to Penn from Rex and Crefeld. In 1973, for instance, Frank Rizzo, the city's first Italian-Catholic mayor, bought a house at 8919 Crefeld Street, overlooking Wissahickon Park. A few years later, Bill Green, the second Irish-Catholic mayor, bought a house on Chestnut Hill Avenue, not far from Rizzo's, and also right on the Wissahickon. My brother Peter still lives in our old place on Rex Avenue and, on Sunday walks in recent years, we've often passed by Mayor Green's place on our way down to the Wissahickon, and by Joseph Sill Clark's place on Rex Avenue on the way home. Every time I visit Chestnut Hill and take those beautiful, wooded walks, I think about how much the entire city has changed in the last fifty years—for better and for worse.

Every civilized society in history has been faced with the twin problems of creating and preserving communal order on the one hand and answering legitimate demands for social justice on the other. As the social forces for order, hierarchy, and authority tend to be antithetical to those for equality and social justice, all societies are actually only relatively orderly and always unjust. Thus when I compare Philadelphia fifty years ago with today, I am bound to conclude that, while social justice has definitely improved, social order and communal authority have just as definitely declined. In 1938 a WASP business class dominated the city, while members of ethnic and racial minorities were more or less second-class and powerless citizens. Today, nobody—no social group or class—dominates the city. As all values are now equal, no values have any real authority. Thus social conflict and disorder reign. Between the two world wars, for instance, the WASP establishment under the leadership of Eli K. Price built most of the beautiful Benjamin Franklin Parkway entrance to the city, including many monumental buildings such as the Museum of Art and the Free Library. Today, a much richer city with a vastly larger municipal budget is almost unable to make decisions, such as the allotment of proper funds to staff either the library or museum. At Penn in 1938, no students questioned the authority of the Gates administration, while today the Hackney administration, hardly possessed of much authority, is forced to spend most of its energies manipulating and pacifying conflicts between sexual, racial, and ethnic minorities. It often seems as if education has taken a second place to battles over social justice.

When I wrote *Philadelphia Gentlemen* in the 1950s, I charted the social and economic power of the city's WASP elite from its founding to 1940. All through that time, a highly cohesive group of upper-class families dominated the city. But in the nearly fifty years since then, our city and nation have undergone a social revolution. Today, Chestnut Hill is no longer entirely WASP, and WASPs no longer control the city. In a real sense, no one does—and that's the problem.

When I was commuting to Penn from Chestnut Hill in 1938, my neighbors included many of the most powerful and affluent men in the city, who were served by a WASP-dominated Republican party that had been in power continuously since the 1880s. The most respected and influential Philadelphian of the day was Thomas Sovereign Gates, who lived on an estate bought from Senator Clark's father. Gates had been a senior partner at Drexel, Morgan and Company when he took over the presidency of Penn (at no salary) soon after the 1929 crash. While he remained the most influential man in town, his successor as senior Drexel partner was another Chestnut Hill resident, Edward Hopkinson, Jr. The Hopkinsons had been leaders since colonial days: Edward's great-great-great-grandfather, Thomas Hopkinson, was a founder of the American Philosophical Society, and his great-great-grandfather, Francis Hopkinson, signed the Declaration of Independence.

Two other powerful bankers lived down in St. Martins: E. Walter Clark (Joe Clark's uncle) was the senior partner of E.W. Clark & Company, investment bankers since 1837, and Joseph Wayne, Jr., a self-made man of great charm, was president of the Philadelphia National Bank, the largest in the city at that time. His salary of over $100,000 a year was rare for the day. In addition to the Chestnut Hill bankers, who, of course, were at the very center of economic power in the city, our neighborhood also included a host of leaders of industrial firms such as Charles E. Brinley, president of the American Pulley Company; John Bromley, head of the family textile firm founded by his grandfather, John Bromley, in 1845; Mahlon Kline, president of Smith, Kline and French Laboratories; and Frederick Rosengarten, descendant of George D. Rosengarten, who founded one of the city's leading chemical firms in 1822.

As might be expected, members of my generation grew up taking power for granted and concentrated on enjoying their privileges. Even though the city and the nation were in the midst of a severe depression, most of them were hardly concerned with questions of social justice. Instead, they were largely preoccupied with private morality and following the code of the Christian gentleman:

- Always play the game according to the rules.
- Never cheat or question umpires' decisions, and always call a questionable shot of one's tennis opponent good.

- Respect the authority of one's parents, elders, and teachers.
- Expect honesty and loyalty among gentlemen.

We were also expected to maintain an honorable and protective attitude toward young ladies, who were definitely different from us—we had to go to college and law or medical school, while most of them did not even go to college. In the interest of class cohesion and continuity through strict marital endogamy, young ladies, after attending various fashionable day and boarding schools, spent their first years after graduation "coming out" or being introduced to the "society" of their family's friends and their children, and we college boys spent four or five years attending debutante parties—during Christmas vacations at all-night balls at the Bellevue, and in June and September at smaller dinners and dances at various suburban clubs and private estates along the Main Line and in Chestnut Hill.

In those Depression days before the tyranny of SAT scores, virtually all one's friends—90 percent—went to either Harvard, Yale, or Princeton; a solid minority of us, impecunious commuters and the sons of loyal Penn families, went to "The University"; a scattered few went north to Williams or Trinity, or south to the universities of North Carolina at Chapel Hill or Virginia at Charlottesville.

In so many ways, we young Chestnut Hillers were as isolated from the rest of the city as ghetto Jews. (And, for that matter, so were Frank Rizzo and his friends, who were growing up at the same time in South Philadelphia. As he once put it: "We considered everything north of Snyder Avenue a trip out of town.")

The Second World War and the GI Bill that followed it were major social forces in homogenizing American society in the direction of more social justice by liberating great pools of talent from the isolation of countless class and ethnic ghettos. As an Italian-American boy who landed on the beach at Anzio put it: "I soon learned over here that I was an American and not an Italian-American."

Soon after Pearl Harbor, I joined the naval air corps. Twenty-twenty vision knew no boundaries of class or creed: I went through primary flight training down at the Navy Yard. At Corpus Christi,

Texas, where I earned my wings, my best buddies were a group of "Flying Hawkeyes" from the University of Iowa and a truck driver from Minneapolis; when a bomb hit the engine room of our light cruiser in the South Pacific, the bravest officer was a Jew from Jersey City. Tragically, the Second World War marked the last time in my generation when Americans of all classes pulled together.

When the war ended, I took advantage of the GI Bill and enrolled in the graduate sociology program at Columbia. After completing the coursework for the Ph.D., I came back to Penn as an instructor in sociology at $2,400 a year, in the fall of 1947, just in time to witness the greatest reform movement in Philadelphia history.

The death of Thomas Gates in 1948 symbolized the beginning of the end of the established authority of the WASP and Republican class in Philadelphia. Many liberal and civic-minded younger members of Gates's class, however, came back from the war and supported the political reform movement led by Joe Clark and Dick Dilworth, prewar socialite lawyers who became friends on the beaches of Southampton, Long Island. Birthright Republicans, they both became Democrats and later decided to go into politics seriously while serving overseas during the war. While Dilworth was defeated in his run for mayor in 1947, Clark won the office in 1951. The Republican machine was replaced by a new Democratic one led by William Green, Sr., longtime boss of the Thirty-third Ward in Kensington.

The spirit of reform was kept alive by the members of the local chapter of the Americans for Democratic Action, which was founded in 1947 in the home of John Frederick Lewis, at 1916 Spruce Street, where members of his family had lived since 1856. The leaders of ADA were largely socialites from Chestnut Hill and wealthy, old-stock German Jews from Mount Airy and the Jenkintown-Elkins Park area. Of the thirteen chairmen (ten men and three women) who served between 1947 and 1968, for instance, seven were listed in the Social Register (one chose not to be, even though his father was); one of the women to be elected chairman was Emily Sunstein, sister-in-law of Jane Freedman, a founder of ADA and a member of the German-Jewish Gerstley/

Sunstein clan, whose family brokerage firm eventually merged with Drexel. Among the patrician chairmen of ADA were Walter Phillips, the unsung hero of the whole reform movement and a resident of Chestnut Hill after the war; L.M.C. Smith, whose wife was the granddaughter of Henry Howard Houston, who once owned and developed the St. Martin's part of Chestnut Hill; and finally Henry W. Sawyer III, a birthright Chestnut Hiller, who has been concerned with social justice and civil rights for minorities since his adolescent days.

When a straw vote was taken at Chestnut Hill Academy in 1936, for instance, Henry and one other student were the only boys in the school to vote for Franklin Roosevelt. After the war, his reform career included serving on City Council (1956–59), presidency of the local chapter of the American Civil Liberties Union, participation in the march from Selma to Montgomery, Alabama, service as a civil liberties lawyer in Mississippi, and so forth. Not a bad record for a Penn Law grad and playboy whom I still vividly remember—red hair, white tie and tails—dancing and drinking till the wee hours in the morning at one of the Bellevue ballrooms. He hasn't done too badly as leading litigator and partner in the patrician law firm of Drinker, Biddle and Reath, where he is the top man on the letterhead as I write these lines.

Finally, I think it is important to note that Sawyer has only recently joined the Philadelphia Club, where such paragons of class authority in the city as Edward Hopkinson, Jr., and Thomas Gates had lunched for many generations; and, on principle, he joined only after the membership had been broadened to include blacks and members of white ethnic minorities (men of accomplishment and natural manners, of course). Such clubs as the Philadelphia and the Union League, which have always included only WASP males of Republican sentiments, have been at the center of the controversies over equality and social justice in recent years.

Joseph Sill Clark, with the arrogant integrity born of social and economic privilege, coldly decided to do what he considered right while in office, regardless of the political consequences. He declined to run for reelection in 1955, even though he was probably the most popular mayor in our history by the end of his term. Richardson Dilworth succeeded him, soundly defeating Thacher Longstreth, a handsome and youthful 6'6" Chestnut Hiller who had grown up on the Main Line and been a BMOC and football star at Princeton before the war. Dilworth was reelected in 1959 and then resigned to run for the governorship in 1962. City Council President James Tate took over, thus becoming the first Irish-Catholic mayor in the city's history (Irish-Catholic mayors had been elected in New York and Boston in the 1880s).

Though Tate started out quoting from the Clark and Dilworth lexicon and retained most of Dilworth's appointees, he eventually turned against the reform movement. An important factor in turning Tate away from reform was the fact that the obsession with social justice among the reformers had, in many subtle ways, atomized the local neighborhoods and the natural societal forces for order and authority. Forced busing was an excellent example of the rational quest for social justice conflicting with the traditional forces for social cohesion. This inevitable conflict was nicely revealed in the 1967 mayoral race between Tate and Arlen Specter (Tate won by a mere 11,000 votes). Specter, now a resident of Mount Airy, was a liberal-Democrat-turned-Republican who had beaten the Democratic district attorney in the election of 1965; Specter had the support of independents, the ADA, and those Jews who admired him as one of the first Jews to seek citywide elective office. As the mayoral race of 1967 approached, Tate saw that law and order was going to be a major issue, so he appointed Frank Rizzo police commissioner. In the summer before the election, Rizzo's police arrested twenty-two demonstrators in front of the Cathedral of Saints Peter and Paul and received the Merit Award of the Chestnut Street Association for his "dedication to the preservation of law and order." For some reason, Specter had underestimated the importance of the law and order issue, especially when he sought and obtained the support of the ADA (all too many white liberals in those days, following the immature slogans of their children and the more radical black leaders, saw police as pigs). Tate won heavily in the black wards as well as among white, blue-collar voters; Specter won the independents as well as both Democrats and Republicans in Chestnut Hill.

The election almost ended the reform movement in Philadelphia. Tate had allowed it to have one last gasp, however, when he appointed Dick Dilworth as president of the School Board in 1965, and reappointed several patrician allies (the ivy mafia) such as Mrs. Albert M. Greenfield, of Chestnut Hill. Surely Dilworth was the most wondrous Philadelphia Gentleman of the century.

My own and Henry Sawyer's generation of Chestnut Hillers was the last to grow up in a privileged class atmosphere. Today our class is gone, and elite status is now measured by money and success instead of lineage. The Gates and Hopkinson generation exerted its class authority over the whole city, while the Clark, Phillips, and Sawyer generation, as we have seen, played a major role in postwar political reform. Where are the members of the third generation, and what are they contributing to the leadership of the city? In the first place, many children of the old families have simply left thc city; while Edward Hopkinson was the end of a long family fine of birthright Philadelphia leaders, his sixteen grandchildren have gone with the wind. None are now living in Chestnut Hill; three live on the Main Line, three in France, three in North Carolina, two in New York City, and one each in Massachusetts, New Hampshire, Michigan, California, and Colorado. This geographical atomization of an ancient family is more or less typical of our children's generation, which came of age in the 1960s.

And their youths had already been dispersed, in a variety of ways. The local private schools, for instance, became more heterogeneous and cosmopolitan, enrolling children from other neighborhoods and from a wide variety of racial and ethnic groups; tolerance was in vogue and overt anti-Semitism taboo. Education in terms of grades and SAT scores gradually overshadowed the traditional moral and mannerly functions of making little ladies and gentlemen; and of course both boys and girls were expected to go to college—and they went to "unheard-of" institutions all over the nation, as such heretofore upper-class institutions as Harvard, Yale, and Princeton became SAT meritocracies. At any rate, the central values of post-1960 Chestnut Hill were increasingly egalitarian, competitive, and extremely atomizing. In the process, parental and religious authority declined at an unusual rate; one's children met their mates (whom they sometimes married) on the campuses of the nation rather than at local ballrooms or cricket clubs. The deans of admissions replaced parents as mate selectors. Meanwhile the Episcopal church had broken away from ancient traditions in its eagerness to assimilate almost every liberal and secular fad of our morally relativistic age into its rituals and theologies. And Assembly Balls have welcomed divorcees since the 1960s.

While we grew up in an isolated and privileged golden ghetto, our children came of age in an even more affluent global village, unprotected by any parental, class, or religious authority. Thus the antiauthoritarian climate of the 1960s produced the lonely present generation of WASP Chestnut Hillers who now watch the power-hungry members of other minority groups competing for political control of the city.

If Dilworth was the last WASP to serve as mayor of Philadelphia, Thacher Longstreth was the last WASP to run for the office, which he did in 1971 against Frank Rizzo. It is enough to say here that Thacher was completely annoyed when the press kept referring to him as "the effete, liberal Chestnut Hill blue blood." The charge was especially ironic, since, as he put it, "*When there was a war, one of us went and the other didn't. I went.*"

The "effete blue bloods" of my generation in Chestnut Hill are now dead or retired. Thacher still hangs on in City Council. Though officially retired from Penn, I am still doing my best to write and think about our age. As I reflect on the lives of such Little Caesars from South Philadelphia as Buddy Cianfrani, Ozzie Myers, and Leland Beloff, all of whom have broken the law in one way or another, or on George Schwartz, perhaps the best president of City Council in modern times, who became an Abscam victim, I have come to one vital conclusion: In our post-1960s obsession with social justice among class, ethnic, and racial (as well as gender) categories, we have witnessed a steady decline in personal morality. Today, it is far worse to be accused of being anti-Semitic, anti-black, sexist, or elitist than to be known as a consummate liar or adulterer. The J-word and the B-word are now more taboo than the F-word, which is now firmly ensconced in liberal living rooms. But, after all, ideological purity has always replaced personal morality in revolutionary ages; perhaps personal morality depends on the existence of a certain degree of social order.

This consideration of morality leads me to the Leland Beloff/ Willard Rouse extortion affair. I think it makes a dramatic comment on the clashing values of South Philadelphia and Chestnut Hill in our age of moral relativity. The important thing about the affair here is that Rouse was horrified and a bit frightened, as he put it at the time, by Beloff's million-dollar bribe, and he immediately reported it to the FBI. For Bill Rouse was cut from the same WASP cloth as those effete Chestnut Hill reformers. Born to considerable wealth and privilege in a family of doers, he was educated at Gilman, Baltimore's most exclusive day school. After graduation from Gilman, he went on to the University of Virginia. There he joined a socially select fraternity, St. Elmo Hall, majored in English, read a lot of literature and developed a taste for Jack Daniels. He could have joined his father and his famous uncle James in the family firm but instead went off to Dallas to seek his fortune on his own. Very much in the tradition of Benjamin Franklin, this auslander WASP is now the leading businessman and all-around civic leader in our city.

The old Chestnut Hill WASP surely seems to have lost his sting. But history never moves in one direction and, as they say, the pendulum may swing back toward some sort of social order. Although there may be all too many money-mad young WASPs and other elite residents of Chestnut Hill today, perhaps some of their children will one day dedicate themselves to revitalizing City Hall in the style of Walter Phillips and Joe Clark.

For their city's sake, let's hope they do.

4

The American Aristocrat and Other-Direction

The ideal-typical constructs of tradition-, inner-, and other-direction are now firmly fixed both in the jargon of social science and in the minds of most modern social critics. They not only provided a useful theoretical point of departure for Riesman's brilliant analysis of American social character; they have also been extremely useful in stimulating other studies of contemporary trends toward conformity in America, such as, for instance, *The Organization Man*, by William H. Whyte, Jr. While Riesman rightly focused his attention, in *The Lonely Crowd*, on middle-class social character, this paper will attempt to apply his theoretical constructs in an analysis of American upper-class social character, especially as it has been changing in central tendency since the Second World War.

According to Riesman, it is "the upper socioeconomic levels in the western democracies today, *except for the aristocracy*, which are most strongly permeated by other-direction."[1] In a recently published monograph, this author tried to show how America had produced a business aristocracy that maintained a continuous tradition of leadership and power, especially in the older cities along the eastern seaboard, from colonial times to the Second World War.[2] As Riesman suggests above, it was apparent that the social character of this prewar aristocracy, especially in Philadelphia, was a blend of tradition- and *inner*-direction.[3] Here it will be our purpose to show, on the other hand, that the postwar generation of "Proper" Philadelphians, along with their peers in Boston,

New York, or San Francisco, may be increasingly tending toward a *new* social character marked by tradition—and *other*-direction. But while the pressures for a new type of conformity are very definitely a part of their postwar social situation, the members of the established upper class are still far more resistant to other-direction than the more mobile members of the new American leadership.

Whereas the members of a hereditary upper class—most of whom have parents, or ancestors, of greater stature than themselves—stand for stability and tradition, middle-class membership means mobility and change. Thus tradition-direction is always the basis of upper-class social character. Moreover in a stable, preindustrial society, both the hereditary aristocracy *and* the people are characterized by tradition-direction. But with the rise of an urban-industrial civilization, middle-class values will eventually permeate the whole social structure. While the style of life of the "old" middle class produced an inner-directed social character, other-direction is a product of the rise of the "new" middle class to a dominant position in modern society. When the entrepreneur and the old middle class produced the typical mobile men, the members of the upper class, in self-defense as it were, took on many of the characteristics of inner-direction. The Protestant business aristocrat in America, and even in England, was always quite different from his counterpart in preindustrial and Catholic Spain. In our era, when the "new" middle class of white-collar employees, led by managers and bureaucrats rather than entrepreneurs, becomes the predominant mobile type, other-direction not only becomes the middle-class mode, it also permeates both the upper and lower classes. The gentlemen of inherited means and traditions who dealt with such new men as Dreiser's Frank Cowperwood were of a very different breed from their descendants who are now dealing with new men of the style of Marquand's Willis Wade. While buccaneering Frank Cowperwood was ostensibly ostracized by Proper Philadelphians because of his irregular private life, sincere Willis Wade had no time for a private life as he fought his way up in a large corporation world. Thus in a country such as America where middle-class values dominate the whole society, one would expect the social character of the upper class to change along with the changing modes of mobility. Of equal importance, however, is the fact that, beginning in the 1930s and accelerated since the Second World War, there has been a gradual but fundamental change in the ethnic composition of America's mobile middle class.

The Rise and Fall of Anglo-Saxon-Protestant Rule in America

Contrary to the melting-pot ideologies, American leadership has been dominated by an Anglo-Saxon-Protestant minority for most of its history. Between the close of the Civil War and the onset of the Great Depression, business gentlemen of Anglo-Saxon descent and Protestant affiliations became the most powerful members of the American community; and they and their children were rapidly assimilated into an already established upper class, composed of the descendants of colonial and pre-Civil War merchants, statesmen and soldiers. In the course of the twentieth century the new upper-class suburbs with their fashionable Episcopalian churches, exclusive country clubs, and country day schools, as well as New England boarding schools and Ivy League universities, all served the purpose of assimilating the sons of the newly rich and powerful into this traditional upper-class way of life. The polished graduates of Groton and Harvard went easily into the best law firms and banks, and eventually on to the Supreme Court, the Senate, the cabinet, or to some choice ambassadorial post abroad; the best medical schools were almost hereditary preserves for these sons of the fortunate; and for those with a less professional turn of mind, there was always the securely held family firm, waiting for heirs to move into top management. And above all, these exclusive institutions were run and supported by families with a nationally recognized monopoly of power and castelike security of social position.

In many ways, of course, this castelike situation in America depended on, and was fostered by, the flood of immigrants, first from Ireland and then later from southern and eastern Europe, who came to these shores each year, primarily to fill the lower socioeconomic positions in our steadily expanding economy. At first these immigrants, who, after all, were used to an inferior and fixed status in Europe, were only too glad to defer to their "betters" here in democratic America. Even though the more ambitious members of these various hyphenated-American groups eventually obtained power and wealth as leaders of our urban political machines, more often than not these machines were subservient locally to the respectable business interests and were represented on the national scene by such men of older stock as Mark Hanna, Nelson Aldrich, or Boies Penrose. "Ed Flynn might boss the Bronx," writes Andrew Hacker, "but he would defer to Franklin D. Roosevelt (of Harvard); Carmine De Sapio rides behind Averell Harriman (of Yale); and Jake Arvey cleared the way for Adlai Stevenson (of Princeton)."[4] Protected by this nationally recognized caste position and assuming a monopoly of ultimate power through a kind of natural rights tradition, it is no wonder that America's business aristocrats of the old regime manifested a strong tradition- and inner-directed social character. In the first quarter of the twentieth century, anti-Semitism and anti-Irish Catholicism were taken for granted among American aristocrats, while any form of ethnic "tolerance"—so characteristic, at least on the surface and in public, of our more other-directed age—was unheard of."[5] After all, it was America's "best people" who strongly supported the tragic decision in the Sacco-Vanzetti trial; upper-class anti-Semitism was perhaps more blatantly displayed in the five decades after 1880 than at any other time in our history; and even more indicative of these last days of Anglo-Saxon-Protestant assumed superiority were the tracts of Madison Grant, himself a product of one of old New York's most patrician families and of the most exclusive clubs in the city.[6] But perhaps the very success of Grant's books during the 1920s was a warning of an era's end and the shape of things to come.

The assumed superiority of this older business aristocracy in America has been seriously challenged, if not defeated, by the revolutionary changes in our society brought on by the depression, the war, and especially the postwar boom. In this connection, the two most important developments have been (1) the unprecedented expansion of our economy since the war and (2) the consequent need for rapidly assimilating new groups, including large numbers of hyphenated-Americans, into the central stream of our national life and *leadership*. We are now witnessing, as never before, the ethnic democratization of plutocracy in America. As a sign of the times, Grace Kelly, of Philadelphia's most eminent Irish-Catholic clan, was not only Hollywood's leading postwar patrician heroine but also went on to marry royalty in the traditional American pattern set by the Vanderbilts and Astors, of the old-stock plutocracy.

This new democratization of plutocracy has created a social situation where the old deference to caste leadership is being replaced by competing ethnic and functional veto groups, to borrow from Riesman's vocabulary. This is so because the new men of power, due to their great number, their interests and values, or their ethnicity, are *not* being assimilated into any traditional upper-class way of life and social organization. With no established tradition of their own, and no traditional group to break into, their social position is probably more slippery than that of any previous group of leaders in our history. In place of the family traditions and the assumptions of Anglo-Saxon superiority which legitimized the power of the old regime, these new men and women (one hesitates to call them families) have had to resort to public relations, manipulation of mass media, and all sorts of social engineering to sell the American public on their new right to rule. The press agent has replaced the genealogist, and the white-collar millions who dream of a place in the sun now prefer the racy style of the gossip columnist to the dreary and dwindling reports of the society editors.

But it is one of the tragic ironies of modern life and leadership that these skillful manipulators of others may themselves have become the most manipulated segment of the population. It is no accident that the hidden persuaders, who have so little respect for the privacy or dignity of the average citizen, are living in an exurban nightmare of insecurity and sophisticated conformity. While Riesman has a charming way (perhaps an other-directed way?) of qualifying and minimizing the unpleasant implications of many of his insights, surely anyone who takes seriously such blunter books as *The Hidden Persuaders, The Organization Man*, or *The Exurbanites* must be impressed and depressed by the other-directed conformity that characterizes the lives of the most talented and ambitious members of America's postwar generation.

Finally, of course, this atomization of American leadership has affected the security of the old upper class, which is now being forced to share its power with others. Both the late Senator McCarthy's rise to power and Madison Avenue's skillful handling of a Republican campaign that focused its attack on the supposed treason of prominent members of the opposition were symptoms of this new power struggle. The tragic tale of Alger Hiss and the well-publicized dismissal of a number of Ivy League diplomats on the grounds of degeneracy were sold as solemn warnings to the American people that proper, Anglo-Saxon Protestants no longer had an exclusive claim on 100 percent Americanism. In the course of this power struggle, Dean Acheson was politically crucified, among other reasons, for his rather inner-directed and hardly public-relations minded definition of what friendship means; and Secretary Stevens, a fellow Yaleman of patrician New England stock, was humiliated before the American public on our most publicized postwar television investigation. But the panic politics of the McCarthy era were only symptoms of much more basic social trends.

The Decline of Family Capitalism

Family power in America has been traditionally based on family capitalism. Yet one of the most important consequences of the postwar economic boom has been the rapid absorption of the family firm by the large corporation. And the decline of family power in America has been an important factor in the growth of other-direction in our managerial society.

The old business aristocracy in America was of course based on families of inherited wealth. And this wealth was produced and preserved by a succession of entrepreneurial founders of family firms. While the modern manager tends to be but a shadow of the established corporation's prestige and power, the old family firm and the upper class upon which it was based to a great extent were the lengthened shadows of these family founders. These family firms were not only a source of wealth and income, they were also the basis of family pride and tradition as well as an important source of parental discipline. Family capitalism fostered paternalism in the home as well as in the factory. Sons and grandsons grew up on the legends of their ancestors' accomplishments; at an early age they were taken to the plant or office, where they often knew many of the employees and sometimes their families; and they were disciplined and inspired by their responsibility as sons and heirs. As an ideal at least, continuity of family ownership created a sense of *noblesse oblige* among the rich and powerful that was not unlike that which went with landed wealth in an earlier era. In vivid contrast to this ideal, which was of course not always lived up to, absentee corporate ownership demands no sense of personal involvement or continuity of responsibility; the dividend playboys who can be found gambling in oil wells around the "brunch" table at El Morocco or the Stork every afternoon are heirs to the modern atomization of ownership.

The current tax structure is of course an important factor in the accelerated postwar decline in family capitalism. The family firm is often sold, not because of inefficiency or lack of competitive success, but rather because inheritance taxes have reached a point where an owner cannot afford to pass on his partnership or firm to his heirs intact; it is far more expedient to sell out to the large corporation in return for stock, which can be divided among the heirs. Although often overlooked, the effect of inheritance taxes in inhibiting the passing on of family enterprises is far more damaging to the heirs psychologically, and to the family sociologically, than is its intended function of limiting large inheritances of more liquid corporate wealth. Whereas, for example, the patriarchal continuity of the Du Pont clan has flourished along with their control of the family enterprise, the publicity-seeking, café society crowd draws many of its most prominent members—such as the divorcing John Jacob Astor III (three wives), Cornelius Vanderbilt, Jr. (five wives), Tommy Manville (nine wives), or the Topping brothers (ten wives between them)—from the ranks of the dividend heirs with no locus of responsibility. In this connection it was interesting to watch the individual members' reactions to the recent sale of one of Philadelphia's oldest and best-known family firms to a Cash McCall type of modern buccaneer. The family patriarch was dead, while the members of the present generation were clamoring for more dividends. Since the sale of the firm, the heirs, now scattered around this country and Europe, with little sense of community roots, are far better off financially, but the family's influence on the business and cultural life of the city is now reduced to a minimum. At any rate, just as the tradition- and inner-direction and family conformity so characteristic of the old upper class in America was fostered by family capitalism, so the new peer, and publicity-dependent, conformity thrives in a social structure that undermines the power of parents and encourages other-directed social situations.

If the inheritance tax atomizes established family power, the income tax makes it far more difficult for the new men of power and ambition to establish new families. While the bank account and community roots create family strength and continuity, corporate loyalty and the expense account life may have quite the opposite effect. The new manager virtually marries the corporation, which, in return, provides him with a generous expense-account life, especially when away from home; retirement benefits replace private savings, make it increasingly hard for him to resign, and encourage an other-directed conformity in his slow struggle to the top. In response to the persistent corporate co-option of the private sectors of modern life, it is not surprising that, since the war, countless numbers of Proper Philadelphians have resigned from promising positions in nationally famous firms. At least one member of an old Proper Philadelphia clan was able to resist, for a time, this modern trend. Possessed of ambition, ability, and drive, this young man was doing very well in the local office of a national corporation. Several years ago, he was moved to New York. Rather than move his family from his beloved Main Line, he arose each morning at five-thirty, took the Paoli Local to the city, where he caught the New York express and arrived promptly at his desk before nine o'clock. But this was not enough for his boss, who felt that he should be available in New York after business hours in order to entertain customers. He refused to move, however, even after several threats from the front office.

About a year later, he was not only still with the firm but had been transferred back to Philadelphia with a raise in salary and a far more responsible position. In relating the story of his corporate life to the writer, he was careful to stress that his peers in the New York office were horrified at what they called his arrogant behavior; he had not, of course, let it be known that he would never have been able to do what he did (he had three children) had he not had ample private means. It is indicative that, since his recent divorce, this ambitious Proper Philadelphian has been working for the same firm out in the West. He is now willing and anxious to travel anywhere they so desire, which of course makes him a far more valuable member of the corporate team.

Corporate Contacts, Family Friends, and Other-Direction

One of the important developments making for an increase in other-direction is of course the fact that modern managers of large corporations, as well as men of affairs in general, have less and less private social life because they spend so many of their leisure hours with contacts within the bureaucratic hierarchy, if not with customers. Inevitably one begins to treat everyone as a customer who is always right and wants to be a friend. This new type of social life, which so often confuses contacts with friends, is reflected in the living language. In the recent past, for example, the inner-directed business gentleman, at least in Philadelphia, carefully structured his human relations in graded levels of intimacy. Thus he addressed his many business contacts in a formal way (Mr. Smith); at a more intimate level of association, business contacts of long standing as well as most of his office colleagues were addressed by their surnames only (Smith); finally given names (Joe) were reserved for his closest associates in the firm, and friends he had known for years, if not since childhood. At the same time, he reserved such terms as "dear" and "darling" for a rather intimate circle of relatives and friends of the opposite sex. Today, when public relations have made private relations old hat, everyone is "Joe" and almost anyone may be "darling." As the gemeinschaft barriers of class, community, and family have largely broken down, even the most patrician businessman or politician must conform to this new pattern of pseudo-gemeinschaft. Although he realizes that resistance to the trend is both ridiculous and reactionary, one can understand his sardonic smile when a new business contact immediately addresses him by his first name when his friends and family have always used his middle name (often an abbreviation of a famous ancestor's surname).

But this new pseudo-gemeinschaft lends warmth to the human relations of a lonely crowd of leaders whose social position is no longer anchored in family, class, or community but is solely due to their status in the corporate hierarchy. Philadelphia, however, sometimes provides a colder climate for new men, especially in those firms where the top executive positions are in the hands of members of the established upper class, who still maintain family and class traditions in their private social life if not in the office downtown. An extremely talented executive from a more progressive city in the Middle West, for example, was brought into Philadelphia recently as president of one of these established firms. He was immediately elected to membership in an elite country club where his new associates entertained customers. But he was surprised that, after about two years as president of this national corporation, he had not yet been asked to join the upper-class golf club to which most of his closest associates in the firm belonged. He had of course assumed that, as was the case with the western branch of the firm, he would automatically take his place in the social group that his high position in the firm warranted.

This unfortunate conflict between upper-class traditions and the new corporate mores illustrates several important things about the new leadership structure in America, and even in Philadelphia. In the first place, this old Philadelphia firm, like many others of its kind in the city since the war, desperately needed new talent at the top. And it is significant that the more progressive Proper Philadelphia members of the firm (the younger rather than the older generation) were extremely upset by the incident and did all in their power to pressure their club's admission committee into accepting their new president.[7] A generation ago, so argued the more traditional and inner-directed older men of the present management, this situation would not have arisen (even if an outsider had been given the presidency, which would have been unlikely).

In our rapidly expanding economy, where new men are needed more than ever before, this incident also serves to emphasize the important function of the new corporate co-option of the social life of its executives. Expense accounts, company-owned country clubs, hunting lodges, and dude ranches are excellent and rapid devices for assimilating new men of talent into the leisure-time aspects of their new station in life. At first, at least, most of these new men do not feel that their private life has been infringed upon by the corporation because they probably have had very little, at least of the kind they are being introduced to. A Proper Philadelphian, for example, recently dined at the home of a talented new executive of the "X" Company, one of the more progressive firms in the city (most of its top executives belong to the same country club, all the officers in which are also officers of the "X" Company). After dinner, he strolled into his host's den and pulled out a blue, leather-bound volume from the small bookshelf. Entitled *Ranching It: 1952*, the little volume contained a snapshot record of a brief vacation his hosts, along with five other executives and their wives from the "X" Company, had spent at a company-sponsored hideaway in the West. Characteristically enough, our Proper Philadelphian, whose family had gone to the same summer resort in Maine for two generations, was surprised that his host not only enjoyed spending his vacation with business contacts but was very proud of this little volume.

Caveat

The postwar economic boom in America has accelerated the decline of the old-family capitalism and increased the importance of the large corporation as well as the other-directed conformity of the new managerial society. At the same time, we have tried to show how the traditional upper-class social organization has been somewhat of a defense against this other-directed trend. It would be entirely misleading, however, to create the impression that the members of the old upper class have in the recent past, or will in the future, remain aloof from these trends. As a matter of fact, they are increasingly taking part and only feel more frustrated because they know what they have to lose in the way of their traditional freedoms.

Moreover, while many of the old established family firms have now been absorbed by large corporations, a host of new and exceedingly prosperous enterprises have grown up during and since the war; these are almost invariably run by rugged new men of the old entrepreneurial mold. But whereas the man of patrician background is most welcome to a modern management that lays such stress on polished human relations in both office and plant, it is the somewhat rougher diamond, often of minority ethnic origins, who is forced to build his own enterprise as the only available way to wealth and power. After a decade of teaching at the Wharton School of Finance and Commerce, for example, one has the definite impression that the *undergraduate* student body has an unusually high proportion of sons of individual entrepreneurs. These boys are not wasting time on "culture" but are preparing to take over from dad (many of the more intellectual among them bemoan the fact that their fathers simply will not pay for the trappings of "culture"). At the Wharton graduate level, on the other hand, polished alumni of the best liberal arts colleges are preparing themselves, by and large, for careers in well-established corporations. Many informal polls in the classroom also reveal that the *undergraduates* at Wharton include a large proportion of second- and third-generation Americans.

Although impossible to document in a brief paper such as this, there is good reason to believe that the individual enterprisers who have produced real wealth in Philadelphia since the war—appliance and automobile dealers, contractors and construction engineers, food-fair magnates, restaurateurs, and so forth, all of whom have benefited from the rising standard of living in our consumer economy—have come predominantly from second- and third-generation American backgrounds. A wartime friend of the newer immigrant stock, for instance, made a small fortune right after the war in secondhand automobiles, sold out at the peak of the boom, and is now on the way to real wealth as a successful manufacturer of storm sash and metal windows, with a lucrative sideline investment in a string of "motels" along a prominent highway leading out of the city.[8] And he has a crowd of affluent friends among the Italian and Irish-American nabobs of South Philadelphia. In describing the elaborate Catholic wedding-party of one of them, to which, as he put it, no one worth less than a million got an invite," this former bombardier for democracy opened up to the writer a prosperous world that we sociologists have not begun to explore systematically. And these inner-directed buccaneers are very different from the other-directed, corporate managers, public relations experts, and Madison Avenue manipulators who are, after all, rapidly rising in somewhat more Brooks-Brothers-suited channels to power.

At the same time, few if any members of the upper class in Philadelphia have started and succeeded in building up their own firms since the war. It is socially acceptable to become a junior executive at General Motors but hardly proper to run the local Buick agency. Even in the law, traditionally the way to power in America, the well-connected young men are usually found in the old established firms. Again, it is rather the new ethnic groups that are contributing the legal entrepreneurs of ability and independent imagination. In 1957, for instance, one of the writer's keenest former students founded his own law partnership. Irish Catholic in background, he remarked while talking over his plans and dreams with his old teacher: "You know that not a single white-Protestant friend (deep in local Democratic politics, this language is second nature) has started a new law firm in the city since the war."

One final point should be made concerning the other-directed leadership that has emerged since the war. The progressive large corporation, with its elaborate devices for acculturating its new executives into the kind of social life proper to their achieved positions in the corporate hierarchy, may *seem* to be far more "democratic" than the community and family-rooted criteria of social position that characterized the way of life of the old upper class. But this new democratic camaraderie cuts two ways: if every new president or vice-president is to be automatically accepted in the company-owned or -sponsored country club life, this very warm and democratic way may have the unanticipated consequence of narrowing the background qualifications for working in the firm in the first place. In other words, in the days when one was not expected to play golf with business contacts, or bring them home to dinner, it made little difference what their backgrounds were so long as they did a good job in the office.[9] But when friends and business contacts are fused, the ground is laid for an even more selective recruitment of management material, on the basis of ethnicity or religion. One often wonders if, in the long run, the new corporate feudalism in America will not eventually prove to be far more socially stultifying than the traditional community, family, and class hierarchies of the past.

The Younger Generation and Other-Direction

The members of the younger generation are always a mystery to their elders, and we shall not attempt to assess the values and attitudes of upper-class youths who are coming to maturity in this postwar era. Nevertheless, there are ascertainable trends in upper-class social organization, especially in the fashionable suburbs, private schools, and colleges, that may be sowing the seeds of other-direction.

In our democracy, ecological stratification has replaced the older, aristocratic barriers of class and family. The fashionable suburb plays such a vital role in modern society primarily because *where* one lives, rather than *who* one is, is a *visible* status referent in an increasingly amorphous social structure. The Main Line, Philadelphia's most publicized elite address today, first became fashionable when the city's leading coal barons, railroad kings, merchant princes, and utility tycoons built houses there around the turn of the century.[10] The tycoons' wives were executive directors of large households staffed with housemaids, chambermaids, parlormaids, waitresses, butlers, cooks, governesses, gardeners, and coachmen. As a result, they were often only indirectly involved with their children and hardly concerned with their social life, which, at the younger ages, usually revolved around the fascinating and congenial life backstairs—in the nursery, in the kitchen, and out in the stable. In this extended-family kind of world, the children's characters were molded largely by the servants who, if anything, overemphasized the patriarchal and class values of their employers. As most of these servants had themselves been reared in the "old country" patriarchal ways, this was inevitable.

This way of life was maintained by many proper Main Line families until the war. As labor was cheap during the depression, even the impecunious genteel usually had a servant or two. With the modern exodus of servants from all but the wealthiest households, however, this world has gone forever. Since the war, most of the old estates have been sold to the Catholic church, been remodeled into modern country clubs, or been subdivided into smaller "estates," more in keeping with a servantless, do-it-yourself age. And even along the prosperous Main Line, these changes have produced a mother-organized and child-centered world, where the smaller household is now served by a host of outside associations, from the diaper service and play school to the country club and summer camp. Before the war, for instance, very few if any upper-class children went to school before the age of six; today all of them go to play school for two or three years (and of course are now far better adjusted to the group). Moreover, as the children grow older, their lives are highly organized in activities outside the home: their personalities are developed by an endless round of dancing, skating, ballet, music, tennis, and golf lessons, and devoted mothers are having nervous breakdowns as they transport Johnny and Joan from one activity to another in the course of each over-steered week.

Modern life along the Main Line has become increasingly organized and competitive because, although it is still an extremely exclusive suburb from the point of view of society as a whole, from the standpoint of old families, it has been democratized to an alarming degree since the war. The members of the new plutocracy, only too glad to pay for this prominent and patrician address, are often avid participants in the social game: there are now five "exclusive" dancing class groups where there used to be one; numerous mutually excluding country club sets are now spread throughout the countryside, and one former Proper Philadelphia mansion has recently been remodeled into the first Jewish country club in the area; and the local social columns report the leisure-time activities of these new families, many of whose names suggest their Irish background.[11] Whereas the Proper Philadelphia clans who built up the old Main Line were servant- and property-protected and could afford to stand aloof from the crowd, today even long-established families are forced by circumstance to be snobbishly selective, especially where their children are concerned. And this new heterogeneous atmosphere, along with the selective and highly organized associational life it fosters, is bound, in the long run, to produce a more other-directed younger generation.

The private schools, always extremely sensitive to social change at the higher levels of society, have of course been flooded with students from both old and newly prosperous homes since the war. Not only have they had to take care of an ever-increasing number of students in Latin, mathematics, and English, they have also had to handle all sorts of extra educational functions that used to be done in the home by parents or servants. Discipline alone has been vastly complicated by the commingling of students from different backgrounds. Several years ago, for example, the school authorities were extremely concerned about the steadily increasing amount of serious juvenile delinquency among teenage children from wealthy and prominent Main Line homes. At an evening class at the University of Pennsylvania that same winter, one of the author's students, a Main Line matron of an inner-directed and intellectual turn of mind, brought the Agnes Irwin School "news" up to the desk after class. Founded by Agnes Irwin, the first dean of Radcliffe College and a well-known Victorian educator, this is Philadelphia's most patrician school for young ladies. At any rate, the school newspaper reported the formation of an association of the leading schools, both public and private, along the Main Line. The purpose of this association was to set up and attempt to enforce a series of rules for parents to follow with their teenage children: when and where they should be allowed to date, when they should be home at night, and the type of chaperonage required at parties. In exercising this kind of authority over modern parents, the private schools have come a long way from the days when, as Riesman put it, the upper-class mother could say to the headmaster: "I don't see why the masters can't get along with Johnny; all the servants do."[12] But in an other-directed age when "Joan's mother allows it, why don't you?" is so often given in to by overworked and distracted mothers, even the most traditional Main Line matron (whose fifteen-year-old daughter can't possibly be prevented from driving forty miles to hear a "name-band" with some new-rich contractor's son in his red Jaguar) must welcome this kind of regimentation by the school authorities. After all, when class lines and values are breaking down, her daughter can ill afford to lose caste with her popular peers.

The New England boarding schools have played an important role in educating the sons of the eastern seaboard aristocracy for several generations. Just as they succeeded in acculturating the sons of the new rich of Anglo-Saxon Protestant stock at the turn of the century, so many of them are now aware of the problems of assimilating the sons of the modern, and often ethnic, plutocracy. Thus, since the war these schools have been changing rapidly. And perhaps St. Paul's School, in Concord, New Hampshire, the favorite Proper Philadelphia school, has changed even more than the rest. Its extremely inner-directed and puritanical traditions, however, remained intact throughout the 1930s.[13] The curriculum was routine and classical, with only the few students who hated Latin majoring in science; there was little if any emphasis on the arts. The masters were often gentlemen of inherited means who found teaching highly rewarding as a way of life rather than as a profession. Their duty was to build character. Intellectual excellence and the rounded personality were secondary, and boys were rarely expelled for scholastic failure. And most of them followed their fathers on to Harvard, Yale, and Princeton.

But it was for its extracurricular programs that St. Paul's was most criticized before the war; they were said to be puritanical, in-breeding, and snobbish. There were, for example, very few athletic contests with other schools. The student body was divided into three clubs, Isthmian, Delphian, and Old Hundred, and all took part in intramural contests. In the fall, everyone, including the more gentle and bookish seniors, was expected to represent his club in football; in the winter everyone played ice hockey; and in the spring, which eventually came after endless, bleak days of New England thaw when the boys had to *amuse themselves* (see below), everyone played baseball, rowed, or ran around the track. While other minor sports were available, they were not encouraged as a major activity. On the whole, four or five years in this rather rigid atmosphere were likely to produce a moralistic, inner-directed, and often unimaginatively snobbish young man. But of course the boys were drawn to begin with from fashionable and conservative homes where the old Republican Protestant values were the norm.

The changes at the school since the war have been far-reaching and progressive. A less puritanical and more permissive atmosphere has been consciously created in order to set a more democratic, tolerant, and possibly other-directed tone to school life. First of all, the curriculum has been broadened and intellectual excellence has been emphasized. Both the sciences and the arts have come into their own. In accord with the times, in fact, science, with excellent new equipment and instruction, has become one of the most popular majors. Music, dramatics, and the plastic arts have assumed a much more prominent place in the whole school community. Honors programs and wide elective choices for the keener students have produced a far more varied intellectual diet. And above all, the postwar faculty appears to be far better trained if not better educated. In place of the traditional gentlemen of inherited means whose primary purpose was to mold character, the new masters are more likely to be specialists in their respective fields, with an increasing number holding advanced degrees. Their social backgrounds are far more diverse, many have graduated from public rather than private schools. As a democratic example to the boys, one of the latest appointments to the faculty happens to be a Negro.[14]

Extracurricular activities are now far more diverse and attractive. To combat the old provincialism and isolation of life at the school, competition with other schools, both public and private, is now being encouraged. Within the school, the boys may now choose between a wide variety of minor sports rather than being forced into playing football or some other major sport each term. There is also a much closer coordination with both private and public schools in the intellectual sphere through increased membership in outside educational associations and participation in interschool programs and contests.[15]

But probably two developments at the school have been most disconcerting to the more traditionally minded parents and alumni. First of all, due to our expanding economy and the consequent increase in the number of newly wealthy and talented families coming to the fore in postwar America, there has been a tremendous pressure both for admission to the school and admission from the school into college. At the same time, both schools like St. Paul's and the prestige universities like Harvard, Yale, and Princeton are definitely attempting to broaden the social base and improve the intellectual standards of their student bodies. One no longer goes to Groton or St. Paul's and then on to Harvard or Yale just because one's father or grandfather did so.

Moreover, to broaden the geographic and social representativeness of the student body, the administrative staff of the school has been enlarged so as to improve its admissions and public relations policies. Among other things, the school sends representatives annually to our major cities, where they meet with specially arranged parent groups. Talks and informal discussions serve to acquaint new families with the advantages of the school and to encourage them to send their sons there. Planned public relations of this sort would have been unheard of during the old regime. Not only are those admitted to the school chosen from a more democratic base; its graduates are also having a much more diverse and democratic college experience. Whereas, for instance, in 1935 all save two or three of the graduating class went on to either Harvard, Yale, or Princeton, approximately the same number of graduates in 1955 went on to some twenty different institutions of higher learning.

As we have stressed before, many of these changes have been forced on a progressive and realistic administration at the school by the profound changes in America's postwar elite structure. Certainly the best forms of tolerance and other-direction must result from this new social situation. But vices lie hidden in all virtues. The overbusy and overorganized life at the school, and the emphasis on personality development and intellectual excellence at the possible expense of character, may not all be to the good. In contrast to Europe, for example, where formal extracurricular activities among students—regular drill and rigid schedules, paid coaches and officials, elaborate and uniform uniforms and equipment, and so forth—are rare, the overorganizing of both school and college life in America is certainly a factor in fostering other-directed conformity. The recently completed indoor athletic building at St. Paul's, costing in the neighborhood of $1 million, is an example of this modern propensity for organized activities. This expensive building now provides efficiently directed activities for boys who previously were forced to spend rainy days and almost the whole New England "thaw" season between February and early April in *amusing themselves*. But perhaps the following anecdote is appropriate here: while talking with an official of the school who was visiting the University of Pennsylvania last spring, the author suggested that the new athletic building was not necessarily a mark of progress. The official replied somewhat as follows: "Many of us at the school might agree with you, but let me tell you a story: two years ago we had two very fine sons of a prosperous, Midwestern industrialist visit the school. We had met the boys the year before and they had excellent records at their local high school. They were just the type we wanted. In the course of looking around the school grounds, however, one of them remarked that we had no indoor athletic facilities. Well, we never got those two boys, as it turned out, because they liked the gym, swimming pool, and baseball cage down at 'X' school. As we had thought we had sold the parents on St. Paul's, we were obviously disappointed. So you can see why those of us who were in favor of the new facilities had a good argument. . . . Anyway the thing is simply built and not too conspicuous, as it is hidden in the woods just above the old baseball field."

Like the boarding schools, the prestige institutions of higher learning are also responding to the postwar democratization of plutocracy. The pressure for admission rises along with the rapid rise in tuition fees. Although the sons and grandsons of alumni are given special consideration, many are being turned down because of increasingly democratic admissions policies, which want intelligent boys from a broad cross-section of American life. The story of the representative from Yale or Princeton who addressed a local alumni group in a large eastern city and ended his talk on the modern pressures for admission by reminding his distinguished audience that two out of three of them would not qualify for admission by today's standards is well known. The sons of disappointed loyal alumni of Harvard, Yale, and Princeton are now getting to know about colleges all over the nation, and even fashionable Foxcroft mothers are having to face the fact that they may lose their dear daughters forever if they can't get into Vassar or Radcliffe and end up instead in the fraternity, courting life at Stanford or California.

This new pattern of college attendance being forced on the eastern seaboard aristocracy will inevitably break down parental power and family continuity, which depends on the maintenance of long-established community roots. Whereas in the 1930s nine out of ten Proper Philadelphia daughters did *not* go to college, and spent their entire postschool year as debutantes in their local community and under parental supervision, today a vast majority of them go to college in various parts of the country where they are on their own in a more or less peer-supervised world. And as Proper Philadelphia sons, before the war, were invariably enrolled at the traditional eastern universities, which were convenient to the debutante functions, class endogamy and family continuity were fostered by a world that has now been modified considerably.

This modern breakdown of class endogamy and parental authority has considerably modified upper-class courting mores. There is reason to believe that the "steady dating" mores in America are partly due to the insecurity fostered by social mobility. Thus the mobile youth substitutes stable emotional ties with his *peers* for the traditional ties with *parents*. Before the war, upper-class youth, by and large, snobbishly looked down on "steady dating" and dismissed it as "middle class." In a parent-supervised and class-protected world, young gentlemen "played the field." On the other hand, it is indicative of the changes in the postwar upper-class world that the present generation invariably follows these same "steady dating" mores that their fathers once looked down upon.

Upper-Class Social Character and Political Leadership

The need for governmental interference in our large corporation economy was first brought home to the American people by the Great Depression and the New Deal; the locus of ultimate power in America moved from Wall Street to Washington, and the days of the indirect control of the reins of government by the all-powerful money-power came to an end. At the same time, Franklin D. Roosevelt and his patrician friends in the Democratic party symbolized the return once more of American aristocrats to positions of direct governmental leadership.

It is perhaps ironic that, just when the assumed superiority of, and traditional deference to, the old-stock aristocracy is being challenged by the postwar democratization of plutocracy, this same aristocracy of overwhelmingly Republican businessmen is now producing great political leaders who, with certain outstanding exceptions, are Democrats, the party in the North of the urban ethnic masses. But America has a long tradition of this kind of leadership: "In a very real sense," writes S.M. Lipset, "the abolitionists and Progressives were American Tory radicals, men of upper-class backgrounds and values, who as Conservatives also helped to democratize the society as part of their struggle against the vulgar *nouveaux riches* businessmen."[16] From Thomas Jefferson, through the two Roosevelts, to Adlai Stevenson, Averell Harriman, and Mennon Williams, the Tory radical in American politics has led the people in their fight for social equality.

But according to Riesman's thesis today and Tocqueville's before him, it is the very triumph of egalitarian values in modern America that has fostered the trend to other-direction. As Riesman writes in *The Lonely Crowd*:

> My general thesis is that the inner-directed character tended and still tends in politics to express himself in the style of the "moralizer," while the other-directed character tends to express himself politically in the style of an "inside-dopester." These styles are also linked with a shift in political mood from "indignation" to "tolerance," and a shift in political decision from dominance by a ruling class to power dispersal among many marginally competing pressure groups.[17]

As everything we have said so far in this paper would suggest, we are in complete agreement with Riesman's thesis relating the rise of other-direction to the decline of class rule in America. On the other hand, it is also our thesis that the modern patrician politician in the Democratic party, to a far greater extent than most members of the class from which they came and now depart in political persuasion, are, by and large, *inner-directed moralizers* with, at the same time, a great respect and sympathy for the so-called tolerance that Riesman finds characteristic of the political public in our other-directed age. It is no accident that the specialists in "inside-dope" along Madison Avenue handled two political campaigns—probably the most other-directed and cynically moralistic in our history—against Adlai Stevenson, who was drawn into politics after the war for deeply moral reasons before leading the Democrats to their first defeat in one of the most inner-directed campaigns since the puritanical Woodrow Wilson ran for office. But, it will be said, these inner-directed moralizers are psychological deviants from their own social backgrounds and from the other-directed political climate that is a vital part of their postwar world.

Psychological deviants only become sociologically relevant when they also form part of a class of persons with a similarly deviant social character. Classes of patrician deviants are usually thrust upon the political scene during periods of rapid social change and class realignment. Such a class of deviants, for instance, grew up in Philadelphia during the early nineteenth century, when talented and wealthy scions of the city's most prominent Federalist families became Republicans, then Democrats, and eventually supported Andrew Jackson. Just as Tocqueville's America witnessed the decline of the once-dominant colonial aristocracy before the surge of frontier egalitarianism, so Riesman's America is now witnessing a similar egalitarian trend as minority ethnic groups are being absorbed into the mainstream of American life and leadership.

Ever since New Deal days, minority aspirations in this country have, by and large, been voiced through the Democratic party. And such men as Stevenson and other patrician leaders who have turned away from their families' traditional Republicanism may be but outstanding examples of a social character characteristic of a whole class of upper-class members who have been workers and supporters as well as leaders in the Democratic party since the war. Of the members of the upper-class generation that came to maturity in America during the 1920s and 1930s, for example, most of those who have had active governmental careers have also been Democrats. And like most of the "do-good" members of the Americans for Democratic Action regardless of background, they have taken a moral rather than an opportunistic approach to politics. It is no accident that former Attorney General Francis Biddle, scion of one of Philadelphia's most patrician clans, was very active in founding ADA, besides acting as its longtime leader in Washington. At the same time, the Philadelphia chapter of ADA was founded in the home of a wealthy philanthropist whose family had continuously occupied that home since 1856, and its president for many years was the overly conscientious heir-through-marriage of one of the city's greatest nineteenth-century family fortunes. On the whole then, this class of deviant patricians is the product of several generations of inherited wealth and social position. The wealthiest among them often feel guilty about their inherited fortunes and are compulsively driven by overly egalitarian convictions. The social character of this whole generation of Tory radicals, however, includes a common conviction in the rightness of accepting persons on their merits and accomplishments rather than their racial, ethnic, or religious backgrounds. Brought up in homes where Jews were rarely seen and never accepted, they are often avidly anti-anti-Semitic.[18]

But what one generation often remembers, the next generation never knew. Thus social change is not only extremely complex; it is also *generationally discontinuous*. It must be remembered that today's patrician Democratic leaders grew up in a traditionally inner-directed and class-protected world. While they are predominantly liberal conservatives with strong egalitarian convictions, the members of the upper class who are now coming to maturity in a more other-directed and far less class-protected world may produce quite different leadership material. Whereas the bright and talented undergraduates in even the best Ivy League colleges tended to be liberal egalitarians during the prewar period, this very well may not be so today. The keenest undergraduate at the University of Pennsylvania since the war, for example, came of a very good family, was senior editor of the newspaper, a campus leader in general, and possessed of a brilliantly conservative turn of mind. And it may be significant that, of the younger generation of gentlemen from old eastern seaboard families who are beginning their political careers today, several are now sitting on the Republican rather than the Democratic side of the House of Representatives. Whatever the character and convictions of this postwar generation, in the long run, they will have to deal with an ethnically mixed society that is no longer dominated by a traditionally inner-directed and property-protected minority of Anglo-Saxon-Protestant patricians.

Both the aristocratic and the egalitarian dreams are inspiring as a hope, but hopeless as a reality. Like Tocqueville before him, Riesman fears the egalitarian trends of his own generation. As egalitarian caesarism marches across our modern world, perhaps the class of deviant patricians in modern American politics will serve a truly conservative function by preserving the best from the past in an other-directed age in which masses of rootless men and their rootless leaders are desperately seeking a brave new world.

Postscript

In this jet-age nation, it often takes some time for one's thoughts to travel from the typewriter to their final resting place on the printed page. The above pages were written over two years ago. Since then there have been on the American political scene new developments that have a direct bearing on our theories about the changing character of national leadership. It is our thesis, to repeat, that the ethnic democratization of leadership is the central fact of American life in the second half of the twentieth century. This change in the ethnic composition of leadership, along with the general decline in family and parental power among the old-stock upper classes, has been largely responsible for much of the falsely tolerant and other-directed national mood. As a sign of the decline in our traditional Anglo-Saxon-Protestant establishment in political leadership, for example, we now have ten state governors, ninety members of the House of Representatives, and twelve senators of the United States who also happen to be members of the Catholic church and descendants of the newer immigrants who came to these shores in the course of the nineteenth century.

When John Fitzgerald Kennedy's great-grandfather settled in the shanty town flats of Boston harbor in the 1840s, along with hordes of his fellow refugees from the Irish potato famines, he may have been founding a new American family in the tradition of the Adamses, Harrisons, Tafts, or Roosevelts. Although Henry Adams would probably squirm in his grave at the thought (and perhaps not, too), President Kennedy sat in the distinguished seat once held by George Cabot, John Quincy Adams, Daniel Webster, Charles Sumner, and the two Henry Cabot Lodges, and like John Quincy went on to the White House.

In an almost mythical sense, the presidency of the United States, at any given time, has usually been a symbol of the mood and makeup of the American population, its values and aspirations, and especially the quality of its leadership as a whole. Just as the Virginia dynasty from Washington to Monroe symbolized the aristocratic nature of our young republic; as Andrew Jackson symbolized the rising tide of frontier democracy, which was challenging eastern seaboard leadership in the early days of the nineteenth century; as Abraham Lincoln has always inspired us as a symbol of our moral struggle with slavery; as Theodore Roosevelt marked the "progressive" revolt of the solid middle classes and the old-stock aristocracy against the rule of the new-rich plutocracy and the trusts; and as Franklin D. Roosevelt's New Deal symbolized the return of aristocratic responsibility to American political life in the form of bureaucratic noblesse oblige; so the choice of John F. Kennedy as the leader of the Democratic party in the recent presidential campaign surely symbolized the type of leadership demanded by our own times. And long after his service in the White House, future generations will remember him as a symbol of an era's titanic struggle for racial, religious, and ethnic democracy, here at home and around the world.

The American people are indeed fortunate that their political traditions are essentially conservative. Just as Andrew Jackson led a rather crude frontier democracy and yet was himself, both temperamentally and sociologically as master of the "Hermitage," so very much in the aristocratic mold of Washington or Jefferson, so, it seems to this author at least, President Kennedy is an ideal blend of the old and the new in American leadership. Thus he sought this high national honor, not as the representative of any local machine dominated by ethnic politicians, not as a man who had risen from humble origins, and, above all, not as a man of *resentment* who tended toward extreme positions of either the left or the right. Born into a family of unquestioned ability, great wealth, and a long tradition of governmental service, and educated at patrician Choate School (which has produced both Chester Bowles and Adlai Stevenson) and at Harvard University, President Kennedy surely follows in the twentieth-century tradition of such Tory reformers as Woodrow Wilson and the two Roosevelts. He is not only essentially conservative politically but, in striking contrast to many modern leaders with no family roots or traditions who have sold themselves through elaborate public-relations techniques and other devices for catering to the crowd, he has, by and large and in spite of his staff's excellent use of these modern techniques, always talked, from deeply rooted historical convictions, in a dry, factual, and typically New England intellectual style. Undoubtedly all this is due, in large part, to his extremely familistic and traditionally religious upbringing, which hardly recognized the modern trend toward peer-directed conformity. But this is, of course, in accord with our central theme to the effect that the inner-directed and parentally inculcated norms of the Protestant ethic have tended to pass from the old-stock families who dominate the corporate dividend world to the typically self-employed ethnics who have been so often excluded from the highest prizes of the more polished and polite ways to wealth. After all, the president's father—Harvard man, bank president at the age of twenty-four, and buccaneering entrepreneur all his life—hardly followed the same ways to wealth, in the large corporations, the established and safe banking houses, or the proper law firms, which so many Proper Protestants of his generation chose as a ready means of supporting a way of life to which they had always been accustomed.

The American people have decided on John F. Kennedy as their choice to lead this nation during the perilous 1960s. The tradition- and inner-directed leadership that he should provide will mitigate, at the very least, the trend toward other-directed conformity that Riesman, and Tocqueville before him, so feared as a consequence of egalitarian democracy. The late John P. Marquand, whose creation of *The Late George Apley* will long remain the classic portrait of the tradition- and inner-directed Anglo-Saxon-Protestant patrician, was apparently convinced of Senator Kennedy's ability to carry on the best American traditions as he (Marquand) understood them. Thus an editor of the *New Yorker* wrote in his last interview with Marquand: "Five days before he died, the week of the Democratic Convention, he surprised us (for we had understood that he was a Republican) by announcing that it was his intention to vote for Senator Kennedy and by contributing, as his share of the talk, a charming and touching personal anecdote about the nominee's grandfather, whom he called Honey Fitz."[19]

Notes

1. David Riesman, in collaboration with Reuel Denney and Nathan Glazer, *The Lonely Crowd: A Study of the Changing American Character* (New Haven: Yale University Press, 1950), 301. (Italics mine.)
2. E. Digby Baltzell, *Philadelphia Gentlemen: The Making of a National Upper Class* (Glencoe, Ill.: The Free Press, 1958). See also E. Digby Baltzell, "Rich Men in American Politics," *The Nation*, May 31, 1958, 493–95.
3. Baltzell, *Philadelphia Gentlemen*, 58.
4. Andrew Hacker, "Liberal Democracy and Social Control," *American Political Science Review* 51, no. 4 (December 1957): 1015.
5. See below for a discussion of Riesman's equation of "tolerance" with other-direction.
6. The works of Lothrop Stoddard also played on the prevalent mood of Anglo-Saxon panic in America. In the March 3, 1923, issue of *Time* (volume 1, number 1) interestingly enough, Charles Scribner's Sons took a full page to advertise Stoddard's books, which were called "An International Sensation." Down through the years, *Time* has continued to reflect middle-class American values.
7. That a prominent member of the upper class from another city, with all the right boarding school and college background, was at this very same time immediately taken into the club after taking over an executive position in another firm in the city did not help matters.

8. It is of passing interest to observe that a Proper Philadelphia lawyer's handling of my friend's legal and tax problems came to an end after the secondhand car business was sold, when it turned out that some $60 thousand in cash profits had somehow not been reported.
9. Isolated instances of this pattern still exist. For example, the heir and president of one of Philadelphia's most ancient publishing houses, a business gentleman of the old school, has never asked his closest associate in the firm either home to dinner or to his club to lunch during more than thirty years of working together in the office.
10. See Baltzell, *Philadelphia Gentlemen*, chap. 9.
11. During an informal show of hands in the audience while I was talking to parent-teacher groups along the Main Line several years ago, it was interesting (especially for the audience) to see that two out of three of the parents had not lived in the community before the war.
12. Riesman, *Lonely Crowd*, 56.
13. As an omen of change, perhaps, it is interesting that the one-man, patriarchal nature of a number of the leading boarding schools came to an end just before, during, and immediately after the Second World War. Drury of St. Paul's, Peabody of Groton, Father Sill of Kent, and Boynton of Deerfield were among the great headmasters who died during this period. Institutionalization has replaced the personal touch today.
14. At Groton, this liberal trend has progressed even further. Negro students have been accepted since the war, and recently a member of the Jewish faith was added to the faculty.
15. In contrast to the past, the school's present effort to influence the mainstream of American life is attested to by the fact that two of its most valued masters recently left the school to take important posts in the public school systems of two major cities in the Midwest.
16. S.M. Lipset, *Political Man* (Glencoe, Ill.: The Free Press, 1960), 299.
17. Riesman, *Lonely Crowd*, 177.
18. Among other reasons, the members of the American upper class during the New Deal days despised Roosevelt for his ethnic and racial tolerance and especially for his so-called philo-Semitism; and the bitter anti-Roosevelt story in those days often referred to "that man" as "Rosenfelt."
19. *The New Yorker*, August 6, 1960, p. 19.

5

The Protestant Establishment Revisited

On July 4, 1963, I completed a book entitled *The Protestant Establishment: Aristocracy and Caste in America*, and sent it off to the publisher for what I hoped would be the last time. Some four months later, after the Kennedy assassination, I revised the book's preface and changed the tenses when referring to the late president and sent it off again on Thanksgiving Day.

The book had a modest success, especially among members of the eastern seaboard establishment as well as among elite Jews who had been more or less excluded from the establishment. Many people, of course, liked it for the wrong reasons. For instance, it detailed rather exhaustively the history and sociology of upper-class anti-Semitism and ethnic prejudice in America. It was highly critical of the WASP establishment, and quite naturally many of the excluded approved. On the other hand, it emphasized, time and again, the need for some sort of establishment, led by men and women from a secure group of upper-class families who were educated together at private schools and universities and belonged to a network of upper-class clubs and voluntary associations. In the closing pages, I wrote that

> this book, of course, has not argued for the abolition of upper-class institutions in the interest of creating a more egalitarian and homogenized society. Quite the contrary. These institutions are vital prerequisites of a secure and organic leadership structure. In an age, moreover, when so many talented Americans are absorbed in success-striving and status-seeking, the institutionalization of a minority community which relieves distinguished men and

> their families from further status struggles is more important than ever—but only when its membership requirements are based on talent and moral distinction rather than ethnic or racial ancestry. Any vital tradition, Biblical warnings to the contrary, requires the continuous pouring of new wine into old bottles.

Perhaps I was overly naive and optimistic at the time, and should have taken the Bible more seriously. Since the book was published, some new wine, as we shall see, has surely been poured. But by and large the wind has turned sour or the bottles have been smashed, and what remains of the Protestant establishment has been watered down beyond recognition.

In the first place, the establishment in America today is not effective, in spite of the fact that it is hated and feared more than ever before. Authority—a hated word in education, in politics, and in all areas of social life—has been more or less replaced by naked power veiled in manipulation and deceit if not downright fraud. Privacy in sexual, social, and political life in America has declined to an alarming degree; class authority has been largely replaced by the manipulation of the mass media, the threat of class ostracism by the threat of public exposure. But most important of all, the American people, as never quite before in our history, are obsessed with one or another conspiracy theory.

Perhaps the most prophetic lines in the *Protestant Establishment* were the following:

> The final protector of freedom . . . may well be a unified establishment from within which the leaders of at least two parties are chosen, who, in turn, compete for the people's vote of confidence, from different points of view and differing standards of judgment, yet both assuming the absolute necessity of using fair means. . . . An establishment, in other words, may be the best protection against a conspiracy theory of history.

Since that was written, conspiracy theories of history have steadily risen among Americans, probably more among the educated classes than among the hardhats. *Time* magazine reported in November of last year that a recent Gallup poll showed that 65 percent of the American people felt Oswald alone had not been responsible for the assassination of President Kennedy. At the same time, former Senator J. William Fulbright felt the need to write an article on the inquisitorial obsessions of the mass media, which, when he was writing, were dredging up every last detail about the conspiratorial activities of the CIA (largely dominated by old-stock WASPs since its founding after the Second World War). In my own experience, the majority of the academic community believed that the Vietnam War, especially under President Johnson, was led by an evil and conspiratorial elite in Washington. "Looking back on the Vietnam War," wrote Fulbright—who was the darling of the intellectuals at the time of his opposition to the war—"it never occurred to me that President Johnson was guilty of anything worse than bad judgment. . . . President Johnson and his advisors were tragically mistaken about the Vietnam War, but by no standards of equity or accuracy did they qualify as 'war criminals.'"

Fulbright was writing at a time when the American people had become so atomized that their mistrust seemed to have no limits. Conspiracy theories of history are the natural outgrowth of a rapidly declining faith in institutions in America. An informal institutionalization of an establishment is but an extension of institutionalization in general—that is, in all areas of social life. The lack of, or declining faith in, an establishment soon spills over into a lack of faith in, and antipathy toward, all institutions. In September of last year, the General Social Survey made by the National Opinion Research Center reported an alarming lack of faith in a wide variety of American institutions. The proportion of Americans surveyed who expressed confidence in major areas of American life, in September 1974 and September 1975, were as shown in table 5.1.

Is it any wonder that one of the most popular men in America today, especially among the younger generation, is Ralph Nader, who makes a profession of sowing mistrust of our major institutions? And he is, of course, not alone. Consider *Time* magazine, for example, which was founded, staffed, and dominated by members of the WASP establishment under the leadership of Henry Luce, and was often accused of Anglo-American chauvinism and biased reporting that favored establishment and (as they say today) "elitist" values. Nowadays *Time* is keeping up with the trend, leveling the elite and exposing the weaknesses of the increasingly

TABLE 5.1
Confidence in American Institutions

	Percent Confident	
	1974	**1975**
Major corporations	31.3	19.2
Organized religion	44.2	24.3
Education	49.0	30.9
Executive branch of government	13.6	13.3
Organized labor	18.2	10.1
Press	25.8	23.4
Medicine	60.3	50.4
Television	23.4	17.8
Supreme Court	33.1	30.7
Scientific community	44.9	37.8
Congress	17.0	13.2
Military	39.6	35.2

midgetlike mighty. Thus if one is seeking an excellent job on the late President Kennedy—in pieces on "JFK and the Mobster's Moll" and a detailed outline, with titillating pictures, of "Jack Kennedy's Other Women"—*Time* provides it. In its first issue of this bicentennial year, it did another excellent job on President Ford's "Ridicule Problem." Such is the compassionate tone of our egalitarian and elitist society, where no authority or conventions of decency exist and where the media are increasingly setting our only standards. But then, *Time* is only reporting, in an objective way, what everybody else is doing and saying.

What an establishment means is that a society is led by a class of men who act according to an agreed-upon code of manners. Certain things are not done; if they are done, they are *not* discussed in public, even when the breaches of convention lead to class ostracism. Without class conventions and class ostracism, on the other hand, everything that happens becomes public property and media exposure is the only remedy. The almost institutionalized "leaks" in Washington today are symbols of a classless elitism.

Two examples from recent history come to mind. In 1936, when the WASP establishment was still dominant and Franklin Roosevelt was leading the nation through one of its great social and political revolutions, Edward VIII abdicated the British throne in order to marry a twice-divorced woman from Baltimore. For three years the king and Mrs. Simpson had carried on their affair under the knowing eyes of her husband and a large part of the British establishment, but without the knowledge of the British public. The affair was discussed with Prime Minister Stanley Baldwin and within the highest circles of the realm. Yet the British press, led by Lord Beaverbrook, kept the news (already making headlines in America) from the public through a gentleman's agreement. This successful suppression of the truth by the establishment was not news control in the style of Nazi and Communist totalitarianism. It was done in a land where most historians would agree that there has been a continuous tradition of freedom of expression, from the days when Karl Marx wrote in the British Museum down to the present.

Another sharp contrast between our media-dominated, egalitarian elitism and established class authority is seen in the comparison of the British Profumo affair with Spiro Agnew's stepping down from his office as vice-president of the United States. Profumo, a British member of Parliament who was found to have lied to his class peers, was so humiliated by his breach of conventions, that ever since the exposé he has been doing penance as a social worker in London's East End. Agnew, on the other hand, is well on his way—thanks to media publicity—toward his first or second million. He has now cashed in further with a novel on the subject of his recent experience. When class authority declines, money talks, echoing in a moral vacuum.

The first open attack on the WASP establishment after the Second World War came when Senator Joseph McCarthy panicked the American people with his cynical and diabolical theories of an upper-class conspiracy to betray America to the Communists. His archenemies were the silver-spooned gentlemen in the State Department, chief among them Dean Acheson. McCarthy's conspiracy theories of course, appealed to an age that had just gone through the case of Alger Hiss, a Baltimorian of impeccable establishment connections who was finally brought to justice by the dogged determination of young Richard Nixon. Dean Acheson—an alumnus of Groton, Yale, and Harvard, who wore striped pants, had a handlebar moustache, and spoke with a phony British accent (as McCarthy called it)—stood up to the demagogue when most of the intellectual elite were running to cover their tracks. At the same time, it was a courageous but mild establishment lawyer from Boston, Joseph Welch, who brought McCarthy to his knees.

No need to rehash the Watergate affair once again; it is enough to say that surely no elite was more deracinated than the men around President Richard Nixon, who himself seemed to come from nowhere and found security only in building his palaces at Key Biscayne and San Clemente. One recalls how Hugh Sidey of *Time*, in one of his brilliant capsules on "The Presidency," contrasted Nixon and his colleagues, sitting around between decisions, forever talking of money, with Adlai Stevenson and other establishment types as late as the Kennedy years. It is hard to imagine men like Stevenson, Acheson, or Harriman even knowing what laundered money was, let alone ordering their minions to carry it from place to place in satchels.

At any rate, it is important to record that two men from the very heart of the WASP establishment finally resigned from the Nixon administration: Archibald Cox and Eliot Richardson. The class code of Cox (of Saint Paul's and Harvard) and Richardson (of Milton and Harvard) would no longer allow them to go along with the team. Richardson's resignation was especially interesting because he has always seemed to put duty to his country above any private ideological or moral convictions. Yet although he seems to have many of the best qualities for sound leadership, few think he has the personal appeal that would get him elected to any national office today. It is media appeal—charisma, in the debased use of that term—that has steadily replaced class authority as the principal characteristic for leadership in our atomized society. Years ago Max Weber saw this only too clearly.

I have concentrated so far on the national consequences of the fact that our society has no secure upper class which is able to dominate our leadership and see that it remains rooted in some kind of tradition or institutional continuity. But what of the WASP establishment itself, which, as far as its effect on our national life is concerned, has gone with the wind? Let us consider this question in light of the "robber barons" and their descendants, particularly their grandsons and great-grandsons.

By and large, the twentieth-century WASP establishment—national, associational, and educational rather than local and familial—and the eastern seaboard upper class in which it was anchored, were founded and financially endowed by the generation of businessmen who came of age during the Civil War and the decade of the 1870s. These men have been called the robber barons, and the time of their ascendancy has been noted as the Gilded Age. Yet they accumulated the great wealth that built up the twentieth-century universities—especially Harvard, Yale, and Princeton, which had been primarily small sectarian colleges throughout most of the nineteenth century. (In the Middle West, John D. Rockefeller's philanthropy almost single-handedly built the University of Chicago.) They also endowed the New England boarding schools and financed the more famous men's clubs at the turn of the century, clubs built by architects like McKim, Mead and White, Horace Trumbauer, and John Russell Pope. While most of the robber barons were self-educated and not necessarily college-bred, their sons went off to the schools and colleges that their fathers had endowed. They went off either before or directly after the First World War, in which many of them fought and some lost their lives. Theirs was the most privileged and opulent generation in American history. They got their jobs through family friends. In business they dealt chiefly with their friends on Wall Street and in the boardrooms of the nation. They trained to be First World War army officers in a gentlemanly group that went to Plattsburgh at the inspiration of Theodore Roosevelt and under the leadership of Leonard Wood. They dominated the first class of naval aviation cadets at Pensacola. And, symbolically enough, the most glamorous of them all, Hobey Baker of Saint Paul's and Princeton, one of the last gentleman athletes of national fame, lost his life flying on the western front.

Most of these men became businessmen and bankers, but many of them were Progressive reformers. Some, like John Reed, who came from an old family in Portland, Oregon, and was a member of the notable class of 1910 at Harvard, became rather famous radicals. Two of Reed's classmates, Walter Lippmann and T.S. Eliot, were of great importance to the intellectual conscience of their era. The two Roosevelts and Woodrow Wilson were, of course, the most eminent political figures of this generation. In many ways it was the generation that produced the last exclusive and still authoritative upper class in America, the class I attempted to analyze in *The Protestant Establishment*.

They were also America's last innocent and utterly confident generation. They fought the First World War to save democracy and led the nation in the Second World War to save civilization from totalitarianism. Their unquestioning faith in money-power and in the American right—indeed, duty—to rule the world came to an end, however, in the period between the stock market crash of 1929 and the close of the Second World War. The vast majority of their wives did not go to college, but were presented to society in class-sheltered debutante rituals and lived out their lives as mothers, hostesses, and volunteers in organizational activities. A few, like Eleanor Roosevelt and Frances Perkins, rose from sheltered debutante backgrounds to the highest levels of American leadership.

While achievement of an upper-class position was most characteristic of the robber-baron era, the scions of this last innocent generation were largely protected by the privileges of ascription in social life, in business, and in sport. The third generation, the grandsons of the robber barons, came of age in the 1930s. Theirs was the transition generation. In their youth they went, almost as a matter of right, to the best eastern boarding schools. Then on to Harvard, Yale, and Princeton, where they joined the best clubs and graduated usually, but not always, with "gentleman *C*'s." While their class position was ascribed as far as school and college were concerned, they came out into a depression world where their families and friends were no longer so easily able to supply them with jobs. Many of them found work at *Time* magazine, which, until the death of Henry Luce, clearly reflected a WASP upper-class point of view. (Both Luce and Briton Hadden, his partner in the founding of *Time*, were Yale men.) Although the depression was a jolt to all these sons of privilege, it was especially hard on those on the fringes of wealth whose fathers lost everything in the crash (and some of whom committed suicide). But at that time, a large proportion of the scholarships at boarding schools and prestige colleges went to the sons of the impecunious genteel, rather than the sons of underprivileged ethnic and minority groups.

While the unquestioned control of the economy passed out of the hands of the WASP establishment after 1929, the Second World War was an even more democratizing experience for the sons of the privileged in this third generation. In many ways, this war was the most leveling and homogenizing war in our history. Meritocracy was firmly in the saddle, particularly in the rapidly expanding army and navy air corps, where twenty-twenty vision was far more important than family connections. Officers came from all walks of life and from every ethnic group. For the first time in their lives, members of the WASP upper class flew and fought and became close friends with Italians, Irish Catholics, and Jews. Actuality, in many instances, shattered stereotypes throughout the various theaters of war. And following the war, the GI Bill of Rights was the first really democratizing agent in the history of college and graduate education. The veterans, on the whole, took education seriously and had little patience with the snobbery of fraternities and other class-excluding institutions on the campus.

Owing to both the meritocratic recruitment of officers during the war and the GI Bill afterward, many talented members of minority groups rose up to challenge the authority of the WASP establishment in the postwar years. Change has a way of creeping up on us, however. The 1950s were a period of seeming stability—except for the McCarthy affair, which in many ways pointed toward things to come in the 1960s, and even more, so I believe, toward our current decade and beyond. Meanwhile various minority groups, especially the Jews, rose to widespread suburban opulence even as the WASP upper class declined in power, affluence, and the influence they had been able to exert through their style of life. In Philadelphia, the city I know best, the major banks and trust companies, the Pennsylvania Railroad, and the University of Pennsylvania used to be dominated and run by members of the city's close-knit and long-intermarried upper class. Today none of these are under such control.

The upper-class style of life was also changing. Whereas most members of the second WASP generation had been able to keep up their ancestral lands and their large houses, the third generation—without servants for the first time in countless decades—was no longer interested or able to do so. Hence they sold off their property to developers of smaller "estates" for the newly affluent. (I recall talking to a parents' meeting at a school on the Main Line after the war and finding out, through a show of hands, that most of the people in my audience had not lived there before the war.) While all the grandchildren of the robber barons had gone to private schools, some were now sending their children to local public schools—not always for economic reasons, but rather because of democratic convictions. Not only that, but many of those children, instead of going to Harvard, Yale, or Princeton, were forced to enroll, as we shall see, in obscure colleges with unfamiliar names.

The great economic changes of the 1950s—the rising affluence of so many and the declining affluence and influence of the upper class—paved the way for the crisis of the 1960s. The Kennedy administration was in many respects the great divide. President Kennedy himself was, of course, symbolically important as the first non-WASP to live in the White House. Although his closest advisers might have been called the Irish Mafia, he had gone to Choate, Princeton, and Harvard, and his administration was the last to be widely staffed with members of the eastern seaboard WASP establishment. However open to question his political effectiveness may have been, I think there can be no doubt that his administration gave Americans in general, and the younger generation in particular, a feeling of confidence and stability. To mention a small example that is nevertheless indicative of how far we have come: just as the press left the American people more or less unaware that President Roosevelt was a cripple, so it also, by tacit agreement, rarely if ever showed President Kennedy on the golf course, although he loved the game. Both he and Roosevelt had the establishment's ability to control the press indirectly in the interest of social stability and traditional authority—a far cry from today, when everyone is so interested in having the mighty revealed with warts and all, to the point where they have become almost all warts. If the press did not photograph John Kennedy on exclusionary golf courses in Palm Beach, today it is gleefully ready to photograph President Ford falling down the ski slopes at Vail, Colorado.

With the assassination of President Kennedy in the fall of 1963 and the outbreak of revolution on the campus at Berkeley in September 1964, the tearing apart of American society, and the bifurcation of all established restraints, began in earnest. This was largely a revolution of the younger generation, but first another word about their parents. Since *The Protestant Establishment* was published, in early 1965, there has been a slow but steady liberalization of the admissions policies of the exclusive urban clubs as well as, to a lesser degree, the suburban country clubs. The rigid exclusion of Jews has broken down to a considerable extent. At the same time, the clubs are having a hard time remaining solvent. Among other reasons for this, bear in mind that when there is at the top a heterogeneous and egalitarian elite rather than a class-dominated society, important decisions are less likely to be made in the anonymous and excluded atmosphere of private clubs. At the elite level, moreover, social life in general is becoming increasingly functional rather than class dominated.

It was not so long ago that business firms first came to have luxurious boardrooms and private dining rooms with modern art on the walls—these replacing the rolltop desk, spittoon, and sawed-off pencils of an earlier day. Today's businessmen have given up home and club entertainment in favor of elaborate conference-room affairs attended by men having common functional interests rather than a common upper-class background. Even when an upper-class businessman does entertain at home, his guests often include his business and functional peers. Before the Second World War, by contrast, the president of an old family firm in Philadelphia had worked with a close associate for fifty years and never once entertained him either at his club or in his home. This would be impossible today in our lonely but more gregarious expense-account society.

Since the war, life at the top has also become less and less place oriented. Before the war, the powerful were to be seen living on their vast estates, with large staffs of servants, on the Main Lines of America, then for two months each year in other luxurious houses at fashionable resorts. Today they are living almost anonymously in unostentatious houses without full-time live-in servants, traveling by air to ski in New England, Colorado, or Europe or to sail the Caribbean or the Mediterranean. They may devote some summers to educational travel with their children, spending no more than a few weeks with their parents who still cling to their old summer homes. The children are then left with their grandparents while husband-and-wife couples charter a boat to get away from it all. What they need to get away from is the great pressure under which they live their functional lives—pressure brought on by democratization, the fear of unfavorable publicity, and increasing government regulation. And perhaps most important of all, since business is now a group operation, committee decisions have replaced the arbitrary individual decisions of the past, a process that is usually time consuming and emotionally exhausting.

Finally, there is another interesting new phenomenon among an increasing number of old-stock Americans in our major cities: internal expatriation. More and more of them are retiring from business while still young and moving to Maine or Vermont, to the Eastern Shore of Maryland, to Virginia. Although their reasons are various, I should judge that many of them have given up on America and on the cities of their birth and heritage. I remember how, going to Virginia for a speaking engagement during the 1960s, I was struck by the great numbers of Goldwater posters I saw along the highways. I was told that the area was filled with Yankee millionaires who had retired there.

But the vast majority of the WASP establishment is not at all reactionary. In fact, although no figures are available, I have the impression that they are becoming more and more liberal. Parlor populism has injected social registerites to almost the same extent as it has the rest of our deracinated and guilty elite. By far the most perceptive review of my *Protestant Establishment* was written by Richard L. Rubenstein, then the campus rabbi at the University of Pittsburgh. He opened it with a description of candidate Barry Goldwater speaking to a WASP audience out the Main Line in Philadelphia. The "Half-Jew" Goldwater, basing his appeal "primarily on a single underlying issue—Protestant nativist racism," told his audience "that the government had been in the hands of 'minority groups' for the past thirty-two years . . . and promised, if elected, to restore it to political power." What Rabbi Rubenstein did not say was that in that election many predominantly old-stock WASP election districts on the Main Line voted the Democratic ticket for the first time since the Civil War. Again, there are no statistics available, but that same old-stock upper class (not the newly rich elites) not only did not vote for Goldwater but did not vote in their habitually large numbers for the Republican party under Nixon.

I happened to spend the fall of 1972 at Cambridge, Massachusetts—the only state that gave more votes to McGovern than to Nixon. Massachusetts is, I should imagine, a state heavily populated with members of the old-stock upper class. The faculties of all the private schools and small colleges are predominantly WASP, and Boston is still basically an establishment city—except for the Irish. At a dinner on election night, I noted that of the owners and staff of a famous Boston newspaper, owned and run by an old-stock fashionable family, all but two were for McGovern. Perhaps when a class is losing power, its social and political attitudes become both more and more liberal and more and more reactionary. This bipolar trend indicates not only a loss of confidence but a certain amount of guilt and self-hate. As Durkheim pointed out years ago, guilt and self-hate are products of a too-rapid rise on the social scale and also a steady decline. No wonder radical chic is espoused by many members of our modern American elite. After all, A. Whitney Ellsworth, the publisher of their favorite sheet, the *New York Review of Books*, is a graduate of Saint Paul's and Harvard.

Finally, it was in the generation of the grandsons of the robber barons that the Protestant establishment lost its intellectual leadership in America. Ideas are infinitely important to all established authority. John Maynard Keynes saw this; "soon or late," he wrote, "it is ideas, not vested interests, which are dangerous for good or evil." Tocqueville noted this even earlier when he wrote of the castelike character of the Old Regime in France: "An aristocracy in the days of its strength does not merely conduct affairs; it still directs opinions, gives their tone to writers and authority to ideas. In the eighteenth century the French nobility had entirely lost this part of its supremacy." The generation of American writers who were born within a decade of 1900, if they went to college, mostly attended Harvard, Yale, or Princeton. Like their spiritual ancestors in the generation of Emerson and Hawthorne, who witnessed the decline of the New England Puritan and Federalist establishment, these writers went on to produce our second American renaissance. And their books, between the lines, foretold the decline of the WASP establishment of which they were a part. F. Scott Fitzgerald—who, in his description of Gatsby's parties, first envisioned the kind of elitist society that is now upon us—was a Catholic by birth, but his father was of old Baltimore stock. Fitzgerald's insights into life within the establishment were perhaps due to his role as a half-insider.

In striking contrast to the WASP supremacy of the 1920s, the intellectual climate of the 1960s was mainly dominated by members of the New York Jewish establishment. True, those Jews were alienated from the WASP establishment by ascription, but the old-stock intellectuals were also alienated from their own inherited class values. Throughout the postwar period, in fact, intellectuals born within the establishment renounced their ancestral allegiance to the Republican party and became liberal Democrats. In Philadelphia, for example, Americans for Democratic Action (ADA) was founded largely by social registerites, in a house where the family of one of the founders had lived for three generations.

In an issue of *Commentary* magazine devoted to the "Failure of Nerve in America," S.M. Lipset brilliantly shows how an adversary intellectual class, or "intelligentsia," has grown up in postwar America. Modeled on the intelligentsia of Old Russia, or of continental Europe between the two wars and today, this class is very different from the traditional British and American pattern in which intellectuals are critical but are not cut off from the establishment by birth or heritage. Lipset quotes the late Lionel Trilling, a man keenly aware of the importance of established manners and civility, who wrote in 1965 that "any historian of the modern age will take virtually for granted the adversary intention, the actual subversive intention, that characterizes modern writing."

The alienation of the intellectuals from the establishment in the third generation of the robber barons' descendants had, in my view, a subtle but profound effect on their sons and daughters. Radical social change is a very slow process. As Walter Bagehot once pointed out, the consequences of the Reform Bill of 1832 were not really felt in England until the 1870s, when a new generation came to power. So although the decline and eventual disintegration of the American Protestant establishment originated with the robber barons' grandchildren, it was *their* children who felt its full force in the 1960s. They knew, as children so often do, what their parents were not ready to tell them.

To begin with, one must see that this fourth generation was media-bred rather than class-bred; these children watched television from their cradles. Yet I, who represent the third generation, can vividly remember hearing a voice talking in a friend's living room, and finding that it came from a newfangled gadget called a radio. The point is that in my generation members of all classes and ethnic groups grew up in various ghettos that were closed off from the rest of the nation and the world at large. For example, a man who several years ago was managing editor of a local Philadelphia newspaper came from a leading family in Independence, Missouri, and went to the University of Missouri during the 1930s. Years later, when he was a Neiman Fellow at Harvard, he kicked himself for not going to Harvard in the first place. But then, he said, he had never heard of Harvard in those days of class, ethnic, and regional isolation. At that same time, there were a lot of things that young men and women leaving Harvard or Yale or Vassar or Smith had never heard of—protected as they were by a class-bound upbringing of dancing classes, private schools, chaperons, debutante parties, and a childhood in the select suburbs of American cities along the eastern seaboard.

The democratization and atomization of the fourth generation of upper-class youth began in the colleges during the 1950s and gradually filtered down to the secondary and elementary schools, even the kindergartens and preschools, by the 1960s. Thus, in the course of the postwar decades, first the colleges and then the lower schools that had been class institutions before the war became elitist meritocracies. Both among the children of the upper class and the children of newly successful families striving to enter the upper class, the conscious and unconscious inculcation of class values was replaced by meritocratic values. The earlier emphasis on character and moral standards slowly gave way to a universalistic and critical attitude that questioned all particularistic values.

The meritocratic changes in education during the 1950s had a great deal to do with the campus revolutions of the 1960s and 1970s. Along with these changes was a growing public awareness that a bureaucratic and highly technical society such as ours needs more well-trained members of the elite and less unskilled labor. While our high school population increased dramatically between the two world wars, it was, as is well known, the college population that boomed in the postwar period. In 1940 Princeton had some 900 applicants for 600 places in the freshman class; in 1960 there were 3,312 applicants for 757 places, and the competition increased throughout that decade. To handle all these applicants, the meritocratic device of SAT scores was adopted, instead of the old class background and "character" (usually WASP or WASP-like), as a major criterion for admission. The result was that the 1960 freshman class at Princeton, with its 650 SAT average, represented the top 2 percent of its age group. No longer could a certain professor say of the freshmen in his class, as he had in 1940, "It was like a room full of siblings." No longer did 60 to 70 percent of first-year Princeton students come from private schools. The freshman class in 1935, of which John Kennedy was a member, included 502 young men from private schools as against 113 from public high schools. By 1960 the proportion of privately and publicly educated students was equal, and by the end of the decade public school graduates outnumbered those from private schools 60 to 40.

As I have said, the great-grandsons of the robber barons were unable to restrict their choices to eastern seaboard colleges. In 1935 all but a handful of the graduating class at Saint Paul's went on to Harvard, Yale, or Princeton. Thirty years later, in 1965, of the 102 boys in the graduating class, 22 went to Harvard, 13 to Yale, and 7 to Princeton. The rest—save 9 who had other plans—went to 24 other colleges. And that class of 1965 was more competitively selected, better educated, and far brighter than their fathers had been in 1935. Thirty-nine percent of them were commended or were semifinalists in the National Merit tests, and Charles E. Bohlen, Jr., was selected as one of the 121 Presidential Scholars for that year.

Until the Second World War, then, Princeton, Harvard, and Yale were still engaged in giving a liberal education to the sons of the upper class, and also assimilating some youth from less privileged backgrounds into that class. At Princeton and Yale, and at Harvard under A. Lawrence Lowell, these young men were, in the words of Woodrow Wilson, being educated to "serve the nation," and many of them, like Kennedy, Stevenson, Chester Bowles, and McGeorge and William Bundy, did. By the end of the 1960s, however, these three class colleges had clearly become nurseries of elitist meritocracies, more in the style of the University of Chicago and the great public universities like the University of California at Berkeley and the University of Wisconsin at Madison. These changes were, of course, all in accord with the national antiestablishment mood of the country, which was bound to replace class and regional diversities with a national egalitarian and elitist uniformity. Conformity to class conventions slowly gave way to a uniformity that was, if possible, enforced by the laws of the state—as Tocqueville would have predicted more than a century earlier. In this other-directed and conforming age of uniformity, it is no wonder that John V. Lindsay, when mayor of New York, found it expedient to refer to his "high school in New Hampshire" rather than Saint Paul's.

While the main reasons for the turmoil on the best campuses in America during the 1960s were the black revolution and the war in Vietnam, it would not be an exaggeration to suggest that the turmoil was also closely related to the decline of the WASP establishment and the rise of other groups, especially the affluent and newly suburbanized Jews, to elite status. Nevertheless, in viewing the generation gap within the old-stock upper class that resulted in its children's radical behavior, let us bear in mind that throughout the 1960s only a small minority of students were, as the saying went, "radicalized." Although in stable times students have always held more or less the same political opinions as their parents, those of the 1960s moved steadily away from the values of the Republican WASP establishment. For instance, in a 1960 presidential straw poll taken at Harvard, John F. Kennedy received 60 percent of the vote—more than Franklin Roosevelt or any other Democratic candidate had ever mustered on that campus since the Civil War.

The trend among Harvard students to pull away from the political party of their ancestors was best illustrated when eighteen-year-olds got the vote in the early 1970s. At the time, according to S.M. Lipset and David Riesman in their *Education and Politics at Harvard*, 80 percent of the Harvard students reported that they were registered to vote: 9 percent of them Republican, 34 percent independent, and 56.5 percent Democratic.

In the late 1960s, the student meritocracy at Harvard was very much like Princeton's—the ratio of students from private and public schools being a similar 40 and 60 percent. Harvard had, of course, been heterogeneous and meritocratic for a longer time, with its proportion of Jewish students higher than at Princeton and far higher than in President Lowell's day. In this connection, it is important to stress one factor in the generation gap within the upper class: the brighter young people were far more opposed to a general, blanket anti-Semitism than were their parents. Indeed, opposition to anti-Semitism was even stronger among the daughters than among the sons. In Philadelphia during the 1960s, upper-class marriages revealed that an unprecedented number of the daughters of the Protestant establishment were marrying Jews. These young women also seemed to be from the more intellectually curious families. As the Scarlett-Rhett romance in *Gone with the Wind* illustrated well, spirited women of a declining class have probably always been attracted to enterprising young men who are rising in the world. The role of women in the 1960s revolution of class relations, during which the deans of admissions at the elite colleges replaced the debutante ritual in deciding who should marry whom, is itself a fascinating story. But for a clue to the values and attitudes of the brightest sons of the fourth-generation WASP establishment, let us look at the behavior of private school graduates at Harvard in the late 1960s.

The Berkeley campus revolution came in 1964, Columbia's in 1968, and Harvard's in the spring of 1969. The book on Harvard by S.M. Lipset and David Riesman includes a study of all the student revolts on that campus since the "Great Rebellion" of 1823, when John Quincy Adams's son John was expelled. "Harvard's year of the 'bust,' 1968–69," write these two authors, "was the most momentous year in the University's history in the century since Eliot took office." The history of that second Great Rebellion in 1969 has been thoroughly documented and need not be gone into here. But one thing is worth stressing: it was the sons of the WASP establishment who finally occupied the central administration building—an act that led to President Pusey's disastrous summoning of the local police.

Student radicalism at Harvard, as on most other campuses, was led by members of SDS. Students for a Democratic Society was founded at Port Huron, Michigan, in 1962, and its Harvard chapter was by 1966 the largest in the nation. One of its founders at Harvard (his father was an ADA Democrat and a member of the Kennedy administration) was a great-grandson of James Stillman, John D. Rockefeller's banker. By the time of the rebellion, the Harvard SDS had broken into two opposing factions, as left-wing movements often do: the more conservative SDS caucus and the more radical PL group, linked to the Maoist Progressive Labor party. From our point of view, the most useful description of the contrasting roles of these two wings in the 1969 "bust" is found in the book *Push Comes to Shove: The Escalation of Student Protest* by Steven Kelman, a student at Harvard between 1966 and 1970. Kelman came to Harvard as a convinced socialist and was the leader of the Young People's Socialist League (YPSL) on the campus. From his first day there, he strongly disapproved of, indeed despised, the "pallid preppies." "On the second day," he wrote in his diary, "I saw a tall, blond, not-quite-fat kid around the dorm. . . . One time he was gazing down at the rest of the world from his pedestal on the ledge of the staircase one floor up, and once again, later in the afternoon, downstairs. His eyes eyed me in a superciliousness so classic that I felt like photographing it. The lips seemed delicately positioned so that he could voice his contempt without saying one audible word . . . Disgusting *prep school* kid!" This reversal of the kike-on-sight syndrome held by private school boys in the 1930s prevails throughout the Kelman book. Young Kelman somehow never seemed to apply the "preppie" epithet, however, to preppies of Jewish background, some of whom were his friends.

"Who's in Harvard SDS?" Kelman asks, and immediately discards the Freudian approach in the Yale psychologist Kenneth Keniston's "sycophantic account in *The Young Radicals*."

> As more of a follower of Marx [Kelman writes], I think it would be useful to apply a class analysis to the sole phenomenon to which SDS refuses to apply this method: themselves, of course. Family income: average for U.S., $8,000 a year; average for Harvard, $17,000 a year; average for SDS, $23,000 a year. (Source: poll of family incomes taken in Soc. Sci. 125, an SDS-run course taken almost entirely by New Leftists.) Secondary school education: of the 150-odd Harvard students arrested after the occupation of University Hall, approximately 50 percent attended prep school, with the largest representation from the most exclusive ones like St. Paul's. Just over 40 percent of the Harvard student body as a whole comes from prep schools.

Kelman divides the affluent SDS membership into the "hereditary left," which dominated the SDS caucus, and the Maoist PL group, made up of preppies whom he calls "WASP" rebels." The SDS at Harvard, according to Kelman, "never could have gotten started without the initial services of the hereditary radicals." This group became radical in the same way a Boston Irishman's son becomes a Democrat—by instinct. Their fathers had come of age in the 1930s and were now members of the increasingly affluent American intelligentsia. According to Kelman:

> Irving Howe estimates that during the thirties and forties a million Americans may have passed through membership in the Communist party. Many are still radicals, if only under the table—or, to put it more accurately, at the dinner table—today. Around these talkative dinner tables the hereditary radicals absorbed from early childhood certain notions about who the bad guys and who the good guys are. . . . The hereditary radicals came to Harvard with their political commitments already well established.

Although the hereditary radicals founded and kept SDS going at Harvard in the 1960s, they lost out to the Maoist PL leaders in the April 1969 rebellion—the taking over of University Hall and the calling of the police by President Pusey. Thus, according to Kelman, "almost none of the leaders of the New Left caucus, up to and including SDS co-chairman Kazin, were arrested. . . . The hereditary radicals tried to conceal their fears in a hocus-pocus of SDS rhetoric, . . . but the real source of their hesitancy was easier to understand . . . they might get jail and expulsion. That was more than Mom and Dad had led them to bargain for."

The hereditary radicals "combined the confidence and optimism of members of a rising social group," says Kelman—and, one might add, the sophisticated caution born of the experience of their fathers. The WASP rebels, on the other hand, seemed to have many of the characteristics (perhaps in the extreme) of most of their declining class. Kelman reflects on his WASP rebel classmates as follows:

> The sight of an aristocrat who has lost the will to live is aesthetically degrading. These declining members of the American aristocracy are not at all similar to the standard aristocratic stereotypes. They are neither self-confident men at the top, uncaring of those below, nor the humane, social-service oriented democratic aristocrats.
>
> The left should normally expect [Kelman continues] good strong hostility and opposition from the upper class—the enemy is nothing if not powerful. If some aristocrats want to rebel, though, that's their right. But the pale, delicate face of the used-up aristocrat who goes into SDS reminds one of nothing so much as Spengler's *Decline of the West*. The American upper class has been an aristocracy produced by primitive dog-eat-dog competition, and it is only now that enough generations have passed for it to begin to produce soft, declining offspring who are not "up" to its standards. . . . It is in the guilty aristocrat that we see clearly politics not for politics' sake, but for self-expression, the possibility of recapturing a lost vitality that one feels too weak to create for oneself.

The "declining aristocrats," as Kelman calls them, were all members of PL, not a "single one of them in the New Left caucus." But it was the PL preppies who carried their convictions—shallow and temporary as they were, and born of their declining self-confidence and frustration—to the ultimate conclusion in taking over University Hall, and being brutalized and arrested in doing so. The occupation of University Hall by the "pallid preppies" was a vital, symbolic event in the history of class relations in this country. Nothing since *The Protestant Establishment* was written,

I should imagine, better illustrates what was happening to the WASP upper class, especially in its fourth generation. Imagine the reaction of the Harvard clubmen in their fathers' and grandfathers' generation had they witnessed "virtually everyone around the exclusive clubs wearing red armbands," as preppie David Bruce, Kelman's roommate in his sophomore year, reported to him during the bust. Kelman's views of his despised preppie classmates may seem to say more about his own relations with his ideological peers than about them. But perhaps his views were not so far off base. Four days after the occupation, the executive editor of the *Crimson* "bared his soul, in the proud *Crimson* tell-it-like-it-is tradition, with a piece entitled 'Non-Politics on the Battlefront.'" The following excerpts cannot be faulted as coming from an anti-prep-school point of view:

> What was most euphoric was us and what we were to each other. We *were* brothers and sisters. We did reach out and hold onto each other . . . we were very human and very together.
>
> None of the above is very political stuff. But there was a group of us in University Hall who were not very political people. It was a strange group, not well-defined at all, that included some girls, some people from the Loeb (Drama Center), a couple of guys from the Fly Club, at least one from the Lampoon, and one in a tuxedo who had just come from a party and was drunk. There were others. Some of us didn't even know what the six demands were.

The executive editor of the *Crimson*, a graduate of Saint Paul's, as was his father before him, had everything that meritocratic Harvard now looks for. He was a good athlete, very popular, and a top scholar. Not long after Kelman's book was written, this wealthy and gifted preppie took his own life. One wonders what will happen to the rest of the gilded-Harvard youth who led the rebellion that spring.

What will happen to freedom in the fourth generation from the robber barons, which dropped out and rebelled in its youth during the late 1960s? Their problem partly reflected a severe crisis of class authority in America, highlighted in a series of tragic events from the assassination of President Kennedy to the Watergate affair. It would be too facile to blame the current decline of authority in America, or the tragic fate of the editor of the Harvard *Crimson* in 1969, entirely on the suicidal, exclusionary values of the WASP establishment. Perhaps the very strengths of an establishment in one generation preclude its functioning successfully in another. At any rate, when I wrote *The Protestant Establishment* during the administration of President Kennedy, I still had faith in the ability of the WASP establishment to assimilate talented men and women of other ethnic and religious origins into its ranks. I have no such faith today. I remain convinced, though, that modern republican, political institutions, in both England and America, have traditionally been based on hierarchical social systems where class authority and the threat of class ostracism have been major agents of social control. A free press is a vital virtue in any democracy; like all virtues, however, it becomes a vice when carried too far and the fear of media exposure becomes the major sanction of a normative system. An authoritative establishment, in the long run, is far more important to the protection of freedom and democracy.

But perhaps it is best to forget about the WASP establishment, and instead cultivate an open but hierarchical society where all men aspire to be like Washington or Jefferson, rather than one in which all men must overtly ape the values of Everyman, all the while covertly coveting the shallow comforts of affluence and power. Not long after the decline of the Federalist establishment (of which the "Rebellion of 1823" at Harvard was a symptom) and the rise of Jacksonian democracy, Tocqueville pointed out the affinities between materialism and egalitarianism, from which the following lines are taken:

> There is in fact a manly and lawful passion for equality which incites men to wish all to be powerful and honored. This passion tends to raise the humble to the rank of the great; but there exists also in the human heart a depraved taste for equality which impels the weak to attempt to lower the powerful to their own level.

6

Upper-Class Clubs and Associations in Philadelphia

"Wherever at the head of some undertaking you see the government in France, or a man of rank in England, in the United States you will be sure to find an association." So wrote Alexis de Tocqueville in his famous book, *Democracy in America*, written a century and a half ago and still the finest interpretation of our democracy ever written. The core of any upper class is, of course, the family, especially of the extended or consanguine variety, which includes not only parents and children but also grandparents, extended cousinages, and ancestors. Family founders are usually ancestors of great distinction or great moneymakers and accumulators. By and large, the Philadelphia upper class was primarily a familistic class for some two hundred years after the colony's founding in 1682. As the upper-class family weakened, especially in the 1920s, clubs became surrogate families which increasingly placed new men and their families in the class structure.

Yet even in the eighteenth century, Proper Philadelphia gentlemen founded several clubs and associations which structured their leisure-time activities. Thus, in 1732, a group of gentlemen-anglers came together to form the oldest men's club in the English-speaking world (White's in London was founded four years later in 1736). This fishing club was called the Colony in Schuylkill, its clubhouse a Castle, on the banks of the Schuylkill River. Today it is called the State in Schuylkill, or the Fish House, and since 1888 the Castle has been located on the Delaware River, near the Nicholas Biddle mansion, Andalusia. Limited to thirty members, it is, after more than two and a half centuries, still the most blue-blooded club in the city. Fish House Punch is, like scrapple for the masses, one of Philadelphia's distinctive contributions to our eating and drinking mores; today the club is primarily an eating place for gentlemen during the summer months. In 1866 a very similar club, the Rabbit, was founded on Rabbit Lane, at the beginning of the Main Line. It serves as an eating club in the winter months. Most members of the State in Schuylkill also belong to the Rabbit.

Perhaps the most important status-ascribing institution within Philadelphia's upper class has been the annual Assembly Balls, which have been held continuously in peacetime since their founding in 1748. Though not strictly a club, the Assembly has been organized and run down through the years by a self-perpetuating committee of gentlemen. Up until the 1960s, it was surely the ultimate index of social position and power in the city. Since that antinomian decade (when, by the way, the ancient traditions of dropping divorced persons from membership was discontinued), it still has some influence among those who still value traditional marks of social position; it is surely irrelevant as an index of either economic or political power.

The man-on-a-horse has been a symbol of gentlemanly authority in many cultures for many centuries. In the aristocratic tradition of horsemanship, a group of Philadelphia's best sporting bloods, in 1766, formed the Gloucester Fox Hunting Club, across the Delaware River in New Jersey. The founders—Chews, Willings, Whartons, Cadwaladers, and endless Morrises—were the leaders of Society in the Revolutionary Era. In 1774, twenty-two members of the Gloucester Hunt were among the founders of the First Troop of Philadelphia City Cavalry, known today as the First City Troop, or just The Troop. The oldest regiment in the U.S. Army, The Troop fought in the Revolution and subsequent wars, and has remained a private club ever since. Christian Sam Morris, the essence of the eighteenth-century Philadelphia gentleman, was captain of the First City Troop in the Revolution, and at the same time governor of the colony in Schuylkill and president of the Gloucester Hunt from its founding till his death in 1812 (the club broke up in 1818).

The fox-hunting tradition in Philadelphia died down in the decades leading up to the Civil War (as it did in England, interestingly enough). After the war and especially in the early twentieth century, the gentleman huntsman went through a revival. The first modern hunt club was formed in the Media area in the now-unfashionable Baltimore Pike area, south of the city. Just on the eve of the Civil War, the Rose Tree Hunt Club was founded in 1859, and is the oldest in America today. In 1883, during the great country-club-forming decades, the Radnor Hunt was established along the Main Line, at Radnor. Today it is farther out on the Main Line, and probably the preeminent social hunt in the city, especially for the members of status-striving new families just learning the ritual. The eminently fashionable and old-money huntsmen in Chestnut Hill and in the Penlyn-Whitemarsh area out along the Bethlehem Pike formed the Whitemarsh Hunt Club in 1903, and in 1914 a group of sportsmen founded the Huntington Valley Hunt Club in the Old York Road area, north of the city in Bucks County. Wharton Sinkler, a wealthy Elkins in-law, and Joseph Wharton Lippincott, son of the founder of the city's most well-known publishing firm, J.B. Lippincott, were masters of fox hounds for many years. Finally, in the beautiful rolling country around Valley Forge, William J. Clothier, national tennis champion and an accomplished all-around athlete, formed the Pickering Hunt Club in 1911 and remained its Master of Fox Hounds for forty years. Hunt club members not only follow the hounds in the fall and winter months; they also hold point-to-point and steeplechase races in which gentlemen-jockeys compete before polite crowds of very proper audiences each year. As Master of Fox Hounds and a gentleman-jockey in his younger years, Bill Clothier broke almost every bone in his body, some more than once.

Next to fox hunting, Philadelphia's indigenous upper-class sport is rowing, immortalized in the brilliant paintings of Thomas Eakins. Just before the Falls and below the old waterworks and the Museum, the so-called Schuylkill Navy includes some ten charming Victorian boat houses, now all outlined in lights at night, which provide one of the city's proudest architectural settings. The most distinguished, of course, is the boat house of the University of Pennsylvania, while the most internationally famous club is the Vespers (Kelly Club). The University Barge Club, founded in 1854, is *the* upper-class rowing club. Its roster of membership down through the years, according to Nathaniel Burt, is "equalled only by the Assembly itself." Many years after its founding, the University Barge Club leased an old broken-down farm house from the Fairmount Park Art Commission in 1887. The farm house, charmingly restored and called the Lilacs, was one of the favorite gathering places of Old Philadelphians up until the Second World War. The Lilacs was hidden in the woods above the West River Drive, while the boat houses were, of course, along the East River Drive, only recently renamed Kelly Drive, after the two Jack Kellys of Olympic rowing fame.

While Philadelphia rowing centers on the placid waters of the Schuylkill, yachtsmen sail on the Delaware where, downriver from Philadelphia, wealthy yachtsmen founded the distinguished and charming Corinthian Yacht Club in 1892. Its commodore in 1894 was the city's most famous banker, A.J. Drexel. The entrance fee that year was $25, as were the annual dues.

The first country club in America was founded in Brookline, Massachusetts, a Boston suburb, in 1882. The two most fashionable country clubs in Philadelphia were founded in the next decade: the Philadelphia Country Club, in 1890, and the Huntington Valley Country Club, in 1892. The Philadelphia Country Club, situated on the old Duhring estate inside the city line at the beginning of the old Main Line, was the center of fashion, polo, and golf, from its founding up until the eve of the Second World War. The valuable property was sold after the war, and a new and opulent Philadelphia Country Club was built at Gladwyne, further out on the Main Line. Today it is an elite, rather than a class country club. The Huntington Valley, not unlike the Philadelphia Country, was once highly fashionable but is now more of an elite club for manufacturing and business families who live in the suburbs out along the Old York Road, which today are also the elite Jewish suburbs in the city. (Elite Jews are members of the Philmont Country Club, founded by Ellis Gimbel in 1906, rather than the Huntington Valley.)

In both Philadelphia and Boston, cricket clubs are older than country clubs. In Boston, the Longwood Cricket Club was founded in 1877 and today is the center of top-flight tennis in the city, as it has been throughout the twentieth century.

After the Civil War, and especially in the closing decades of the nineteenth century, the Philadelphia upper class produced the finest cricket ever played in America. In 1896 Proper Philadelphia cricketeers scored their finest victory, defeating the Australian stars 282 to 222 at the Merion Cricket Club in Haverford. Cricket was brought to Philadelphia by wool weavers from the north of England who settled in Germantown in the early nineteenth century. The first all-American-born cricket club in the city was at Haverford College in 1834.

The three leading cricket clubs in Philadelphia were the Philadelphia Cricket Club in Chestnut Hill, founded in 1854, the Germantown Cricket Club, founded in 1855, and the Merion Cricket Club, founded in Merion on the Main Line in 1865 and later moved to its present location at Haverford. The Newhall family of Philadelphia, which once fielded a whole cricket eleven with three generations of the family, has generally been regarded as the first family of American cricket (much like the immortal Grace family of England). Family continuity in Philadelphia's upper class is suggested by the fact that there are some twenty Newhall conjugal family units listed in the current *Social Register*. The Philadelphia, Germantown, and Merion cricket clubs still exist today but largely as centers of tennis and squash. Four United States Lawn Tennis Champions, Tilden of Germantown, R. Norris Williams of the Philadelphia Cricket, and William J. Clothier and E. Victor Seixas, Jr., both of Merion, were Philadelphians. The city not only produced Big Bill Tilden, the greatest tennis player in history, but also four national champions, the only city to have done so.

While both the Philadelphia Cricket in Chestnut Hill, and Merion on the Main Line, have excellent golf club annexes (the Merion course is of world-class stature), the inner core of Proper Philadelphia families have played at less-crowded facilities ever since the First World War: at the Gulph Mills Golf Club on the Main Line, and at Sunnybrook in the Whitemarsh Valley, just over the city line from Chestnut Hill. Sunnybrook was founded in 1913 and Gulph Mills in 1916.

While hunt clubs, cricket clubs, country clubs, and golf clubs have structured social life and social status in the suburbs, the ultimate class authority and power has been centered in the halls of the urban men's clubs. The oldest men's club in the city is the Philadelphia Club, founded in 1834, and the oldest of its kind in the nation (the comparable Union Club in New York, and the Somerset in Boston were founded in 1836 and 1851, respectively).

Since its founding in 1834, the Philadelphia Club has marked the inner core of Proper Philadelphia prestige and power. The first chairman of the club was George Cadwalader (1834), the first president was Commodore James Biddle (1845–48), and the president at the club's 100th anniversary was the famous novelist, Owen Wister, author of *The Virginian*. Through the years, Philadelphia Club members have, of course, dominated the management of the Assembly Balls. Of the eighteen directors of the Assembly between 1820 and 1840, eight were founding members of the club; in 1940 five of the six managers of the Assembly were club members. Since 1940 most of the managers have also been club members. An inspection of the names of the 2,101 members of the club between 1834 and 1940 reads like an economic and cultural history of the city; old-family members of the club have included 35 Biddles, 17 Morrises, 16 Coxes, 14 Peppers, 13 Cadwaladers (including 3 presidents), 12 Whartons, 11 Ingersolls, 10 Broies, 10 Willings, 10 Woods, 7 Merricks, 7 Rushes, 6 Drexels, as well as several Pembertons, Penroses, Chews, Hopkinsons, Walns, Ridgeways, Dallases, Meades (including the great Civil War general), Lippincotts, Harrisons, Rosengartens, and Cassatts. Such members as Anthony Drexel Cassatt, A.J. Drexel Paul, and two A.J. Drexel Biddles suggest the consanguinity of the membership and the prestige of the great banker's name, as well as the ancient Biddle proclivity for marrying money.

Just as the Rabbit is less ancient and distinguished than the Fish House, so the Rittenhouse Club compares to the Philadelphia Club. Founded in 1875 by such leading Philadelphians as S. Weir

Mitchell and William Pepper (both Philadelphia Club members), the Rittenhouse Club is located in one of the few remaining Victorian mansions on Walnut Street opposite Rittenhouse Square. It is appropriate that the younger club, founded when Rittenhouse Square was in its greatest days as the most fashionable address in the city, should be located uptown on Walnut Street, while the older club has remained downtown at 13th and Walnut. Originally founded as the Social Art Club (changed to Rittenhouse in 1888), the members of the Rittenhouse have always been somewhat more intellectually and artistically inclined than their more sporting peers at the older club. The differences are of course subtle, but real nonetheless. The fact that until the 1960s revolution (in the 1970s), the Diocesan Headquarters of the Episcopal Church was located across the Square in the old Cassatt mansion, next to Holy Trinity Church, and that the club is nearer the University out in West Philadelphia may have contributed to this atmosphere; in the old days, at least, one was far more likely to see men of the cloth and professors lunching at the Rittenhouse.

Although the core of upper-class Philadelphia lunched at the Philadelphia and Rittenhouse clubs, there has always been a solid group of athletic gentlemen at the Racquet Club, which was founded in 1889 by some of the best players of racquet and ball games in the city. For decades, for instance, one found the brothers Clark eating together every day at the same table; they were, next to the Newhalls, one of the leading cricket families in the great days at the turn of the century, and Joseph Sill (father of the reform mayor in the 1950s) was first intercollegiate champion in tennis, while his brother, Clarence, was first national doubles champion of the United States along with his brother-in-law-to-be, Frederick W. Taylor, founder of scientific management. Joseph and Clarence Clark were also the first Americans to play at Wimbledon.

Just as gentlemen athletes founded the Racquet Club, so a group of the city's leading, turn-of-the-century intellectuals, led by the famous novelist-physician, S. Weir Mitchell, founded the Franklin Inn Club in 1902. The Inn, as it is often called by its members, is comparable to the Tavern Club in Boston, or the well-known Century Club in New York. It is housed in a charming old house on Camac Street, a narrow alley running south from Walnut Street below Thirteenth. At one long, masculinely simple table, one meets at lunch the city's leading writers, artists, book collectors, librarians, and professors from the local colleges and universities, as well as a group of publishers and editors of newspapers, periodicals, and books (sons of such famous Philadelphia houses as Lippincott, Lea and Febiger, Curtis and Bok). Charm is in the mind rather than the pocketbook, and the conversation is lively, except when the loquatious club bore holds sway.

Among fashionable Philadelphians of the old school, both of the birthright and social-climbing variety, the only two clubs that counted in the city were the Philadelphia and the Rittenhouse. At the same time, the vast majority of the city's solid citizens, as well as most historians, were convinced that the most powerful, snobbish, and conservative club in the city was the Union League (it is *never* called a club—only the Union League or just the League). Founded during the Civil War by reforming idealists who supported the antislavery cause and the new Republican party, the League became the heart of Philadelphia's business establishment and the seat and symbol of the rock-ribbed Republicanism which ruled both city hall and the state capital, except for brief reform periods, between Appomatox and Pearl Harbor. The first Republican Convention was held in Philadelphia's Music Hall in 1856 and nominated John C. Fremont; at the time, both Philadelphia and the state were still Democratic, and James Buchanan, the only son of Pennsylvania to ever reach the White House, defeated Fremont in a surprisingly close presidential election. Soon afterwards, 331 Philadelphians who supported the Republican platform founded Philadelphia's first Republican Club. Fifty-one of the more wealthy and prominent among them eventually became members of the Union League, which was founded in 1862. The fifty-five men who were founding members of the League were surely among the most distinguished members of the Civil War business establishment. Their social position was indicated by the fact that thirty of them were members of the Philadelphia Club during the nineteenth century—fifteen members when the League was founded, and fifteen joining later. Two of the League founders had been president of the Philadelphia

Club: General George Cadwalader, first chairman, and Adolph E. Borie, fourth president. George Boker was a Philadelphia Club member at the League's founding and served as president of both the League and the Philadelphia Club during the 1870s and 1880s.

The Union League clubhouse is certainly the most distinguished in the city as far as architecture and location are concerned. The original building was designed by John Fraser in French Renaissance style. Its mansard roof and brick and brownstone facade on Broad Street, only a block and a half south of City Hall, remind all passersby of business and Republican power in the city since the General Grant era. The League eventually outgrew its original clubhouse, and an addition was finally made in 1906–10. Built of granite and limestone in the Georgian style, it was designed by the city's most famous architect at the time, Horace Trumbauer. The addition was more than twice as large as the original building, and the present clubhouse covers almost half a block, running along Sansom Street; the impressive main hallway runs for a whole city block between Broad and Fifteenth. The clubhouse today is surely the most distinguished in the city and probably the nation.

In 1940, at the very end of the pre-atom-bomb era in world history, the pattern of mobility within the social, economic, and political power structure of the city was clearly articulated within the halls of the Union League and the Philadelphia and Rittenhouse clubs, as I outlined in the following paragraph in *The Philadelphia Gentlemen* (1958):

> As new men succeed in business, they join the Union League as a matter of course. If they eventually join the Rittenhouse, often at advanced ages, they retain membership in the Union League. If they then go to the Philadelphia Club, however, they may drop out of the League. One gentleman in the 1940 elite, for example, was quite a clubman back before the First World War. His club listings in a prewar *Social Register* amounted to ten clubs in all, including the Union League, University and Rittenhouse Clubs. With his entrance into the Philadelphia Club in the late thirties, however, his club listings in *Who's Who* in 1940 included the Philadelphia and Rittenhouse only.

Although the Philadelphia Club, in 1940, stood at the pinnacle of economic and social power in the city, the membership of the

Union League has probably always been the most distinguished in the city and state, in an *elite* (*Who's Who*) or accomplishment sense, even though the Philadelphia Club members held more secure and inherited *class* positions (*Social Register*). Before the Second World War, however, both the elite and the upper class—the League and the Philadelphia Club memberships—were almost exclusively white Anglo-Saxon Protestants (WASPs).

Today Philadelphia, and American society as a whole, is a more or less classless bureaucracy. There are quite naturally the usual elite positions in business, banking, advertising, law, medicine, and a host of other fields, but they are not held together by any clearly defined upper-class family structure. There still are hundreds of old-stock, upper-class families living out on the Main Line and in Chestnut Hill. But their men are no longer in control of the powerful functional elites in the city to anywhere near the same extent as before the Second World War. The Philadelphia and Rittenhouse clubs are becoming less and less relevant to the power struggles in the city, which today are centered in the halls of the Union League, now the most relevant club in the city. How and why this is so is another story, too long and complicated to be told here. It can be briefly said, however, that the WASP male's dominance of the city, and his wife and family, is now a thing of the past; WASP males and females, Irish and Italian Catholic males and females, black males and females are all in the elitist race today. The class is irrelevant, which, after all, depended on the family and a set of moral standards set by women, who still stood above the competitive battles of the marketplace, as Tocqueville wrote 150 years ago.

In the prewar days when male clubdom ran the city, Proper Philadelphia ladies formed the Acorn Club in 1890; it was the first of its kind in the nation (older than the Colony in New York or the Chilton in Boston). Many years later, in the more feminist 1920s, fashionable and unfashionable Philadelphia ladies founded the Cosmopolitan Club, in 1928. The Acorn has been the female counterpart of the Philadelphia Club down through the years, while the more intellectual and careerist members of the Cosmopolitan Club are more like the members of the Franklin Inn (within the past decade, women have been taken into the Inn).

Back in 1915 the creative elites in the city formed the Art Alliance, which has been open to both sexes since the beginning. With a membership more interested in culture than mere power, the club has been congenial but hardly a center of the social and economic struggles in the city.

7

Social Mobility and Fertility Within an Elite Group

The existence of an inverse relationship between social class and fertility in the more industrialized nations of Western civilization has been regarded as a confirmed sociological fact for some decades.[1] Within the social structure as a whole, parents with more education, higher incomes, and various other indexes of "high" socioeconomic status tend to have smaller families than parents in less fortunate circumstances. In the 1930s, however, the findings of empirical research, both in this country and in Europe, indicated that this inverse relationship was reversed at the higher socioeconomic levels.[2] The topmost socioeconomic groups, for example, were shown to have similar and/or higher fertility rates than those immediately below them. With each successive study reaffirming these relationships, the question of "why" has become more pertinent. The evidence of the Indianapolis Study, for example, has raised many questions concerning the reasons why social-class position persistently colors all other associations between various social and psychological variables and fertility.

In interpreting this relationship between fertility and socioeconomic position, differential social mobility and its various social and psychological consequences may be an important intervening variable. Westoff, for example, has emphasized the hypothesis that the *process* of achieving a given class position may exert equal if not greater influence on family size than the sociological consequences of the position itself.[3] In other words, fertility declines as one ascends the social-class hierarchy mainly because the requirements of a more expensive pattern of consumption militate against having children and partly because of the internalization of small-family norms already existing in the cultural definitions of the class of destination. Consequently, fertility should be expected to decline at successively higher levels in the social-class hierarchy partly because those persons in higher positions are, on the average, more mobile than those below them. On the other hand, as the top of the hierarchy is approached, this inverse differential may be reversed precisely because, in contrast to those immediately below them, social mobility may be less characteristic of persons at the top levels. The following analysis of the fertility patterns of a small group of persons of high socioeconomic status in Philadelphia should be conceived of as an exploratory attempt to test the existence of an inverse relationship between upward social mobility and family size.

In 1940, 770 residents of Philadelphia were listed in *Who's Who in America*.[4] On the basis of selected criteria of social mobility, this comparatively homogeneous Philadelphia elite will be divided into various subgroups in order to test the hypothesis that the less mobile parents have the largest families. There are, of course, both advantages and limitations in using these *Who's Who* biographies to test this relationship. In the first place, the fact that persons listed in *Who's Who* are, from the standpoint of society as a whole, a relatively homogeneous socioeconomic group is a decided advantage. On the other hand, the inferential nature of the various indexes of social mobility used below is, of necessity, a limiting factor. The fertility data, in addition, suffer from omissions which are characteristic of *Who's Who* biographies (see below). As a result of these and other considerations, the present analysis is intended more to suggest the potential value of the fertility/mobility hypothesis than presuming to confirm or reject it.

In most societies, there are people at the top of the class pyramid who, coming from "old family" backgrounds and often possessing inherited wealth, may be considered of high *ascribed* social-class position. In Philadelphia, the *Social Register* is a convenient listing of families whose members, on the whole, possess these attributes of high ascribed position.[5] On the other hand, there are the so-called self-made men who presumably have *achieved* their high occupational status largely through their own efforts and sacrifices.[6] In order to test the fertility/mobility hypothesis, the 770 Philadelphians who were listed in *Who's Who* in 1940 may be divided into two groups—the 226 persons who were also listed in the *Social Register* in that year and the 544 persons who were not so listed.[7] While both of these groups within the Philadelphia elite were composed of persons with high occupational, educational, and income positions in the city, the 226 listed also in the *Social Register* were more likely, on the whole, to have been of high ascribed position (less mobile), whereas the high positions of the remaining 544 were more likely to have been achieved (more mobile). For example, it is reasonable to infer that a private, secondary school education, Protestant religious affiliation, and the ties of place and tradition are, among other things, useful indexes of high ascribed social-class position in America; the evidence in table 7.1 indicates that persons also listed in the *Social Register* are more likely to possess these attributes than the remaining persons listed only in *Who's Who*.[8]

The 770 Philadelphians listed in *Who's Who* in 1940 were older men and women. Of those reporting age (719 or 94 percent), all were over thirty-six years of age in 1940, a large majority (83 percent) were over fifty, and their mean age in 1940 was 61.6 years. Those persons listed in the *Social Register* were somewhat older (mean age in 1940 *Social Register* group, 64.3; non *Social Register* group, 60.5). Thus, assuming that wives tend, on the whole, to be only slightly younger than their husbands, most families in this study have passed through the child-bearing period. As females constituted only a small proportion (7 percent) of the Philadelphians listed in *Who's Who* in 1940, they will be discussed separately below.[9]

What are the marital and family characteristics of the two groups of males within this listing of distinguished Philadelphians? In the first place, while 92 percent of the total report ever having been married, those also listed in the *Social Register* are more likely

TABLE 7.1
Philadelphians Listed in Who's Who in 1940: Schooling, Religious Affiliation, and Birthplace by Social Register Affiliation.

Inferred Indices of High Ascribed Status	Social Register Affiliation	Non Social Register Affiliation
	Per Cent	Per Cent
Private Secondary Schooling*	41	15
Protestant Religion	64**	58**
Born in the United States	97	91
Born on the Eastern Seaboard***	87	64
Born in Philadelphia	52	29
Total Number	226	544

*Private Schooling does not include the Catholic Parochial School.

**As these figures include those not reporting on religion, it is pertinent to note that, of the 513 persons reporting on religious affiliation, 99 percent of the Social Register group, in contrast to 86 percent of those listed only in Who's Who, were Protestant.

***Eastern Seaboard includes the Middle Atlantic, New England, and South Atlantic Census areas.

to report marriage (95 percent ever married) than the remainder (90 percent ever married). This differential in the proportion married is the first clue to the more familistic nature of the former, less mobile group.

As the under-reporting of children in *Who's Who* biographies makes any estimate of the number of childless marriages in this sample extremely hazardous, the fertility patterns of parents, rather than married couples, will be analyzed below. From other sources, there is some evidence that, if anything, there are fewer childless couples within the *Social Register* group. For example, it was found that at least six "Social Registerite" fathers in this study (all with more than three children) failed to report the names of their children in *Who's Who*.

The fertility rates of 501 male parents are presented in table 7.2. The parents also listed in the *Social Register* tend to have larger families, and are less likely to have only children and more likely to have large families (three or more children) than the

TABLE 7.2
Philadelphians Listed in Who's Who in 1940: Family Size of Male Parents by Social Register Affiliation.

Number of Children	Social Register Affiliation	Non Social Register Affiliation
	Per Cent	Per Cent
1 Child	14	21
2 Children	30	36
3 Children	31	21
4 or more Children	25	22
Number of Male Parents	149	352
Children Per 100 Male Parents	280	262

remaining parents listed only in *Who's Who.*[10] Here, then, are two groups of male parents of high socioeconomic status in Philadelphia; those parents who have been apparently less mobile than the rest are more likely to report large families.

As an additional test of the fertility/mobility hypothesis, education, religious affiliation, and birthplace of parent—presumed indexes of ascribed status and mobility—will now be viewed in relation to differences in family size.

In the first place, perhaps a private secondary school education, which depends almost entirely on the socioeconomic position of one's parents, may be an even more valid index of high ascribed social-class position than *Social Register* affiliation. If this is true, privately educated parents, regardless of *Social Register* affiliation, should be expected to have more children than those parents without the advantages of this start in life and all that it implies in the way of wealth and social contacts.[11] The inverse relationship between fertility and social mobility is suggested once again in table 7.3, which indicates that privately educated parents tend to have the largest families. Moreover, family size remains the same within the group of privately educated parents, regardless of *Social Register* affiliation.

TABLE 7.3
Philadelphians Listed in Who's Who in 1940: Fertility of Male Parents by Social Register Affiliation and Secondary Schooling.

Secondary Schooling of Male Parents	Social Register Affiliation		Non Social Register Affiliation	
	Number of Male Parents	Children Per 100 Male Parents	Number of Male Parents	Children Per 100 Male Parents
Private Schooling*	66	300	51	300
No Private Schooling	83	264	301	255
Total	149	280	352	262

*Private Schooling does not include the Catholic Parochial School.

In America, Protestants, on the whole, tend to have higher social origins than non-Protestants. As shown in table 7.4, for example, there is only one non-Protestant parent in the *Social Register* group. Within this Philadelphia elite, Episcopalians have the highest ascribed social class positions.[12] Consequently, it is pertinent to note that (see table 7.4) the Episcopalian parents tend to have larger families than the other Protestant parents.[13] Furthermore, the Episcopalian parents who are also listed in the *Social Register*, presumably the least mobile parents, have larger families than even the non-Protestants. In other words, using religious affiliation as an index of differential mobility, table 7.4 indicates that, at least within the Protestant group, fertility is inversely related to social mobility.

Upward social mobility often coincides with horizontal mobility. Especially in the small town, one rarely "crosses the tracks" within the same community where everyone knows "who" one is. On the contrary, one must move out, and usually to the large city, in order to escape previous social definitions. In Philadelphia in 1940, almost two-thirds (64 percent) of the persons listed in *Who's Who* were born outside the metropolitan area. Thus persons who have achieved success in the city are presumably more

TABLE 7.4
Philadelphians Listed in Who's Who in 1940: Fertility of Male Parents by Social Register and Religious Affiliation.

Religious Affiliation of Male Parents	Social Register Affiliation		Non Social Register Affiliation	
	Number of Male Parents	Children Per 100 Male Parents	Number of Male Parents	Children Per 100 Male Parents
Episcopalian	70	304	53	263
Other Protestant	36	258	177	261
Catholic-Jewish	1*	—	30	293
No Religion Reported	42	256	92	246
Total	149	280	352	262

*One Catholic with two children.

mobile than the residents of Philadelphia as a whole. It has been shown that members of the *Social Register* group are less horizontally mobile than the remaining persons listed only in *Who's Who* (table 7.1). In table 7.5, there is apparently a consistent inverse relationship between horizontal mobility, which may imply upward mobility, and family size.

To some extent, of course, *Social Register* affiliation is achievable. In order to ascertain the hard core of "old family" Philadelphians, the 226 persons who were listed in both *Who's Who* and the *Social Register* in 1940 were traced back to the turn of the century. It was found that, of the 149 male parents listed in the *Social Register* in 1940, only forty-five were listed, or had parents who were listed, in the Philadelphia *Social Register* as of 1900. These forty-five parents, the hard core of old family Philadelphians and as such neither horizontally nor vertically mobile, should be expected to have larger families than any other group in *Who's Who*. That these "Proper" Philadelphia parents, many of them descendants of Philadelphia's colonial aristocracy, reported an average of over three children, and that no less than

TABLE 7.5
Philadelphians Listed in Who's Who in 1940: Fertility of Male Parents by Social Register Affiliation and Birthplace.

Birthplace of Male Parents	Social Register Affiliation		Non Social Register Affiliation	
	Number of Male Parents	Children Per 100 Male Parents	Number of Male Parents	Children Per 100 Male Parents
Philadelphia	73	290	97	272
All other Areas	76	270	255	257
Total	149	280	352	262

40 percent of them reported four or more children, tends to substantiate further the fertility/mobility hypothesis.

In Philadelphia in 1940, there were 770 persons listed in *Who's Who in America*. In terms of several logically inferred indexes of upward social mobility, the 501 males who reported the names of their children were divided into various subgroups. A consistent inverse relationship between upward mobility and family size was found to obtain within this Philadelphia elite (table 7.6). In a sense, the tabulations in table 7.6 may be conceived of as a summary of a series of logically manipulated, "ex post facto" experiments.[14]

Do the fertility patterns of the small number (54) of women listed in *Who's Who* tend to support the fertility/mobility hypothesis? In the first place, one hardly would expect the "emancipated" or career-oriented women listed in *Who's Who* to be familistically inclined. These women in the Philadelphia elite, for example, are much less likely to have ever been married than the men; while over 90 percent of the men report ever having been married, only 44 percent of the women so report. The women also listed in the *Social Register*, however, are more likely to report marriage (64 percent ever married) than the remaining

TABLE 7.6
Philadelphians Listed in Who's Who in 1940: Fertility of Male Parents by Inferred Indexes of Social Mobility.

Indices of Social Mobility	Number of Male Parents	Children Per 100 Male Parents
(1) Male Parents Listed in Who's Who But Not in the Social Register	352	262
(2) Male Parents Listed in Who's Who And Also in the Social Register	149	280
(3) Philadelphia Born Male Parents Listed in Who's Who and Social Register	73	290
(4) Privately Educated Male Parents Listed in Who's Who and Social Register	66	300
(5) Episcopalian Male Parents Listed in Who's Who and Social Register	70	304
(6) "Old Family" Male Parents: Listed in Philadelphia Social Register in 1900	45	313
All Male Parents in Who's Who	501	267

women (37 percent ever married). Moreover, the mothers listed in the *Social Register* report considerably more children than the rest (266 as against 162 children per 100 mothers). Although this elite contains only a small number of women, the less mobile group, like the men, appear to be more familistic.

Social mobility and the attendant decline in traditional, family values characterize the modern world where there are few fixed landmarks and where most men are "constantly spurred on by a desire to rise and a fear of failing." This paper has attempted to indicate how, within a group of distinguished Philadelphians, fertility tends to be inversely related to upward social mobility. While the evidence is limited quantitatively, the consistent differences in fertility, as between the various subgroups within this relatively homogeneous elite, provide some insight into the nature of differential fertility. Any conclusions drawn from so limited a source must, of course, remain highly tentative.

Notes

1. In America, the pioneer publication in this field appeared in 1930. See Edgar Sydenstricker and Frank W. Notestein, "Differential Fertility According to Social Class," *Journal of the American Statistical Association* 25, no. 169 (March 1930): 9–32.
2. See Karl Edin and Edward P. Hutchinson, *Studies of Differential Fertility in Sweden* (London: P. S. King and Son, 1935); and Clyde V. Kiser, *Group Differences in Urban Fertility* (Baltimore: Williams & Wilkins, 1942).
3. Charles F. Westoff, "The Changing Focus of Differential Fertility Research: The Social Mobility Hypothesis," *Milbank Memorial Fund Quarterly* 31, no. 1 (January 1953): 24–38. See also, Jerzy Berent, "Fertility and Social Mobility," Population Studies 5, no. 3 (March 1952): 244–60.
4. *Who's Who in America*, vol. 21 (Chicago: A. N. Marquis, 1940). This paper is part of a more complete analysis of the biographies of the 770 Philadelphians listed in *Who's Who* in 1940. See E. Digby Baltzell, "The Elite and the Upper Class in Metropolitan America: A Study of Stratification in Philadelphia." Ph.D diss., Columbia University, 1952.
5. The *Social Register*, first published in New York City in 1888, is currently published, in November of each year, by the Social Register Association for the following large cities in America: New York, Philadelphia, Chicago, Baltimore, Boston, St. Louis, Cleveland, Pittsburgh, Buffalo, Cincinnati-Dayton, San Francisco, and Washington, D.C. See my dissertation for a more thorough analysis of the *Social Register* as an index of high ascribed social-class position in America.
6. For the classic discussion of "ascribed" and "achieved" status, see Ralph Linton, *The Study of Man* (New York: D. Appleton-Century, 1936).
7. As there is no demographic or biographical information available for persons listed in the *Social Register* but not in *Who's Who*, this paper must, of necessity be limited to an analysis of the 770 Philadelphians in *Who's Who*.
8. Chi squares were computed to test the statistical significance of the relationships between these attributes of social mobility and *Social Register* affiliation (table 7.1). The tests revealed that all the relationships, except "Protestant Religion," were significant. The values for P were .001 for "Private Secondary Schooling," "Born on Eastern Seaboard," and "Born in Philadelphia"; .01 for "Born in the United States"; and .10 for "Protestant Religion."
9. It is of interest to note that Kiser and Schacter found that "women comprise only about 6 percent of all persons listed in the last edition (1948–1949) of *Who's Who*." Clyde V. Kiser and Nathalie L. Schacter, "Demographic Characteristics of Women in *Who's Who*," *Milbank Memorial Fund Quarterly* 27 no. 4 (October 1949): 395.
10. A comparison of the distributions in table 7.2 by chi square analysis indicates a statistically significant degree of association between family size and *Social Register* affiliation (P = .02 – .05).
11. There is, of course, no way of ascertaining the differences in inherited wealth between these various subgroups in *Who's Who*. There is reason to believe, however, that inherited wealth, perhaps more than wealth per se, is an

important variable in fertility differentials within the higher socioeconomic stratum. This factor may be especially important where professional education demands sacrifices during the child-bearing period.

12. Episcopalian religious affiliation as an index of high ascribed social-class position in Philadelphia is thoroughly documented elsewhere. See my unpublished dissertation. Research in this area has found that Episcopalians tend to have a high socioeconomic rating. See, for example, Liston Pope, "Religion and the Class Structure," *Annals of the American Academy of Political and Social Science* 256 (March 1948): 84–91; and Ronald Freedman and P. K. Whelpton, "Social and Psychological Factors Affecting Fertility," *Milbank Memorial Fund Quarterly* 28, no. 3 (July 1950): 319.
13. The relatively high fertility of the "Other Protestant" parents who are not listed in the *Social Register* (table 7.4) is partially explained by the presence of three Swedeborgian parents who report eight, ten, and twelve children respectively.
14. Approximately the experimental model, we have attempted to test a hypothesis in a set of contrasting situations; the variable of "social mobility" was injected, as it were, into a succession of partially controlled situations. See Ernest Greenwood, *Experimental Sociology: A Study in Method* (New York: King's Crown Press, 1945), chap. 4.

8

Thorstein Veblen: Scientism and the Modern Mood

All human actions and social relations are concrete. Men, on the other hand, and especially intellectuals, have always been highly adaptable and creative in relation to both their human and natural environments, largely because of their ability to abstract from reality in the form of generalized concepts. This is true of all language and particularly the language of science. For the scientist, consciously and purposely, makes no attempt to describe the world in all its concrete chaos but rather to order and make sense of it by simplifying its complexities in a series of abstract laws, or, best of all, in quantitative equations. Thus Einstein once touchingly confessed that he was really an escapist by nature who had always shunned the muddled and confusing world of affairs by seeking shelter in the ordered world of scientific abstractions. Just as language can be both a vehicle and an obstacle to understanding, so, I think, the language and logic of science, when applied to human affairs rather than the natural world, may have certain undesirable consequences. In other words, I should like to suggest that there is an ever-present danger in the social sciences of moralizing abstractions, of turning concepts into epithets, and, above all, of downgrading the dignity of man.

Though the history of natural science, even since its coming to maturity in the ages of Galileo and Newton, has been full of examples of brilliant men who have become emotionally involved in defending outworn and erroneous concepts, it is in the social sciences that concepts are constantly evolving into ideologies which whole classes of men have loved or hated and have been willing to live and die for. Thus the Darwinian concepts of "natural selection" and "survival of the fittest" certainly involved no invidious comparisons or moral judgments among oysters, dogs, or dinosaurs, yet they easily, and perhaps unavoidably, became epithets and ideologies when races, classes, or national honor were involved. While the concept of the inheritance of acquired characteristics, believed in by Darwin, was eventually replaced by new concepts in biology, it was instructive to see that the Lysenko controversy raged in a culture founded on the ideology of science rather than in the West where men were still living, as moral rentiers to be sure, on the older, Judeo-Christian tradition.

It is indeed no accident, as more than one anthropologist and student of race has noted, that the liberating and enlightening Darwinian concepts in the field of biology have, at the same time, contributed to the intensification of class and racial conflicts and many other forms of social Darwinism which have marked our liberal and scientific age with unprecedented examples of man's inhumanity to man. (Tocqueville immediately saw that his friend Gobineau's classic work on race was fundamentally opposed to Christian teachings and predicted that it would one day be taken up by the Germans.) All of which is to suggest that, while new concepts in the social sciences begin by shedding light on the causes of human behavior and the nature of the historical process, they also, in turn, all too often end up by influencing, and causing, the behavior they once conceptualized. The concept of gravity, for instance, has no effect on the behavior of the tides of the sea, nor natural selection on the behavior of dinosaurs. Yet, as soon as the average man learns that life is no longer a moral journey in preparation for an afterlife but rather a competitive struggle for survival among higher animals (individual in classical, and classes in socialist, social theory), he will begin to behave quite differently towards his neighbors. Nor will he necessarily possess more dignity if he believes that his leaders are merely capitalist exploiters or members of a leisure class rather than God's elect or apostles of Christ. By their faiths in abstractions ye shall know them.

Not only do concepts in the social sciences eventually become causal factors in the historical process; they also, especially those modeled on natural-science concepts, exhibit a tendency to belittle, dismiss, and debunk the higher motives, dignity, and aspirations of men. Thus such psychological terms as rationalization or projection, along with such sociological abstractions as capitalist or bourgeois, begin as neutral, and useful, conceptualizations of reality but soon become ways of dismissing the values, motives, or rational arguments of those one dislikes or disagrees with. The altruism or Christian charity of a great lady like Jane Addams, or the motives of Lady Bountifuls in general, are cleverly dismissed by the initiated as merely projections of their sexual frustrations or rationalizations of their leisure-class guilt; all the virtues of thrift, cleanliness, good manners, punctuality, parental responsibility, deferred gratification, and sexual restraint, whether practiced by pharisees, philistines, bourgeois, or the modern squares, all too easily become, to the bohemians of one age or the beatniks of another, merely ways of avoiding truly authentic and healthily human emotions or spontaneously natural human contacts, rather than the inevitable disciplines practiced by most solid citizens in all civilized communities.

And of course the United Fund, the YMCA, and the Church become merely ways of perpetuating the power of the vested interests or, as Veblen would have it, the kept classes. Thus it follows that one of my Veblenian colleagues (who never contributes to the United Fund drive because it offends his sincere socialist convictions that the government could handle these problems more efficiently) dismisses the building of Mont Saint Michel or Chartres, as well as the atom bomb, as merely examples of how the leisure classes in two historical cultures have engaged in conspicuous consumption. A faithful follower of Feuerbach, Freud, and Durkheim in their scientific studies of religion, he also dismisses the concept of God as merely the projection of man's frustrations or a useful symbol of communal solidarity. But then, as sociological surveys have shown, we social scientists are less likely to believe in God than our less sophisticated natural-science peers. Perhaps my friend is himself merely an example of what Veblen called the "trained incapacity" which characterizes the faithful practitioners of all disciplined ways of thinking.

Though he was hardly of the stature of Marx or Freud, whose concepts have now become common coin in the language of all literate (and not so literate) men, Thorstein Veblen was certainly one of the American masters at coining abstract epithets. After reading a recently published biography of Veblen,[1] I reread his classic work, *The Theory of the Leisure Class*. I was particularly interested in rereading this one book of his because I have had the impression that its theme was causally related to the pervasive decline of authority in America today, as manifested in the rising rates of juvenile delinquency (especially among the upper and middle classes), the lack of leadership and widespread avoidance of leadership roles by many of the most talented members of the younger generation, and, perhaps most interesting of all, the radical revolt from authority on our college campuses and among the beatnik sons and daughters of some of our more concerned and affluent citizens. I should like, then, to briefly outline just enough of Veblen's theory of the leisure class to suggest how its debunking tone—much of which still forms part of the tacit assumptions of many of our leading intellectuals and academicians, as well as their brighter students—may have contributed to this modern mood.

To understand Veblen, I think, one must see him as a brilliant and ironic essayist, using the language of science to hide his own passions and frustrations behind a wealth of anthropological and historical detail which was, in turn, ingeniously ordered in highly abstract concepts. In fact, he conceptualized the history of human evolution in terms of his own hatred for the predatory and crude capitalism of the Gilded Age and, like his contemporary, Mark Twain, ended up in a mood of pure despair. Unlike Twain, he left us a host of abstractions rather than Huck Finn or Tom Sawyer (both innocents in the Garden of Eden before the knowledge of science and industrial technology transformed the face of America).

Veblen had his own highly abstract Eden, which he conceptualized as the stage of "savagery," and saw all the evils of civilization as variations on the theme of "barbarism," the next higher stage in the evolutionary process. Thus private property, conspicuous consumption, leisure classes, idle curiosity, good manners, and especially predatory sports and capitalism were all examples of man's Fall. In many ways, Veblen was a feminist (as was Marx except when he found that his favorite daughter was living in "sin" with one of London's most notorious "bounders"). He definitely preferred the feminine to the masculine elements in society. The Fall came when the predatory patriarchal principle replaced the peaceful and egalitarian matriarchal one. Thus he wrote that "a leisure class coincides with the beginning of ownership . . . the earliest form of ownership is the ownership of women by the able-bodied men of the community . . . the ownership of women begins in the lower barbarian stages of culture, apparently with the seizure of female captives . . . who seem to have been useful as trophies."

Veblen was also the extreme egalitarian. All distinctions were "invidious" ones. His ideal was the "masterless man," and he saw no need for leaders or differentiation of function within institutions (he saw college and university administrations as examples of "total depravity"). In fact he was actually against all institutions (he was in the habit of rewarding all his graduate students at Chicago with an equal grade of "C," partly because of his egalitarian values and partly to confuse the administration). He idealized the simple stage of savagery largely because both men and women are still engaged in productive labor and living in small, static, and egalitarian communities.

Being somewhat of a technological determinist, Veblen naturally saw the Fall as the result of the invention of the tool, and its counterpart the weapon, which allowed for the rise of the predatory and barbarian stage of culture. Distinctions were now possible and a leisure class, "conspicuously exempted from all useful employment," developed; the normal occupations of this class were "government, war, sports and devout observation," all examples of predatory, not productive, employment; yet all were honorable pursuits and engaged in, incidentally, by men rather than women.

As Civilization "advanced," this leisure class of predatory males (women were mainly "trophies") developed all kinds of hierarchical devices. Veblen, in his own inimitable style, describes the process as follows: "As the population increases in density, and as human relations grow more complex and numerous, all the details of life undergo a process of elaboration and selection; and in this process of elaboration the use of trophies develops into a system of rank, titles, degrees, and insignia, typical examples of which are heraldic devices, medals, and honorary decorations."

Conspicuous leisure, "closely allied with the life of exploit," was of course the ultimate test of high rank. For leisure allowed for all kinds of unproductive accomplishments which, according to Veblen, included "knowledge of the dead languages and the occult sciences; of correct spelling; of syntax and prosody; of the various forms of domestic music and other household art; of the latest proprieties of dress, furniture and equipage; of games, sports, and fancy-bred animals, such as dogs and race-horses." One of the most important consequences of leisure and the predatory culture was the growth of good manners or "breeding, polite usage, and decorum." Thus manners, according to Veblen, "hold a more important place in the esteem of men during the stage of culture at which conspicuous leisure has the greatest vogue"; and "manners have progressively deteriorated as society has receded from the patriarchal stage, as many gentlemen of the old school have been provoked to remark recently." But naturally to Veblen, a clean functionalist long before houses were conceived as "machines for living," the "pervading principle and abiding test of good breeding is the requirement of a substantial and patent waste of time."

At least as of Veblen's publication of *The Theory of the Leisure Class* in 1899, this leisure class of predatory gentlemen of good manners and some grammar was still in the habit of keeping both its ladies and its "lackies," as well as its children, in their proper places. Veblen ingeniously illustrates this in a discussion of the differential use of intoxicating beverages and narcotics, some of which I must quote directly:

From archaic times down through all the length of the patriarchal regime it has been the office of women to prepare and administer these luxuries, and it has been the prerequisite of the men of gentle birth and breeding to consume them. Drunkenness and the other pathological consequences of the free use of stimulants therefore tend in their turn to become honorific, as being a mark, at the second remove, of the superior status of those who are able to afford the indulgence. Infirmities induced by overindulgence are among some peoples freely recognized as manly attributes. . . . The same invidious distinction adds force to the current disapproval of any indulgence of this kind on the part of women, minors, and inferiors. . . . Where the example set by the leisure class retains its imperative force in the regulation of the conventionalities, it is observable that the women still in great measure practice the same traditional continence with regard to stimulants.

How far have we progressed, at least in the democratization of drunkenness, since Veblen's day!

It is of course not my purpose to give a complete outline of Veblen's theory of the leisure class in all its wealth of fascinating detail and debunking epithets. I hope to have given enough, however, to show that, behind all his bitterness and brilliant irony, he was trying to show how all advanced civilizations (in their various stages of barbarism, including the Gilded Age) depend on a class of men who have been able to rise above the purely productive level which traps all men, women, and children in the egalitarian stage of savagery. And the barbarian stages of civilization depend on the differentiation both of function and style of life. Most important of all, I think, was his realization that, at least in his day, the leisure class style of life still possessed authority as far as the rest of the community was concerned. Thus he wrote:

The leisure class stands at the head of the social structure in point of reputability: and its manner of life and its standards of worth therefore afford the norm of reputability for the community. The observance of these standards, in some degree of approximation, becomes incumbent upon all classes lower in the scale.

Veblen is remembered primarily as the man who debunked gentlemen of the leisure class who bought clothes, lived in correct neighborhoods, cultivated good manners and good grammar, went to church, and built cathedrals purely to impress others, especially those beneath them. But he was interested in far more. He was interested in no less than a comprehensive theory of civilization, in an age when he didn't like very much what it had produced. And due partly to his own temperament and partly to the intellectual climate of opinion in his day, he was led to debunking all civilized institutions, which must inevitably involve hierarchy and leadership, as barbaric departures from the peaceful, stagnant, and egalitarian stage of savagery, a point of view which has of course had a long tradition ever since the days of the eighteenth-century philosophs.

In many ways this tradition of debunking institutions and institutionalized authority in general has been successful. There is hardly a leisure class in Veblen's sense in America today (surely the nervous pleasure-seekers in the jet set do not know what either leisure or manners mean), and what leisure and conspicuous consumption there still is has slowly slid down the socio-economic scale since the Second World War. And it is not beyond the realms of possibility that the behavior of the beatnik is inspired by folk values of the stage of savagery idealized by Veblen, or that the recent Berkeley and Columbia revolutions against the modern and permissive Captains of Erudition could have used Veblen's *Higher Learning in America* as their bible. All civilization may be sinful, but the longing to return to Eden is pure folly.

But more than this, I think there is a possibility that Veblen and so may others of his school, both before him and since, have somehow missed the point. It is not, in other words, that conspicuous consumption (the behavior might have been conceptualized as "setting an example") is wrong, but rather whether men seek to impress others by building cathedrals or atom bombs, by inspiring us with the Seagram's building or depressing us with the Pan American monstrosity atop Grand Central; whether the young aspire to emulate Liz Taylor or the idealized ladies of Charles Dana Gibson, Frank Merriwell or Elvis Presley, the Beatles or the queen, their peers or their parents.

Similarly, I suppose, sexual frustration will always be with us in spite of the modern permissive and hedonistic temper. Yet is makes all the difference in the world whether these frustrations are projected in one way rather than the other; in creating Hull

House or decorating the Sistine Chapel rather than in rabid racism, pornography, or blatant homosexuality; in the idealization of sexual satisfaction as in the art of D.H. Lawrence rather than in its degradation in the theatre of Tennessee Williams or Edward Albee. Thus a leisure-class inheritance and the frequency of guilt which goes with it has produced Jane Addams, Eleanor Roosevelt, and Adlai Stevenson as well as Marx and Engels, Leopold and Loeb, and even Veblen himself, who married well and never held a full-time job until he was thirty-five. On the other hand, the frustrations which go with less fortunate choices of parents produced both Lincoln and Adolf Hitler. It is, then, not necessarily the class of abstract pathologies, whether psychological or sociological, which are the main problem but rather how concrete individuals, influenced by the values of their time, class, and culture, of course, are inspired to handle them. It is, after all, the injured and not the healthy oyster which produces the pearl. The modern passion for perfect social justice or psychological adjustment through the materialistic means of social equality and permissiveness may well prove as undesirable as it surely is utopian. No well-rounded man ever produced anything of lasting value, and surely there are more well-rounded and happy men living in the stages of savagery today than there are along Madison, Park, or Pennsylvania Avenues here in the United States.

But perhaps, after all, Veblen himself had a clue to our problem, which may lie in the "trained incapacity" of the scientific mind to go beyond the analysis of the material causes of our troubles to the theology of hope and the art of inspiration.

Note

1. Douglas F. Dowd, *Thorstein Veblen* (New York: Washington Square Press, 1966).

9

W.E.B. Du Bois and *The Philadelphia Negro*

In an appendix to his famous study of the American Negro, *An American Dilemma*, Gunnar Myrdal discussed the need for further research in the Negro community. "We cannot close this description of what a study of a Negro community should be," he wrote, "without calling attention to the study which best meets our requirements, a study which is now all but forgotten. We refer to W.E.B. Du Bois, *The Philadelphia Negro*, published in 1899."[1] One would hardly expect a greater tribute to this early classic in American sociology. It is no wonder that there has not been a scholarly study of the American Negro in the twentieth century which has not referred to and utilized the empirical findings, the research methods, and the theoretical point of view of this seminal book.

A classic is sometimes defined as a book that is often referred to but seldom read. *The Philadelphia Negro* written by a young scholar who subsequently became one of the three most famous Negro leaders in American history, surely meets this requirement. Though always referred to and frequently quoted by specialists, it is now seldom read by the more general student of sociology. For not only has the book been out of print for almost half a century; it has been virtually unobtainable, as my own experience of almost twenty years of searching in vain for a copy in second-hand bookstores attests. Even at the University of Pennsylvania, under whose sponsorship the research was undertaken and the book published, although one copy has been preserved in the archives and one on microfilm, the sole copy listed in the catalogue and available for students in the library has been unaccountably missing from the shelves for several years. In writing this introduction, I am using a copy lent me by my good friend, Professor Ira Reid of Haverford College, a one-time colleague and friend of the late Professor Du Bois at Atlanta University. Modern students, then, will certainly benefit from a readily available paperback edition of this study of the Negro community in Philadelphia at the turn of the nineteenth century.

In order to gain a full understanding of any book, one ought to know something of the life and intellectual background of its author, the place of the book in the history of the discipline (in this case sociology), as well as the climate of intellectual opinion and the social conditions of the era in which the book was written. Because *The Philadelphia Negro*—like all his other writings—was so intimately a part of the life of W.E.B. Du Bois, I shall begin this introduction with a brief outline of his career. Du Bois himself wrote in his seventies: "My life had its significance and its only deep significance because it was part of a problem; but that problem was, as I continue to think, the central problem of the greatest of the world's democracies and so the problem of the future world."[2]

It is one of the coincidences of American history that in the year 1895, Frederick Douglass, a crusading abolitionist and the first great leader of the Negro people, died, and Booker T. Washington rose to national leadership, with his "compromise" speech at Atlanta, in which he made the famous statement that "in all things that are purely social we can be as separate as the fingers, yet one as the hand in all things essential to human progress." In that same year, which marked the passing of Negro leadership from the fiery and moralistic Douglass to the compromising and pragmatic Washington, a young New Englander, W.E.B. Du Bois, obtained the first Ph.D. degree ever awarded a Negro by Harvard University.

William Edward Burghardt Du Bois "was born by a golden river and in the shadow of two great hills," in Great Barrington, Massachusetts, in 1868, the same year "Andrew Johnson passed from the scene and Ulysses Grant became President of the United

States."[3] He was a mulatto of French Huguenot, Dutch, and Negro ("thank God, no Anglo-Saxon") ancestry. The Burghardt family had lived in this area of the Berkshires ever since his mother's great-grandfather had been set free after having served for a brief period in the Revolution. (In 1908, Du Bois was accepted by the Massachusetts branch of the Sons of the American Revolution but was eventually suspended from membership by the national office because of his Negro ancestry.) Du Bois grew up in a community of some five thousand souls which included between twenty-five and fifty Negroes. Social position in the small town was more a matter of class than of color. The rich people in town, mostly farmers, manufacturers, and merchants, were "not very rich nor many in number." Like the wealthier white children whom he "annexed as his natural companions," young Will Du Bois judged men on their merits and accomplishments and felt, as was natural in that day, that the rich and successful deserved their position in life, as did the "lazy and thriftless" poor. He "cordially despised" the immigrant millworkers and looked upon them as a "ragged, ignorant, drunken proletariat, grist for the dirty woolen mills and the poorhouse."

As his father, apparently a charming but irresponsible almost-white mulatto, died when he was very young, Du Bois was brought up by his mother. Though always very poor, she did her best to pass on to her only son her own pride of ancestry and old established position in the local Negro community. Fortunately, young Will was a precocious and brilliant boy, possessed of an infinite capacity for work and an abiding passion to excel. His stern New England upbringing was reflected in the following description of his values as a senior at Fisk: "I believed too little in Christian dogma to become a minister," he wrote many years later. "I was not without faith: I never stole material or spiritual things; I not only never lied, but blurted out my conception of the truth on many untoward occasions; I drank no alcohol and knew nothing of women, physically or psychically, to the incredulous amusement of most of my more experienced fellows: I above all believed in work—systematic and tireless."[4]

From an early age, Du Bois planned to go to college and was fortunately encouraged to do so by his friends and teachers. "A wife of one of the cotton mill owners, whose only son was a pal of mine," he wrote more than half a century later, "offered to see that I got lexicons and texts to take up the study of Greek in high school, without which college doors in that day would not open. I accepted the offer as only normal and right; only after many years did I realize how critical this gift was for my career."[5]

Among the Negroes of Great Barrington, young Will Du Bois soon came to have a very special place. He was the only Negro in his high school class of twelve and one of the two or three boys in the whole class who went on to college. After school and on weekends he worked at all sorts of jobs. Through his friendship with the local newsdealer, he obtained, for a brief period, a position as local correspondent for the *Springfield Republican*. He also contributed local news to two Negro newspapers, one in Boston and the other in New York. With a few harsh exceptions as he reached adolescence, he was accepted on his merits by his peers. Though not particularly good at sports, he was highly respected intellectually. At fifteen, he began annotating his collected papers, a practice he scrupulously followed until his death, in Ghana, at the age of ninety-five.

Du Bois was, of course, aware of the color line as he grew up, but he had his first experience with a large Negro community at the age of fifteen, when he went to visit his grandfather in New Bedford. "I went to the East to visit my father's father in New Bedford," he later wrote, "and on that trip saw well-to-do, well-mannered colored people; and once, at Rocky Point, Rhode Island, I viewed with astonishment 10,000 Negroes of every hue and bearing. I was transported with amazement and dreams; I apparently noted nothing of poverty and degradation, but only extraordinary beauty of skin color and utter equality of mien, with absence so far as I could see of even the shadow of the line of race."[6]

Du Bois graduated with high honors from high school in the spring of 1884. His mother died soon after graduation day. Too poor—and also thought to be too young—to go to college, he finally took a job as timekeeper for a contractor who was building a fabulous "cottage" for the widow of Mark Hopkins, whose father-in-law had made a fortune in railroads and founded one of the first families in San Francisco. He learned a great deal about the ways of men on this responsible job, and was also able to save a little money. In the fall of 1885, he obtained some scholarship aid and entered Fisk University in Nashville, Tennessee, as a sophomore. He would have preferred Harvard, but Fisk in many ways proved to be a very valuable experience. Here for the first time he lived among, and learned about, his fellow Negroes. Though he did learn about a certain segment of the Southern Negro community at Fisk and in Nashville, he was, nevertheless, determined to see it whole. "Somewhat to the consternation of both teachers and fellow students," he obtained a job teaching school in the summer months in West Tennessee. "Needless to say, the experience was invaluable," he wrote. "I traveled not only in space but in time. I touched the very shadow of slavery. I lived and taught school in log cabins built before the Civil War. My school was the second held in the district since emancipation. I touched intimately the lives of the commonest of mankind—people who ranged from barefooted dwellers on dirt floors, with patched rags for clothes, to rough, hard-working farmers, with plain, clean plenty. I saw and talked with white people, noted now their unease, now their truculence and again their friendliness. I nearly fell from my horse when the first school commissioner whom I interviewed invited me to stay to dinner. Afterwards I realized that he meant me to eat at the second, but quite as well-served table."[7]

His years at Fisk, in contrast to his youth in New England, left Du Bois with a strong and bitter sense of the "absolute division of the universe into black and white." Yet it was probably a good thing that he went there before finally realizing his boyhood dream of going to Harvard, which he entered on a scholarship, as a junior, in the fall of 1888. "I was happy at Harvard, but for unusual reasons," he wrote much later. "One of these unusual circumstances was my acceptance of racial segregation. Had I gone from Great Barrington high school directly to Harvard I would have sought companionship with my white fellows and been disappointed and embittered by a discovery of social limitations to which I had not been used."[8]

On the whole, his days at Cambridge were very lonely. He made friends with only a very few of his classmates and reserved his social life for the stimulating Negro community in and around Boston: "I asked nothing of Harvard but the tutelage of teachers and the freedom of the library. I was quite voluntarily and willingly outside of its social life."[9]

Fortunately, the members of the faculty were far more friendly than the students:

> The Harvard of 1888 was an extraordinary aggregation of great men. Not often since that day have so many distinguished teachers been together in one place and at one time in America. . . . By good fortune, I was thrown into direct contact with many of these men. I was repeatedly a guest in the house of William James; he was my friend and guide to clear thinking; I was a member of the Philosophical Club and talked with Royce and Palmer; I sat in an upper room and read Kant's Critique with Santayana; Shaler invited a Southerner, who objected to sitting by me, out of his class; I became one of Hart's favorite pupils and was afterwards guided by him through my graduate course and started on my work in Germany. It was a great opportunity for a young man and a young American Negro, and I realized it.[10]

Apparently, even the haughty Anglophile and defender of Anglo-Saxon traditions Barrett Wendell knew a good man when he saw one. And Du Bois never forgot the following experience:

> I have before me a theme which I wrote October 3, 1890, for Barrett Wendell, then the great pundit of Harvard English. I said: "Spurred by my circumstances, I have always been given to systematically planning my future, not indeed without many mistakes and frequent alterations, but always with what I now conceive to have been a strangely early and deep appreciation of the fact that to live is a serious thing. I determined while in school to go to college—partly because older men went, partly because I foresaw that such discipline would best fit me for life. . . . I believe foolishly perhaps, but sincerely, that I have something to say to the world, and I have taken English 12 in order to say it well." Barrett Wendell rather liked that last sentence. He read it out to the class.[11]

W.E.B. Du Bois did indeed have something to say to the world and he soon went on to write and speak more eloquently in behalf of his race than any other man of his generation. But first he finished his work at Harvard, obtaining an A.B. in 1890, an M.A.

in 1891, and completing most of the requirements for the Ph.D. before going abroad for two years on a scholarship. Du Bois set sail for Europe on a Dutch boat in the summer of 1892, a year, as he put it, which marked "the high tide of lynching in the United States, when 235 persons were publicly murdered." He studied at the University of Berlin, where he listened to Max Weber and was accepted into "two exclusive seminars run by leaders of the developing social sciences." During the vacations, he traveled all over Europe where he was pleased to find far less racial discrimination than in the United States. He later summed up his experiences in Europe as follows:

> From this unhampered social intermingling with Europeans of education and manners, I emerged from the extremes of my racial provincialism. I became more human; learned the place in life of "Wine, Women, and Song"; I ceased to hate or suspect people simply because they belonged to one race or color; and above all I began to understand the real meaning of scientific research and the dim outline of methods of employing its technique and its results in the new social sciences for the settlement of the Negro problems in America.[12]

Du Bois returned from Europe in 1894 with an almost blind faith in science and a determination to engage in a career of research, writing, and teaching. He had originally wanted to be a philosopher but "it was James with his pragmatism and Albert Bushnell Hart with his research method, that turned me back from the lovely but sterile land of philosophic speculation, to the social sciences as the field for gathering and interpreting that body of fact which would apply to my program for the Negro."[13]

After spending a year teaching the classics at Wilberforce, where he was frankly horrified at the low standards and especially the overly emotional religious atmosphere (as contrasted to his own rearing in the Congregational Church in Great Barrington), he was called to the University of Pennsylvania, where he was given an opportunity to carry out his program of applying the methods of science to the Negro problem. In the meantime, he received his Ph.D. from Harvard and had his thesis, *The Suppression of the African Slave-Trade to the United States of America, 1638–1870*, published as the first volume in the Harvard Historical Series, in 1896, the year he began his research on the Philadelphia Negro.

W.E.B. Du Bois was brought to Philadelphia largely on the initiative of Susan P. Wharton, a member of one of the city's oldest and most prominent Quaker families. She had long been interested in the problems of Negroes and was a member of the Executive Committee of the Philadelphia College Settlement, which had been founded in 1892. It is important to see that *The Philadelphia Negro* was a product of the New Social Science and Settlement House movements, both of which grew up in this country and in England during the closing decades of the nineteenth century.

"The best account of this new period," writes Nathan Glazer, "and indeed the most important book, to my mind, for an understanding of the rise of the contemporary social scientific approach, is Beatrice Webb's *My Apprenticeship*. Beatrice Webb describes the rise of her interest in social problems, and the unique vantage point afforded to her by the Potter family (she was Beatrice Potter) and its connections to further this interest. Although the most distinguished visitor to her home was Herbert Spencer, two other distinguished Victorians who played a central role in the development of social science were often there. One was Francis Galton, whose discoveries in correlation were to be largely responsible for moving social statistics from the level of simple enumeration to that of a scientific tool of great precision and value. The other was Charles Booth, who, with his own fortune acquired from industry, was to conduct, beginning in the 1880's, the first great empirical social scientific study, an investigation into the conditions of life among all the people of London."[14]

It was in 1883, the year Karl Marx died, that young Beatrice Potter deserted the social life of fashionable Mayfair and went to the East End of London to work on her friend Charles Booth's famous and seminal study of the life and living conditions of the London poor. The next year, a group of Protestant clergymen, followers of Charles Kingsley and Frederick Dennison Maurice and their Christian Socialism, along with some young college men from Oxford and Cambridge, founded Toynbee Hall, which was an important landmark in the Settlement House and Social Gospel movements in England and also in this country. At the same time, Jane Addams, who had just graduated from college and was traveling abroad, made her first visit to the slums of London's East End. She was so horrified by what she saw there, and so impressed with the work being done at Toynbee Hall and with her newly acquired friend Beatrice Potter, that she came back and founded Hull House, in 1889, in the heart of the Chicago slums. Other settlement houses soon sprang up in most of the major cities along the eastern seaboard. In the meantime, the famous *Hull House Papers and Maps* were published in 1895, based directly on Charles Booth's methods of research; even the colors on the maps, which indicated different degrees of poverty, were the same.

While the more famous founders of sociology, such as Auguste Comte, Karl Marx, and Herbert Spencer, were predominantly armchair theorists in their approach to understanding the causes and consequences of the industrial and urban revolutions, the rise of capitalism, and the problems of labor, it was the more empirical and pragmatic tradition of Charles Booth in England and the Hull House work in this country, as the following paragraph suggests, that inspired young Du Bois when he came to Philadelphia.

> Herbert Spencer finished his ten volumes of Synthetic Philosophy in 1896. The biological analogy, the vast generalizations, were striking, but actual scientific accomplishment lagged. For me an opportunity seemed to present itself. . . . I determined to put science into sociology through a study of the condition and problems of my own group. I was going to study the facts, any and all facts, concerning the American Negro and his plight, and by measurement and comparison and research, work up to any valid generalization which I could.[15]

It was in this same spirit that Susan P. Wharton went out to the Wharton School, which a member of her family had founded at the University of Pennsylvania, and prevailed on the Provost, Charles C. Harrison, to undertake a study of the Negro problem in the city's Seventh Ward (where, incidentally, Provost Harrison, Miss Wharton, and many of Philadelphia's more fashionable families lived at that time). Provost Harrison, heir to one of the great sugar fortunes in America, had turned away from business in his later years to devote himself to education and social reform. He was immediately receptive to her plans. (The project was outlined at a meeting at the Wharton residence, 910 Clinton Street, situated only a few blocks from the heart of the Negro ghetto and the College Settlement House at Seventh and South Streets. It was indeed fortunate for the University, Miss Wharton, and the city as a whole, that a young scholar of Du Bois' ability, background, education, and scientific point of view was obtained for the job by a member of the sociology department of the Wharton School, Samuel McCune Lindsay. Du Bois came to the city in August 1896, and, except for a brief period of two months during the summer of 1897, when he studied rural Negroes in Virginia because so many of them had recently migrated to Philadelphia at the time of the study, he remained in the city until January 1898. Many years later, Du Bois described his call to Philadelphia and his stay there:

> In the fall of 1896, I went to the University of Pennsylvania as "Assistant Instructor" in Sociology. It all happened this way: Philadelphia, then and still one of the worst governed of America's badly governed cities, was having one of its periodic spasms of reform. A thorough study of causes was called for. Not but what the underlying cause was evident to most white Philadelphians: the corrupt, semi-criminal vote of the Negro Seventh Ward. Everyone agreed that here lay the cancer; but would it not be well to elucidate the known causes by a scientific investigation, with the imprimatur of the University? It certainly would, answered Samuel McCune Lindsay of the Department of Sociology. And he put his finger on me for the task.
>
> There must have been some opposition, for the invitation was not particularly cordial. I was offered a salary of $800 for a limited period of one year. I was given no real academic standing, no office at the University, no official recognition of any kind; my name was even eventually omitted from the catalogue; I had no contact with students, and very little with members of the faculty, even in my department. With my bride of three months, I settled in one room over a cafeteria run by a College Settlement, in the worst part of the Seventh Ward. We lived there a year, in the midst of an atmosphere of dirt, drunkenness, poverty and crime. Murder sat on our doorsteps, police were our government, and philanthropy dropped in with periodic advice.[16]

These are bitter words. And apparently Du Bois was not quite true to the facts of the case. There was no evidence in the minutes of the University's Board of Trustees of any "opposition" to the appointment. On a request for information on the case from a Du Bois biographer, the late Professor Lindsay replied that Du Bois was "quite mistaken about the attitude of the Sociology Department. It was quite friendly, I am sure, and as far as I know that was true of the entire Wharton School faculty."[17] I have quoted this passage from Du Bois' writings, nevertheless, because it suggests his own bitterness in 1944, when he wrote the passage, at the general neglect in this country of the Negro problem in the four decades following his publication of *The Philadelphia Negro*. More important, I think, it may very well reflect the spirit if not the letter of the thoughtless rather than malicious attitudes of whites of that era toward an educated and fastidious Negro like Du Bois. For Du Bois was very sensitive to the climate of opinion at that time which, by and large, assumed the inferiority of all Negroes, whether educated or not.

The life and thought of every age, one would suppose, is always marked, like the life of every individual, by ambivalence, paradox, and contradictions. In other words, just when many men and women like Beatrice Webb, Jane Addams, or Miss Wharton were dedicating their lives trying to understand and alleviate the horrible conditions that surrounded the lives of the downtrodden at the turn of the century, the dominant values of the comfortable and complacent middle classes were crudely materialistic, smugly racist, and somewhat self-righteous, to say the least. In short, the 1890s were indeed marked by materialism at the top and misery at the bottom of both the class and racial scales. Thus Du Bois, for instance, noted that the year 1892 marked the high tide of lynching in the United States; it was also the year of the bitter and cruel Homestead Strike. In 1894, Coxey's Army marched on Washington. In 1895, South Carolina, following the lead of Mississippi, and under the leadership of the extreme racist Ben Tillman, disfranchised its Negroes; in the same year, the Supreme Court of the United States, in the Plessy vs. Ferguson case, sanctioned the "separate but equal" standard that Booker T. Washington compromised with in his Atlanta speech; and between 1895 and 1909, the Negro was systematically disfranchised throughout the South. It is no wonder that many Americans responded to Bryan's plea, in the campaign of 1896, that Wall Street should not "crucify mankind upon a cross of gold." Perhaps Kelly Miller, the son of former slaves who rose to become a professor of sociology at Howard University, caught the spirit of the "Gay Nineties," as seen from the Negro point of view, in the following summary of the distinction between Frederick Douglass and Booker T. Washington:

> The two men are in part products of their times, but also natural antipodes. Douglass lived in the day of moral giants; Washington lived in the era of merchant princes. The contemporaries of Douglass emphasized the rights of man; those of Washington, his productive capacity. The age of Douglass acknowledged the sanction of the Golden Rule; that of Washington worships the Rule of Gold. The equality of men was constantly dinned into Douglass' ears; Washington hears nothing but the inferiority of the Negro and the dominance of the Saxon.[18]

The Anglo-Saxon complex Kelly Miller was referring to was, of course, a reflection of the inevitable racial implications of Social Darwinism, which was the overwhelmingly dominant ideology in America at that time. In an age when men thought of themselves as having evolved from the ape rather than having been created in the image of angels, the Negro, it was almost universally agreed among even the most educated people, was definitely an inferior breed and situated at the very base of the evolutionary tree. "Now as to the Negroes," Theodore Roosevelt wrote to his friend Owen Wister, "I entirely agree with you that as a race and in the mass they are altogether inferior to the whites." And Roosevelt never repeated his "mistake," as he called it, of asking Booker T. Washington or any other Negro to the White House. For he was very sensitive to the opinions of an age in which, as the historian Rayford W. Logan has written, "both newspapers and magazines stereotyped, caricatured and ridiculed Negroes in atrocious dialect that shocks the incredulous reader today. Few newspapers in the Deep South today portray the Negro in such outlandish fashion as did the spokesmen for the 'Genteel Tradition in the North,'"[19] Nor must we forget that very distinguished and objective social scientists, almost without exception, agreed with the "Genteel Tradition" and Roosevelt's point of view. With calipers and rulers and all sorts of statistical devices, they were busy building up elaborate classifications of the "inborn" mental and psychological traits of Nordics, Aryans, Semites, Teutons, Hottentots, Japs, Turks, Slavs, and Anglo-Saxons—with Negroes of course at the very bottom of this biological hierarchy.

Finally, it is important to place this dominant American ideology in a larger frame. For it was between the publication of Darwin's *Origin of Species by Natural Selection, or The Preservation of Favored Races in the Struggle for Life*, in 1859, and the Boer War in 1902, that white Western men conquered, explored, fought over, and partitioned among themselves the continent of black Africa below the Sahara. The year of 1896, when Du Bois went to Philadelphia, also witnessed Queen Victoria's Diamond Jubilee celebration, a symbol of the high tide of "white supremacy" throughout the world.

It was, then, in the most discouraging and deplorable period in the history of the American Negro since the Civil War that young Du Bois came to Philadelphia and set about doing a thorough and objective study of the Negro community. That the book, when finally published in 1899, succeeded in being objective, most modern readers, I think, will recognize. But even at the time of its publication, its reviewers were equally impressed with the author's critical and thorough methods of research. In the *Yale Review*, a reviewer found the book to be "a credit to American scholarship . . . the sort of book of which we have too few. . . . Here is an inquiry, covering a specific field and a considerable period of time, and executed with candor, thoroughness and critical judgment."[20] The reviewer in the *Annals of the American Academy of Political and Social Science* (a Southerner) found the book to be "exceptional and scholarly. . . . It is a critical, discriminating statement of the conditions and results of Negro life in a large, northern seaboard city a little more than thirty years after the Civil War . . . and its permanent national value to the scholar and the statesman is predicted."[21] The reviewer in *The Nation* was especially impressed with the historical material included in the book and only criticized the author for taking "too gloomy a view of the situation."[22] The *Outlook* review was long, detailed, and filled with praise: the historical background alone, thought the reviewer, "would of itself give this volume exceptional value."[23] And he went on to praise Du Bois' objectivity: "In no respect does Dr. Du Bois attempt to bend the facts so as to plead for his race . . . he is less apologetic than a generous-minded white writer might be. . . . Professor Du Bois' aim is always to keep well within the field where his generalizations cannot be disputed."[24]

Thus the reviews at the time of publication invariably praised the book and remarked on the objectivity of the author. In fact, between the lines one has the impression that most of the white reviewers were rather surprised that a Negro author could have been capable of a work of such careful scholarship and objectivity. In spite of this, one is amazed to find that the reviewers did not come out openly and criticize Du Bois' definitely environmental, rather than racial, approach to the problems of the Philadelphia Negroes. There was only a hint of this in the *American Historical Review*, in which the reviewer praised the book but questioned the author's optimism in regarding the Negro problem as soluble, in the long run, in terms of status and environmental improvement. The reviewer also, incidentally, appeared to be worried about "race pollution." The tone of the review is suggested by the following lines:

> The book is not merely a census-like volume of many tables and diagrams of the colored people of Philadelphia. The author seeks to interpret the meaning of statistics in the light of social movements and the characteristics of the times, as, for instance, the growth of the city by foreign immigration. . . . He is perfectly frank, laying all necessary stress on the weaknesses of his people. . . . He shows a remarkable spirit of fairness. If any conclusions are faulty, the fault lies in the overweight given to some of his beliefs and hopes.[25]

After praising Du Bois' fairness and outlining some of his findings, the reviewer criticizes Du Bois' hopes:

> This state of things is due chiefly, in Dr. Du Bois' judgment, to a color prejudice, and this he believes can be done away with in time, just as the class prejudices of earlier centuries in Europe are being wiped out gradually . . . but we need, what Dr. Du Bois does not give, more knowledge of the effects of the mixing of blood of very different races, and the possibilities of absorption of inferior into superior groups of mankind. He speaks of the "natural repugnance to close intermingling with unfortunate ex-slaves," but we believe that the separation is due to differences of race more than of status.[26]

The hereditarian or racial, as against the environmental or cultural, approaches to the causes of the differences between Negroes and whites, both in America and in other parts of the world, divide men to this day. Perhaps the ultimate truth lies in a "both/and" rather than an "either/or" approach. Nevertheless—and especially in an age such as our own which tends to assume, often dogmatically, the greater importance of environment and culture—one must look back on *The Philadelphia Negro* as a pioneering attempt to objectively advance this modern approach in an era when most men deeply and sincerely felt that fixed hereditary aptitudes differentiated the races of men and consequently precluded any possibility of eventual integration on a plane of social, cultural, and political equality. Thus, in answer to his hereditarian opponents such as the reviewer in the *American Historical Review*, Du Bois fell back on his own broad historical perspective by reminding his readers in the closing pages how many once-held hereditarian dogmas had already been eroded by the passage of time and the changing social situation:

> We rather hasten to forget that once the courtiers of English kings looked upon the ancestors of most Americans with far greater contempt than these Americans look upon Negroes—and perhaps, indeed, had more cause. We forget that once French peasants were the "Niggers" of France, and that German princelings once discussed with doubt the brains and humanity of the *bauer*.

It was, then, not only Du Bois' painstaking methods of research and his objective interpretations of the evidence that has given *The Philadelphia Negro* a permanent place in the sociological literature. It was also the fact that Du Bois brought a thoroughly sociological point of view to bear on this carefully collected evidence. In other words, the book, in emphasizing an environmental point of view, made a definite theoretical contribution. Some four decades later, for example, the authors of an important modern study of the Negro community in Chicago, *Black Metropolis*, explicitly referred to this contribution as follows:

> In 1899, Dr. W. E. B. Du Bois published the first important sociological study of a Negro community in the United States—*The Philadelphia Negro*

> (University of Pennsylvania). At the outset, he presented an ecological map detailing the distribution of the Negro population by "social condition," and divided his subjects into four "grades": (1) the "middle classes" and those above; (2) the working people—fair to comfortable; (3) the poor; (4) vicious and criminal classes. Despite the economic emphasis in this classification and his extensive presentation of data on physical surroundings, Du Bois concluded that "there is a far mightier influence to mold and make the citizen, and that is the social atmosphere which surrounds him; first his daily companionship, the thoughts and whims of his class; then his recreation and amusements; finally the surrounding world of American civilization." This emphasis upon the *social* relations—in family, clique, church, voluntary associations, school, and job—as the decisive elements in personality formation is generally accepted. The authors feel that it should also be the guiding thread in a study of "class" . . . All serious students of Negro communities since Du Bois have been concerned with the nature of social stratification . . . In the Thirties this interest was given added stimulus by the suggestive hypotheses thrown out by Professor W. Lloyd Warner and by a general concern in anthropological and sociological circles with social stratification in America.[27]

As this quotation from *Black Metropolis* suggests, there has been a direct intellectual line between Du Bois' emphasis on class and social environment as major causal agents in personality formation and a whole subsequent tradition in American sociology. Thus, for example, Franz Boas in his Lowell Lecture, *The Mind of Primitive Man* (1911), was echoing the findings and conclusions of Du Bois when he wrote that "the traits of the American Negro are adequately explained on the basis of his history and his social status . . . without a falling back upon the theory of hereditary inferiority."[28] And the tradition continued through W.I. Thomas and Florian Znaniecki's classic and pioneering study of the adjustment to the urban environment of Polish peasants in Chicago and Warsaw (*The Polish Peasant in Europe and America 1918–21*), through the whole school of urban sociology which Robert E. Park (for some time an assistant and colleague of Booker T. Washington at Tuskegee) inspired at the University of Chicago during the 1920s, to the later W. Lloyd Warner school of community studies at Harvard and Chicago, which inspired *Black Metropolis* and *Deep South* as well as the classic "Yankee City" series. The origins, in both method and theoretical point of view, of all of these studies are to be found in *The Philadelphia Negro*.

In many ways, Du Bois' whole life experiences before coming to Philadelphia in 1896—his youth, when he competed on his merits with his peers in the white community in Great Barrington, his observations of the faculty and students at Fisk as well as the poorest and most primitive Negroes in West Tennessee, his own achievements at Harvard as well as his contacts with great teachers like William James, and his witnessing the attitudes of educated Europeans toward himself—all combined to prepare him to see that racial inequality was partly a matter of class inequality and to emphasize the need for stratification and the creation of an open and talented elite class within the Negro community. And, above all, he emphasized the fact that this class, already existing in nascent form in Philadelphia, must be recognized by members of the white community, who were forever judging all Negroes on the basis of the behavior of the "submerged tenth." "In many respects it is right and proper to judge a people by its best classes rather than by its worst classes or middle ranks," he wrote in the excellent chapter on "The Environment of the Negro." "The highest class of any group," he continued, "represents its possibilities rather than its expectations, as is so often assumed in regard to the Negro. The colored people are seldom judged by their best classes, and often the very existence of classes among them is ignored." Thus Du Bois saw very clearly that the white community's propensity to see all Negroes as part of one homogeneous mass served as a rationalization for their own racist thinking. Much of the charitable work among the depressed classes of Negroes, moreover, only served to reinforce white prejudices: "Thus the class of Negroes which the prejudices of the city have distinctly encouraged," wrote Du Bois, "is that of the criminal, the lazy and the shiftless; for them the city teems with institutions and charities; for them there is succor and sympathy; for them Philadelphians are thinking and planning; but for the educated and industrious young colored man who wants work and not platitudes, wages and not alms, just rewards and not sermons—for such colored men Philadelphia apparently has no use."

While Du Bois was rightly critical of the white community, he also criticized upper-class Negroes for not taking the lead among their own people:

> The aristocracy of the Negro population in education, wealth and general social efficiency . . . are not the leaders or the idealmakers of their own group in thought, work, or morals. They teach the masses to a very small extent, mingle with them but little, do not largely hire their labor. Instead then of social classes held together by strong ties of mutual interest we have in the case of the Negroes, classes who have much to keep them apart, and only community of blood and color prejudice to bind them together. . . . The first impulse of the best, the wisest and richest is to segregate themselves from the mass . . . they make their mistake in failing to recognize that however laudable an ambition to rise may be, the first duty of an upper class is to serve the lowest classes. The aristocracies of all peoples have been slow in learning this and perhaps the Negro is no slower than the rest, but his peculiar situation demands that in his case this lesson be learned sooner.

In emphasizing the need for a properly functioning class structure within the Negro community, Du Bois was anticipating one of the major themes of the late E. Franklin Frazier's classic study of the emerging Negro middle class in America. Half a century after Du Bois' study of Philadelphia, Professor Frazier (the first Negro to be elected president of the American Sociological Society) wrote in his *Black Bourgeoisie*:

> Because of its struggle to gain acceptance by whites, the black bourgeoisie has failed to play the role of a responsible elite in the Negro community . . . they have no real interest in education and genuine culture and spend their leisure in frivolities and in activities designed to win a place in Negro "society." The single factor that has dominated the mental outlook of the black bourgeoisie has been its obsession with the struggle for status.[29]

In the long run, one of the most important contributions of this book, as more than one reviewer at the time of its publication noted, may well be the fact that it is the best documented historical record of an urban and northern Negro community in existence. Fortunately, Du Bois was well trained in, and devoted to, the historian's craft. But it was also fortunate that the city of Philadelphia possessed the oldest and, in 1896, the largest Northern Negro community in the nation, exceeded in population only by the three southern Negro communities of New Orleans, Washington, D.C., and Baltimore (a border city).

In fact, Negroes had been brought up the Delaware by the Swedes before Penn founded the colony in 1682. In the city where the Declaration of Independence was written and the nation founded, the Negroes also had an important history, which Du Bois carefully documented: here in Philadelphia was the first expression against the slave trade, the first organization for the abolition of slavery, the first legislative enactments for the abolition of slavery, the first attempt at Negro education, the first Negro convention, and so forth.

Since Du Bois himself, in this study and in many others, contributed so much to the understanding of his people's history, it seems most appropriate to close this introduction with a brief history of some of the more important sociological changes in the Philadelphia Negro community since the turn of the nineteenth century.

The Philadelphia Negro Since Du Bois

The most striking thing about the development of the Philadelphia Negro community since Du Bois' day is its steady increase in size. In fact, the steady migration of southern Negroes to Philadelphia began in the decade of the 1890s (see table 9.1) and kept up throughout the twentieth century. Du Bois saw this increasing pace of migration and consequently went to Virginia during the first summer of his study in order to see how the Negroes lived in the rural areas, the better to understand their problems of adjustment to urban life. The pace of migration, of course, was greatly increased during World War I and the 1920s. At the same time, anti-Negro attitudes increased, producing racial strife, increasing segregation in public places, and a rapid rise in residential ghettoization. Migration slowed down during the 1930s, then increased again during World War II and the postwar years, until today the Negroes constitute over one fourth of the city's residents in contrast to the less than 5 percent minority of Du Bois' day.

With the steady increase in the size of the Negro population, the pattern of residential distribution also changed. In contrast to 1890, when most of the city's Negroes lived in the center of the city and close to their white neighbors, by 1960 a majority of Negroes had moved to the southern, northern, and western sections of the city (table 9.2). In 1960, for the first time in the city's

TABLE 9.1
Philadelphia Negro Population Increase by Decades (1890–1960)

Decade	Population	Increase: Number	Increase: Per Cent
1880	31,699		
1890	39,371	7,672	24
1900	62,613	23,242	60
1910	84,459	21,846	33
1920	134,229	49,770	58
1930	219,599	85,370	63
1940	250,880	31,281	14
1950	376,041	125,161	50
1960	529,239	153,198	30

history, one whole city section contained more Negro than white residents (table 9.2: 70 percent Negro in North Philadelphia). The changing size and residential distribution of the Negro population has, of course, been both cause and result of changing social relations between the races.

TABLE 9.2
Philadelphia Negro Population Distribution by City Sections in 1890 and 1960

	1890				1960			
	Number Negro	Number Total	Per Cent Negro	Per Cent of Negro Total	Number Negro	Number Total	Per Cent Negro	Per Cent of Negro Total
Center City	15,627	104,154	(15)	(40)	7,476	38,323	(18)	(1)
South Phila.	7,914	218,506	(4)	(20)	66,621	260,767	(30)	(13)
West Phila.	4,080	99,182	(4)	(10)	169,100	402,161	(42)	(32)
North Phila.	7,504	267,044	(3)	(20)	234,646	342,857	(70)	(44)
Kensington	1,329	250,555	(1)	(3)	8,148	257,508	(3)	(2)
Northwest-Far North	1,891	72,229	(2)	(5)	36,506	347,464	(10)	(7)
Greater Northeast	1,026	35,294	(3)	(2)	6,742	353,432	(2)	(1)
City Total	39,371	1,046,964	(37)	(100)	529,239	2,002,512	(26)	(100)

Source: Population of Philadelphia Sections and Wards 1860–1960, Philadelphia City Planning Commission, 1963 (Mimeo.).

In Philadelphia in the 1890s, the largest concentration of Negroes was in the Seventh Ward, which Du Bois studied in detail. But this ward was, at the same time, the center of the city's "silk stocking" or upper-class neighborhood. The majority of the Negroes in the ward were employed as domestic servants, and lived in close proximity to (if not in the homes of) their employers. Social relations between whites and Negroes, therefore, were marked by clear status differentials and high social interaction, rather than by the residential segregation and low social interaction which characterizes the relations between the races today. In 1960 the Seventh Ward, as in its heyday of fashion in the 1890s, is still about one-third Negro. But most of the members of the white upper class have migrated to the suburbs. Though there are still a few fashionable white blocks, many of the old mansions have long since been converted into cultural institutions, apartments, rooming houses, and offices for physicians and other professional people. Both the white and Negro populations have steadily declined in absolute numbers: In 1890, the Seventh Ward had 30,179 residents of whom 8,861 (or 30 percent) were Negroes; in 1960, there were only 17,079 residents in the ward, of whom 6,308 (or 35 percent) were Negroes.[30] And of course, in our modern, mechanized world of smaller middle-class households, live-in domestic servants are no longer fashionable or economically feasible, producing a consequent decline in social relations between the races.

Following a pattern set by the Georgetown community in Washington, D.C., in an earlier day, the Seventh Ward has been witnessing, during the 1960s, a steadily increasing pattern of white invasion of the Negro areas of the ward. Though the ward has recently been absorbed into one all-inclusive center-city ward, its traditional area will be largely white by 1970. More and more white, suburban families are now moving back to the city, both those who have raised their children and those of the younger generation who are disenchanted with the suburban way of life. But they will be moving back to a more and more segregated city, as the figures in tables 9.2 and 9.3 clearly show.

Fortunately for the historian and the sociologist, there were three major ghettoized Negro wards in the city in 1960 which had

TABLE 9.3
Three Negro Ghetto Wards in Philadelphia 1890–1960

	30th Ward South Phila.			32nd Ward North Phila.			24th Ward West Phila.		
Year	Number Negro	Number Total	Per Cent Negro	Number Negro	Number Total	Per Cent Negro	Number Negro	Number Total	Per Cent Negro
1890	1789	30614	6%	382	30050	1%	930	42556	2%
1900	5242	28874	20%	962	39889	2%	2193	53200	4%
1910	9999	29209	34%	1517	40293	4%	3958	54370	7%
1920	15481	29471	51%	3926	47540	8%	8152	60408	13%
1930	19537	27783	70%	14476	45663	31%	13041	54947	24%
1940	22185	27605	82%	24975	50062	–50%	18343	53803	34%
1950	23789	27208	88%	44872	60860	73%	36741	63391	58%
1960	21587	23527	96%	52191	54497	96%	45666	57987	80%

Note: These three wards, whose boundaries have remained unchanged since 1890, lay in the heart of the three Negro ghettos of Philadelphia as of 1960 (see Table 9.2). The 30th, the oldest ghetto ward in the city, became half-Negro for the first time in 1920; the 32nd, over half foreign born or foreign stock in 1920 (largely Jewish), first became over half Negro during World War II. In 1960, the 32nd was the largest Negro ward in the city.

Source: Population of Philadelphia Sections and Wards 1860–1960, Philadelphia City Planning Commission, 1963 (Mimeo.).

not had their boundaries changed since 1890 (table 9.3). The changing racial composition of these three wards reflects the history of the Negro community in the city in the twentieth century. As an inspection of the figures in table 9.3 will show, all three of these wards contained a small minority of Negro residents in 1890. But as the size of the Philadelphia Negro community steadily increased in the twentieth century, each ward eventually became ghettoized in a definite historical pattern. The Thirtieth Ward, which lies just to the south of the Seventh, became the city's first Negro ghetto (51 percent Negro in 1920). It was no accident that Philadelphia's first race riot in the twentieth century, in the summer of 1918, took place on the southern boundary of the Thirtieth Ward. Thus in her Ph.D. dissertation at the University of Philadelphia published in 1921, Sadie Tanner Mossell (now Mrs. Raymond Pace Alexander, wife of a noted jurist and herself a lawyer and chairman of Philadelphia's Commission on Human Relations) wrote that "a colored probation officer of the Municipal Court, a woman of refinement and training and an old citizen of Philadelphia, purchased and took up residence at the house numbered 2936 Ellsworth Street. The white people in the neighborhood resented her living there and besieged the house. A race riot ensued in which two men were killed and sixty injured."[31] The steady migration of Negroes into the city during the war years and the 1920s not only contributed to the ghettoization of the Negro community, it also contributed to the segregation of Negro children in the schools and the closing of most of the city's commercial and entertainment centers to Negroes. As Miss Mossell noted, "such social privileges as the service of eating houses and the attending of white churches and theaters by Negroes, were practically withdrawn after the influx of Negro migrants into Philadelphia."[32] The older Negro residents of the city were naturally upset by this new segregation. The Mossell study continued:

> The old colored citizens of Philadelphia resented this. Placed the blame at the migrant's door and stood aloof from him. Negro preachers invited the new arrivals into the church but many of the congregations made him know that he was not wanted. In some cases the church split over the matter, the migrants and their sympathizers withdrawing and forming a church for themselves.[33]

South Philadelphia, especially the southern part of the Seventh Ward running along Lombard and South (the oldest Negro commercial street in the city) streets, together with the whole Thirtieth Ward, was Philadelphia's first Negro ghetto. And it remained so from the 1920s through World War II. Beginning in the 1920s, however, another Negro ghetto began to develop in North Philadelphia (see tables 9.2 and 9.3). Thus in 1920, the Thirty-second Ward was composed primarily of residents of foreign-born and foreign-stock (mostly Jewish) origins. In the course of the next decade, however, the Negro population increased almost fourfold, and by 1930 made up nearly one-third of the ward's residents (table 9.3). By 1940, the Thirty-second Ward was about half Negro, as was the Forty-seventh, an immediately adjacent ward to the south (the Forty-seventh was cut out of the eastern half of the Twenty-ninth after the 1910 census, and hence not used for table 9.3). By 1950, the Thirty-second, the Forty-seventh, and three other North Philadelphia wards were over half Negro; by 1960, this whole section became the city's major ghetto (70 percent Negro).

During the long, hot summer of 1964, a series of race riots broke out in major American cities, beginning in Harlem in July and ending in Philadelphia on the last day of August. Just as the riot of 1918 had broken out along the boundary of the Thirtieth Ward ghetto, so it was no accident that the racial disturbance in 1964 broke out on the boundary between wards Thirty-two and Forty-seven, along Columbia Avenue at 22nd Street, when a husband and wife, both intoxicated, were found quarreling by the police. Rioting soon spread throughout the North Philadelphia ghetto, killing two persons, injuring 339, and producing some $3 million worth of property damage.

The causes of any riot are many and complex. But Du Bois would have agreed that one of the important causes in 1964 was the fact that the Negro masses in North Philadelphia were almost completely cut off from the more affluent and successful members of their own race. Most of the solid Negro citizens live in more suburban areas of the city and, like their counterparts whom Du Bois criticized in his day, are more concerned with their own careers than with the problems of racial leadership. An exception was the local head of the NAACP, Cecil Moore, a flamboyant, charming, but often irresponsible individual who has stepped into the leadership vacuum left by the more solid Negro establishment. For unlike the establishment Negroes, Moore resides within the North Philadelphia ghetto and was on the scene during the riots, doing his best to calm his neighbors down. Lenora E. Berson, in her study of the riot, wrote:

> Today, only the National Association for the Advancement of Colored People (NAACP) has any real following in North Philadelphia. The Student Non-Violent Coordinating Committee (SNCC) and the Congress of Racial Equality (CORE) have made little headway in the city.

Since his ascension to the presidency of the Philadelphia branch in January 1963, Cecil Moore has transformed the NAACP from a conservative institution into a mass-membership action organization.

Much of Moore's strength within the local NAACP comes from its North Philadelphia members, whom he recruited into the organization. Unlike most Negro leaders, Moore lives in the riot area. He calls the North Philadelphians "my people," and many feel they are just that. In a poll of residents conducted by Radio Station WDAS, Moore was found to be far and away the best-known Philadelphia Negro.[34]

The last Negro ghetto to develop was that of West Philadelphia. By 1950, the Twenty-fourth Ward had more Negro than white residents for the first time. It has never reached the high proportion of Negroes which marks the Thirtieth in South Philadelphia, or the Thirty-second in North Philadelphia, largely because, since the 1950s, the southern part of the ward has developed into a bohemian and intellectual community. Once an elite residential neighborhood containing some of the finest examples of Victorian architecture in the city, this part of the Twenty-fourth, known as "Powelton Village," has become a more or less integrated and middle-class community, made up largely of graduate students and faculty members of the University of Pennsylvania and other local institutions, as well as other professionals possessing liberal or bohemian values. There is a great deal of neighborhood pride in this area and some civic concern for life in the neighboring ghetto to the north.

By 1960, fourteen wards in the city—eight in North Philadelphia, three in South Philadelphia, and three in West Philadelphia—contained a majority of Negro residents. Indeed, the racial composition of the city and the residential distribution of its Negroes had changed beyond recognition since Du Bois' day.

And so in many ways had the economic position of the Negroes, both for the better and for the worse. Du Bois was vitally concerned with the depressed and segregated economic plight of the Negroes in the last decade of the nineteenth century, which was probably worse than it had been during the first decade of the century. He considered freedom and political rights to be a mere sham unless Negroes were also able to take their rightful place in the city's economic life. He was, for instance, horrified to find that the depressed economic plight of his people pushed them into close social relationships with the most corrupt elements of machine politics. Above all he stressed the fact that the lack of opportunity to advance by education or hard work corrupted the Negro and drove him into the psychological environment of "excuse and listless despair." Thus he wrote: "The humblest white employee knows that the better he does his work the more chance there is for him to rise in business. The black employee knows that the better he does his work the longer he may do it; he cannot hope for promotion." Aware of his own position in spite of his educational qualifications, Du Bois saw that educational attainments of Negroes only led to frustration: "A graduate of the University of Pennsylvania in mechanical engineering, well recommended," he wrote, "obtained work in the city, through an advertisement, on account of his excellent record. He worked a few hours and then was discharged because he was found to be colored. He is now a waiter at the University Club, where his white fellow graduates dine." A graduate in pharmacy applied for a job and was given the following answer: "I wouldn't have a darky to clean out my store, much less stand behind the counter." Clerks and white-collar jobs were, of course, unobtainable, but so were both skilled and unskilled jobs in industry. Du Bois noted one exception to this at the Midvale Steel Works, where the manager, dubbed a "crank" by many of his peers, had employed some 200 Negroes who worked along with white mechanics "without friction or trouble." (Though Du Bois did not mention it, the "crank" at the Midvale Steel Works was Frederick W. Taylor, who eventually became world famous as the "father of scientific management.") Finally, Du Bois deplored the fact that, unlike other minority groups, Negroes were rarely found running their own businesses. Those that did exist were marginal. In short, the vast majority of Negroes in the city in Du Bois' day were relegated to domestic service or allied personal services such as catering or hotel jobs as waiters, porters, shoe-shine boys (some in their fifties and sixties), and so forth.

As of the 1960s, though Negroes are surely a long way from obtaining equal opportunity with whites, there is no question that opportunities for Negro employment in the city have improved greatly since the 1890s when Du Bois painted a dismal picture of their plight. Perhaps the first wave of improvement in employment opportunities in the city, as well as all over the nation, came during World War I—incidentally, a mixed blessing. While, as noted above, there was virtually no industrial employment of Negroes in 1896, Miss Mossell estimated that some 30,000 Negro laborers were employed by Philadelphia firms as of 1917. The Midvale Steel Company, which was the exception in 1896 when it employed some 200 Negroes, employed some 4,000 Negroes in 1917. While this new employment was a change for the better in some ways, it also had unfortunate consequences. "The Pennsylvania Railroad," wrote Miss Mossell at the time, "was the only industry which provided any kind of housing for the migrant. The camps in which it lodged him, however, proved to be of little assistance, since the camps themselves, consisting of ordinary tents and box cars, did not provide adequate shelter."[35] The living conditions of the Negro migrants were miserable enough during the war. But things were even worse when the war came to an end. Unemployment, idleness, racial riots, and continual strife marked Negro-white relations during what Eugene P. Foley has called "the warring Twenties."[36] In fact, racial unrest was continual up to and after the time of the passage by Pennsylvania of its first Civil Rights Act of 1935. Though Negroes were now employed in industry, their inferior position and pay was taken for granted. For example, the city went through the most crippling transit strike in its history in the early 1940s. The strike, which cost the taxpayers more than $10 million, was due to the fact that white workers refused to go back to their jobs as long as Negro workers were given equal pay for equal work. On the whole, then, it can be said that Negroes made very little headway in breaking down discrimination in employment throughout the 1920s and 1930s. Employment in industry, of course, picked up during World War II, but real gains awaited the postwar period.

The 1950s were definitely years of increasing opportunities for Philadelphia Negroes, even though in 1960 Negroes were twice as likely to be unemployed as whites (10 percent versus 5 percent). In the first place, there was a great decline in the proportion of Negroes engaged in domestic service. (Du Bois was very concerned about the low sex ratio (80) among Negroes and its effect on the family. It is consequently of interest that, in 1960, the sex ratio of Negroes in the city had increased to 90, partly a reflection of the decline of domestic service as the main Negro occupation). Du Bois found that 88.5 percent of the females, and 61.5 percent of the males in the Seventh Ward were domestic servants. By 1960, these proportions had declined on a city-wide basis to 0.6 percent of the males and 3.3 percent of the females.[37] The big change came in the 1950s, when male domestic service declined by 61.2 percent, and female by 29.9 percent, in the course of a single decade. In contrast to this decline in the proportion of Negroes in these occupations which stigmatized their inferior position, white-collar employment among Philadelphia Negroes increased in a relatively spectacular fashion. Between 1950 and 1960, for example, the proportion of Negro males employed as clerical workers increased by 58.9 percent, that of females by 221.8 percent. At the same time, the proportion of Negro males in professional occupations increased by 45.9 percent, of females by 90.9 percent; salesmen increased by 30.7 percent, saleswomen by 88.4 percent.

These statistics showing the quantitative increase in the proportion of Negroes in white-collar occupations during the 1950s reflect unprecedented changes in the quality of race relations in the center city. As of the 1930s, for instance, one rarely saw a Negro in the major downtown department and clothing stores, in banks, moving-picture houses, theaters, or other public places. No major department store or bank had Negroes in white-collar positions dealing directly with the public. No Negro lawyer could obtain office space in the center-city business district. Negroes sat in the balconies of the big movie palaces. Hotels and restaurants were strictly segregated. Most of these strict taboos came in during and immediately after World War I; all of them were removed in the decade of the 1950s.

Du Bois was particularly interested in the poor record of Negroes as businessmen. In 1896, there were no more than 300 Negro-owned businesses in the city. The majority of them were barbershops, catering establishments, and restaurants—all extensions of the servant role. And most of them were marginal, with the exception of a few well-known caterers. There is a direct relation, according to Eugene P. Foley, who has studied the Negro businessman in Philadelphia and elsewhere, between the ghettoization of the Negro and the growth of Negro businesses. In fact, among Negroes, as among whites, immigrants to the city seem more likely to go into business for themselves than older residents. Thus in 1964, there were over 4,000 Negro-owned businesses in the city, most of them located within the boundaries of the three Negro ghettos. Unfortunately, however, most of these businesses were pretty much of the same marginal character as those of Du Bois' day. Along with the absence of responsible leadership, this lack of success in business enterprise was certainly an important factor in the North Philadelphia riots of 1964. In her study of the riots, for example, Lenora E. Berson found this to be true.

> The history of the Jews and of North Philadelphia combined to make the Jewish merchants the major representatives of the white establishment in the area. But it was as whites and as merchants and realtors rather than as Jews per se that they bore the brunt of the Negroes' attack. Anti-Semitism was not a primary factor in the rioting.
>
> Nevertheless, the Jews do have a special and ambiguous position in the Negro ghetto. In every large city, Jewish organizations and individuals have long been in the forefront of the civil rights campaigns. In Philadelphia, two white board members of the NAACP are Jews, as is the only white elected official from North Central Philadelphia, State Senator Charles Weiner. The two Negro-oriented radio stations in the city are owned by Jews. It is likely that many, if not most, of North Philadelphia's residents are treated by Jewish doctors, advised by Jewish lawyers and served by Jewish community agencies.
>
> But the landlord, too, is likely to be Jewish, as is the grocer and the man who owns the appliance store on the corner. All too often the Negro sees himself as a victim of their exploitation, and the contrast between himself and the more affluent businessmen of the community generates bitterness and resentment.[38]

The living conditions in the North Philadelphia ghetto are still deplorable and probably getting worse; and they are so dehumanizing largely because of the moral myopia of white residents of the City of Brotherly Love. At the same time, there is cause for hope if one takes Du Bois' position that the ultimate salvation of the Negro community depends on its "Talented Tenth." He opened his famous essay on the "Talented Tenth" as follows:

> The Negro Race, like all races, is going to be saved by its exceptional men. The problem of education, then, among Negroes must first of all deal with the Talented Tenth; it is the problem of developing the Best of this race that may guide the Mass away from the contamination and death of the Worst, in their own and other races.[39]

Opportunities for the Talented Tenth within the Philadelphia Negro community have opened up at an increasing rate since the end of World War II. Of nonwhite Philadelphians aged twenty-five and over, for example, the proportion that had finished high school tripled, the proportion that had finished college doubled between 1940 and 1960. Furthermore, in contrast to Du Bois' day when employment for educated Negroes was almost nonexistent, there are now more jobs available for educated Negroes than there are educated Negroes to fill them. Finally, Du Bois would have been most gratified that, since World War II, talented Negroes have moved into elite positions on the local bar and bench, in business, in politics, and on the faculties of the local colleges and universities.

In closing, perhaps the best way to gain a historical perspective on the dramatic changes in the opportunities that have opened for talented Negroes since Du Bois' day, might be to speculate how he himself would now be received by the University of Pennsylvania. And certainly there is no question that today, if a gifted young Negro with a recent Ph.D. from Harvard, a book published in the Harvard Historical Series, and two years study abroad should apply for a position in the sociology department, he would be welcomed with open arms as an assistant professor at least, and at a salary of over $10,000 a year. In fact, he would hardly need to apply; for he would have been vigorously recruited; and he probably would not even consider Pennsylvania because of the great demand for young Negro sociologists at the very best sociology departments in the nation.

Notes

1. Gunnar Myrdal, *An American Dilemma* (New York: Harper and Brothers, 1944), 1132.

2. W.E.B. Du Bois, *Dusk of Dawn* (New York: Harcourt, Brace & World, 1940), vii.
3. In writing of Du Bois's life, I have tried to quote him directly where possible. I have profited greatly from the following biographical studies: Francis L. Broderick, *W.E.B. Du Bois: Negro Leader in a Time of Crisis* (Stanford: Stanford University Press, 1959); and Elliott Morton Rudwick, "W.E.B. Du Bois: A Study in Minority Group Leadership." Ph.D. diss., University of Pennsylvania, 1956.
4. W.E.B. Du Bois, "My Evolving Program for Negro Freedom," Rayford W. Logan, ed., *What the Negro Wants* (Chapel Hill: University of North Carolina Press, 1944), 38.
5. Ibid., 34.
6. Ibid., 35.
7. Ibid., 37–38.
8. Du Bois, *Dusk of Dawn*, 34.
9. Ibid., 35.
10. Ibid., 37.
11. Ibid., 38–39.
12. Logan, *What the Negro Wants*, 42.
13. Ibid., 39.
14. Nathan Glazer, "The Rise of Social Science Research in Europe," in Daniel Lerner, ed., *The Human Meaning of the Social Sciences* (New York: Meridian, 1959), 58–59.
15. Du Bois, *Dusk of Dawn*, 51.
16. Logan, *What the Negro Wants*, 44.
17. Rudwick, *Du Bois: A Study*, 32.
18. Quoted in E. Franklin Frazier, *The Negro in the United States* (New York: Macmillan, 1949), 545.
19. Rayford W. Logan, *The Negro in the United States: A Brief History* (Princeton, N.J.: Van Nostrand, 1957), 54.
20. *Yale Review* 9 (May 1900), 110–11.
21. *Annals of the American Academy of Social and Political Science* 15 (January–May 1900), 101.
22. *The Nation* 69 (1899), 310.
23. *Outlook* 63 (1899), 647–48.
24. Ibid.
25. *American Historical Review* 6 (1900–1901), 163.
26. Ibid., 184.
27. St. Clair Drake and Horace R. Cayton, *Black Metropolis* (New York: Harcourt, Brace & World, 1945, 1962, 1970), 787–88.
28. Franz Boas, *The Mind of Primitive Man* (New York: Macmillan, 1911), 272.
29. E. Franklin Frazier, *Black Bourgeoisie* (Glencoe, Ill.: The Free Press, 1957), 235–36.
30. *Population of Philadelphia Sections and Wards 1860–1960* (Philadelphia City Planning Commission, 1963).
31. Sadie Tanner Mossell, "The Standard of Living Among One Hundred Negro Migrant Families in Philadelphia." (Ph.D. diss., University of Pennsylvania, 1921), 9.
32. Ibid.
33. Ibid.

34. Lenora E. Berson, *Case Study of a Riot* (New York: Institute of Human Relations Press, 1966), 30.
35. Mossell, "Standard of Living."
36. Eugene P. Foley, "The Negro Businessman: In Search of a Tradition," in Talcott Parsons and Kenneth B. Clark, eds., *The Negro American* (Boston: Beacon Press, 1965), 573. This is an excellent study of Negro business in America and is most relevant here because most of the empirical data was taken from the Philadelphia community.
37. *Philadelphia's Non-White Population 1960* (Philadelphia City Planning Commission, 1963), tables 5 and 5a.
38. Berson, *Case Study*, 46.
39. W.E.B. Du Bois, "The Talented Tenth," in *The Negro Problem* (New York: James Pott, 1903), 33.

10

Reflections on Aristocracy

Men have always been concerned with the social and political organization of leadership and the proper distribution of power and authority. The dictionary defines aristocracy as the "rule of the best." All men everywhere would surely agree that this was the ideal toward which every society should strive. But they have never been able to agree on who were the "best," how the "best" were to be selected and elevated to positions of leadership, nor in whose interests the "best" should rule. All and each of these perennial problems concerning the "best" assume, of course, that except in small and homogeneous communities such as the tribe, the village, or the New England town where self-rule or direct democracy is possible and practical, all civilized societies—especially as they become larger and more heterogeneous—have been oligarchical in fact if not in theory. Even the classic Athenian democracy was actually oligarchical in that out of a heterogeneous population of over 300,000, the voters comprised a homogeneous minority of some 20,000 citizens (no votes for women, minors, aliens, or slaves). At the same time, the Golden Age was ruled by the noble statesman, Pericles, who was reared in one of the great "Whig" families of Greece, the Alkmonidai and their allies, while most of the spiritual leaders of the fifth and fourth centuries, with the exception of the Sophists and Euripides, were on the side of aristocracy. Pindar, Aeschylus, Heraclitus, Parmenides, Herodotus, and Thucydides were aristocrats themselves, and the middle-class Sophocles and Plato identified completely with the nobility.

As traditionally defined in political and social theory, oligarchical systems have been called *aristocratic* when leadership has been drawn from a hereditary class of landowners, usually originating in military conquest and calling forth the virtues of honor and loyalty; *plutocratic* when based on more liquid wealth, economic conquest, and the trading virtues of honesty in fulfilling the obligations of contract; and *theocratic* when based on priestly or magical powers, religious or ideological conquest, and demanding the virtues of adherence to creed or doctrine. Who are the "best," then, will tend to vary as between aristocratic, plutocratic, or theocratic societies.

While all concrete historical societies of any complexity are in one sense oligarchical, it is also true that all viable societies are at the same time democratic. It is at just this point that the traditional definitions of oligarchy are somewhat confusing. Yet some clarification is possible if one asks the questions (a) how are the "best" to be chosen? and (b) in whose interests are they to rule? To answer these questions, we may postulate two continuums (rather than either-or concepts) as follows: (a) the "best" may be chosen on the basis of *more or less democratic* (achievable) or aristocratic (ascribed) principles, and (b) the "best" may rule in a *more or less autocratic* (in their own interest) or representative (in the interest of all) way. In the Western liberal tradition one would suppose the ideal society would be both democratic and representative. The abolition of entail and primogeniture and the institution of inheritance taxes and universal and free education, for example, are all efforts to mitigate the advantages of birth, and foster democracy, while parliamentary representation, the two-party system, and universal suffrage (ascribed on the basis of adult citizenship and not of achievement) are all devices for fostering accountability and representativeness in leadership. Yet in spite of men's designs, it is safe to say that the aristocratic and autocratic principles will always play more or less active parts in all historical situations. As a matter of fact, as will be brought out below, stability and continuity of social structures have favored the aristocratic and representative principles, whereas democracy and autocracy have come to the fore together in periods of more rapid social change. The Roman Republic and the British parliamentary monarchy, for instance, have been two of the world's most stable and free societies; both were more or less aristocratic and also representative. During the golden age of Republican Rome (the two hundred years before the Gracchi) of the 200 consuls, 159 were drawn from 26 noble families, and 99 from only 10. Similarly, the parliamentary leadership of Britain during its greatest days of world leadership was drawn largely from the ranks of a hereditary class. On the other hand, with the decline of the Roman Republic and the rise first of military dictatorship and eventually the Empire, leadership was chosen more on ability and merit according to democratic principle, while freedom declined and autocracy reigned. Caesarism was and still is autocratic and democratic, as we are using the terms here. On the whole, the aristocratic principle stresses stability, the democratic principles stresses ability and change. Who would deny that, at that classic historical catastrophe at Munich, Hitler, who achieved rather than inherited his power, was more of a natural leader than Chamberlain, who was drawn from a hereditary class. Heredity breeds the gentleman, while the new and old Caesars qualify on the basis of their merits. A celibate priesthood, fascinatingly enough, is the only case in history where pure democracy, as the term is used here, has been possible; at the same time, both the Church hierarchy and particularly the Jesuit order have been strictly autocratic, ruling in the interests of God as his vicars or appointees. We shall return to this theme below, but in the meantime, for the purposes of this article, it is most useful to think of the term *aristocracy* as *referring to the hereditary principle or to a class of leaders of more or less ascribed position.*

Plato and Aristotle

In any discussion of the traditional theories of leadership in the West, one must go back to Plato and Aristotle, upon whom all Western political and social theory has often been called a series of footnotes. For in many ways, according to aristocratic assumptions, political and social theory, like art and unlike physics or chemistry, is *not cumulative*. All students of politics and art can learn from Aristotle and Leonardo, respectively, while men of classical antiquity or the Renaissance have nothing to teach even a young freshman about the science of modern chemistry.

On the whole, the aristocratic assumptions about the nature of society and government go back to Aristotle, while the more mechanistic and utopian traditions of social theory go back to Plato. For Plato had a rational blueprint of the ideal and completed society which was to be ruled by scientifically chosen experts or Guardians; property was to be held in common, the family obliterated and art suppressed. In this utopian and essentially totalitarian Republic, however, order, justice, and stability were purchased at the cost of freedom, creativity, and change. Aristotle, on the other hand, emphasized the fact that the *best* government was *second best*, at least in this world. In other words, he saw the need for a compromising balance, or an evolving tension, between the principles of monarchy, aristocracy, and democracy, judiciously combining the advantages of all with the inevitable drawbacks of each. Like Aristotle, the aristocrat mistrusts the scientific expert, prefers the amateur connoisseur, and is always a trimmer.

In accord with another aristocratic assumption to the effect that social theory should be empirical and critical rather than rational and creative, it is of particular interest that Aristotle spent far more time analyzing the drawbacks of each form of government than he did in pointing out their advantages. After carefully observing at first hand the constitutions of more than one hundred and fifty communities in the ancient world, he came to the conclusion that, while good government must be in the interests of all citizens, all rulers have a tendency to rule in their own, rather than the public, interest. Thus monarchy becomes perverted into tyranny (government in the arbitrary interest of an individual), aristocracy into oligarchy or plutocracy (in the interest of the few), and democracy into demagoguery (in the arbitrary interest of the many) or anarchy (which inevitably leads back to the despotic rule of the one). In order to avoid these perversions, Aristotle emphasized the necessity for compromise, mixed forms, and the golden mean; no form should be carried to its logical conclusion in the name of absolute justice; a wise civility will always be satisfied with relative justice and the second best. Above all, Aristotle saw the need for curbing the arbitrary wills of men through the instrument of law. The law, not king, aristocrats, or people, must be the final sovereign: thus he wrote that "in democracies that obey the law there are no demagogues . . . and where the laws are not sovereign there is no constitution." In a world that is constantly changing (stability is always a relative term), it is vitally important that no one group, class, or form of rule should be completely victorious, no victory total, no surrender unconditional. In this connection, playing the game for its own sake is an aristocratic value, while playing to win is more in accord with so-called democratic values, as the well-known American baseball slogan, "nice guys finish last," attests; similarly, "unconditional surrender" is a twentieth-century and democratic, rather than an eighteenth-century and aristocratic, view of war.

Aristotle, perhaps the first "Whig" trimmer, took a compromising and constitutional stand primarily because he had a less optimistic view of human nature than had Plato; he saw the inevitable injustices of this world as the product of a corruptible human nature and not, as with Plato, in the corrupting influences, on essentially good men, of imperfect institutions. Accordingly, Aristotle devoted much of his thought on politics to pointing out the unanticipated consequences of Plato's utopian and rational blueprint: "Legislation such as Plato proposes," he wrote in *Politics*, "may appear to wear an attractive face and to argue benevolence. The hearer receives it gladly . . . all the more as the evils now existing under ordinary forms of government are denounced as due to the absence of a system of common property. None of these evils, however, is due to the absence of communism. They all arise from the wickedness of human nature." In contrast to Plato, Aristotle thought that private property and the family were basic institutions in all healthy and free societies: "What is common to the greatest number gets the least amount of care. Men pay most attention to what is their own . . . the scheme of Plato means that each citizen will have a thousand sons . . . and the result will be that every son will be equally neglected by every father."

Aristotle's emphasis on private property and the family is, of course, in accord with the aristocratic principle. For aristocracies are never planned but are always the inevitable products of historical continuity and tradition in all more or less stable social structures which do not unduly tamper with the family or private property. The origin of rank in ancient Rome, for instance, began with the separation of the top from the rest of the people. A man who had distinguished himself was able to transmit his distinction to his descendants, who were in turn called *patricii*; that is, "children of the father." Thus, according to the most ancient law, only persons of noble descent had a legal father, all others being plebeians or atomized "people." All complex and fully developed societies are patriarchal systems. This is especially true of the top levels which, at the same time, tend to continue to be consanguine rather than conjugal—top ascribed position depending on the consanguine rather than the conjugal relationship. This is still true even in such a mobile and atomized society as modern America, where Roosevelts, Tafts, Adamses, Du Ponts, or Rockefellers stand for consanguine-status continuity in a land where the conjugal family unit is overwhelmingly dominant throughout the rest of society.

Aristocracy and Leadership

Though varying in detail in an infinite variety of ways, the leadership principle in history has asserted itself somewhat as follows: in the beginning of all social organization it has almost always taken the form of the rule of one (*dux*, or the natural leader). In agricultural societies, the leader is most likely to obtain his position through the possession of religious or magical powers with relation to the unknown world (God or gods) upon which the community depends for rain or good harvests. Among hunting or nomadic people, on the other hand, the leader stands out or is chosen on the more secular basis of superior skill, strength, and power of command. One of the safest and least disrupting ways of passing on leadership positions is through the hereditary principle; thus the natural leader in the first generation (*dux*) becomes the institutionalized or hereditary king in succeeding generations (*rex*). At the same time, both *dux* and *rex* need friends, flunkies, companions, cohorts, or courtiers, most of whom will have families and children. Consequently, there evolves, inevitably and organically rather than rationally, a hereditary class of families whose ancestors have been kings' men and whose gradually acquired wealth and authority are passed down from generation to generation. Monarchy and aristocracy usually go hand in hand and are the products of natural ability or naked power, gradually becoming institutionalized in the form of hereditary authority and privilege. As history inevitably involves heredity, in a very important sense, all rational systems are both ahistorical and mechanistic, and from Plato's utopian *Republic* to Aldous Huxley's distopian *Brave New World*, the nonrationality of family continuity has had to be done away with by their authors. Perhaps this is why almost all utopias are authoritarian, as the aristocratic Tory, Aristophanes, saw so clearly when he satirized Plato's utopian schemes in the *Birds:*

> No girl will of course be permitted to mate
> Except in accord with the rules of the state
>
> All bars and partitions forever undone,
> All private establishments fused into one.

Aristocracy and War

Throughout history, aristocracies and aristocratic values have, perhaps, been most closely allied with war and the warlike virtues. Classless societies come at the beginning, and not the end, of history; simple, homogeneous and unstratified societies have usually remained at low technological and cultural levels. Population growth, the increasing complexity of the division of labor, and the extension of the territorial size of the political unit, on the other hand, have all been the products of war. The first economic (slavery) and political (state) revolutions were the products of war and conquest, which, in turn, divided societies into roughly three classes or estates—the conquerors at the top and the slaves at the bottom, with the ordinary citizens in between. ("Progress" began when conquerors first spared the lives of the conquered and absorbed the women into a patriarchal system as wives, concubines, and servants, and the men into slavery.)

War requires leadership and the habit of command. While in agricultural societies the king and court were primarily of religious and ceremonial importance, hunting and nomadic people already possessed the virtues which war demanded, as Aristotle saw when he wrote that "a pastoral people is the best trained for war, sturdy of physique and used to camping out." War meant mobility, rapid transportation, and communications over ever-larger areas, and its acceleration in history began with the introduction of the horse. While the first horses were probably of the small pony type found wild in the Russian steppe country, the Arab nomads of the desert tradition took the lead in their breeding and development. In many ways the Crusades brought horse-breeding and horsemanship, and the ideals of chivalry, into the main stream of European culture. Chivalry, or magnanimity toward the defeated and downtrodden, is a desert attitude of mind. Much like the code of the sea, where even enemies are rescued, the desert mores, bred in a world where the real enemy of both the victors and the vanquished was cruel nature itself, quite naturally produced a code like chivalry. And in many languages—knight, cavalier, chevalier, caballero, and so forth—horsemanship has always symbolized the gentleman.

Monarchy creates nobility, but war contributes to its growth and influence as men of experience, courage, and ability are constantly added to the king's men of purely ceremonial, religious, or birth distinctions. The noble horseman is literally looked up to, just as he literally looks down on others. Being subject to greater risk and requiring greater skill and daring than the common foot soldier, however, he is more often respected than envied. And as war is surely no woman's game, aristocracies are dominated by men, who eventually decline in influence along with the rise of urban affluence and plutocracy, and the consumer-dominated world of women.

Aristocracy and the Decentralized Society

On the whole, the principle of monarchy comes to the fore in periods of centralization, while aristocracies thrive during periods of decentralization. It was Louis XIV and Henry VIII, both autocrats of great natural ability, who led their people out of feudalism into the modern centralized nation-state. Though feudalism, the classic case of warring decentralization, is usually associated with the medieval period in Europe, approximately similar forms of social organization have been found at other times and places. Thus at the close of the Chou Dynasty, China was ruled by some five or six thousand warlords or hereditary nobles. Before the coming of the modern state under Western influence, Japan went through a similar experience during the Samurai period. In India, the caste system grew out of conquest and a long period of decentralized feudalism. The originally dominant caste, the Kshatriyas, were aristocratic warriors superior to the Brahmins (priests), Vaishyas (commoners), and Sudras (originally slaves). Eventually, in the course of some five centuries, the Brahmins rose to the top position. This rigidly aristocratic or ascribed and decentralized system based on an agricultural economy has been one of the most stable the world has ever known. Incidentally, the caste system today, with all its anachronistic and antidemocratic characteristics so abhorrent to Western progressive minds, may be one very important reason why India has not yet fallen prey to the atomized totalitarianism which has been the fate of so many other peoples who are coming into the industrialized state system in the twentieth century. Traditional social theory usually overlooks the fact that African tribalism has much in common, both historically and sociologically, with feudalism; witness the weakness of the conjugal family and the virtues of tribal loyalty, honor, courage, and so forth.

Aristocratic Values Grounded in Feudalism

Many of the aristocratic values which have been carried down into the modern period are products of feudalism. In the feudal code of the horseman, breeding and descent, for horse and man, played a central role. But the stud book and heraldry were also accompanied by the need for training and discipline. Young men who aspired to knighthood were rigidly trained in the arts of war, the hunting and sporting virtues, and the chivalric codes of courage and honor. There was no promise of comfort or affluence, and there was always the risk of death. Yet war was limited and, in a sense, ritualized: fighting took place on a chosen field, often at appointed hours; individual enemies were killed, but women, children, and members of the clergy, as well as families of noble birth, were spared; the knightly or noble order must, above all, be maintained; the code of honor among gentlemen was much like the sportsmen's code of a later day in that enemies were treated more like opponents, according to rules, with courtesy and even friendship and, of course, with respect. It follows, above all, that the feudal system was one of order and law. Manners and morals, in so many ways unlike our own age, stood securely above and beyond mere whim and will. The chivalric code was not entirely unlike that of monasticism: men who cannot live without war, like those who must live without women, cannot afford to live without rules. And both in the knightly and monastic orders there was a rigid etiquette of equality among the qualified. Monk and knight were bound by the norms of chastity and poverty, or honor and courage. Witness, for example, the Samurai code which demanded suicide, and the gentlemanly code which demanded the duel when honor was threatened. (In Durkheim's sense, *suicide altruiste* is an aristocratic virtue, while *suicide egoiste* is a democratic vice.) Though America is not supposed to have had a feudal past, it is interesting that the gentlemanly code of the cowboy in the decentralized horse culture of the old West, as well as that of the gentleman-master of the decentralized plantation system of the old South, were not unlike that of the desert nomads or the knights of medieval Europe.

Probably one of the most important ways in which the feudal social order differed from our own was that, while the former was hierarchical in both fact and theory, ours is surely hierarchical in fact but often dogmatically not so in theory. The hierarchy of feudalism, recognized in theory, was also strictly regulated by law.

Political theory was primarily legal and theological (pertaining to the laws of God). The law, in other words, came to have a higher authority than either the king, the nobles, or the people. Feudal freedom, unlike that of our own day, was freedom within a hierarchical system of rigid codes and not a freedom of arbitrary whim or will. It was freedom to serve an order of peers. The rule of law is one of our most precious heritages from the Middle Ages. Even today, aristocratic values imply freedom from the arbitrary will of others, above all the tyrant and the totalitarian, but certainly *not* freedom *from* a code. Feudalism imposed a hierarchy of duties rather than rights. Duty obligates one in dignity; submission to arbitrary power enslaves and impoverishes the soul. Institutionalized authority dwells in hierarchies grounded in theory and law, while arbitrary power thrives in existential hierarchies divorced from theory and law.

Aristocracy and the State

One of the most useful theories of political and social science is that which analytically distinguishes between *state* and *society*. Thus people in a given territory acting cooperatively (i.e., the nation) behave on two levels, or orders, concurrently and simultaneously (a) in a voluntary way, as a social order, or society, and (b) in a legal or compulsory way, as a legal order, or state.

By and large, at the beginning of all human social organization, the societal principle predominates. The individual, in a sociological sense, simply does not exist, and the ascriptive units of family, tribe, clan, caste, or estate are all-inclusive. Manners and mores, and social ostracism, are the major elements of social control; the legal principle of the state has not yet emerged. This is the age of honor, of the heroic epic, of the family feud; the aristocratic principle rules. The second stage of social organization is that of the city and civilization and the rise of political forms, or the state. In a very important sense, the emergence of the state is in accord with the democratic principle in that the individual gradually becomes the central sociological unit. The reforms of Solon (a centralizer like Louis XIV and Henry VIII—or Napoleon) centered on the abolition of the clan as the central sociological unit and paved the way for fifth- and fourth-century democracy.

Though the major dividing line in history may well have been the emergence of the state from society or, as Oswald Spengler or Alfred Weber have put it, the advance from culture to civilization, it is important to stress the fact that this division which exists at all higher levels of social organization is always a conceptual one and, therefore, never a matter of either/or but rather a matter of more or less. Hence throughout historical time, there has been a swinging of the pendulum, as it were, between the forces of aristocracy and decentralization (society) and democracy and centralization (state). State and society have remained in a condition of dynamic tension, with neither one completely victorious, except perhaps in the case of modern totalitarianism, whose coercive and centralized direction of change is reflected in the new distopian literature such as *Brave New World* and *1984*. This literature is born of the fear that, while civilized man had long ago escaped from the tyranny of custom and all-inclusive society, our age may be falling back into a new barbarism, born of the atomization of society and the total victory of the all-inclusive state.

It is just at this point that we may find a clue to why the ideals of socialism have so often led to some form of totalitarian autocracy. To return to our earlier discussion of the democratic-aristocratic and representative-autocratic continuums, it will be seen that both the aristocratic and representative principles are reflections of a strong society, while the democratic and autocratic principles come to the fore when society is weakened, or unable to cope with changing circumstances, and the state is perforce led to take command. Now, by and large, socialism has concentrated its attack on the evils of the aristocratic principle rather than the autocratic; this is quite in contrast to nineteenth-century liberalism, which centered its attack on the autocratic principle in favor of representative democracy. Socialism stresses classlessness; liberalism, open classes. But—and this may be the clue to the problem—classes are merely the reflection of a strong family and society. Hierarchical rank, especially bureaucratic rank, on the other hand, is an inevitable characteristic of a centralized state. In this sense, then, Russia is actually a classless society, possessed nevertheless of a rigid and articulate hierarchy of rank. Former Presidents Truman and Eisenhower still possess authority in America because of their societal or class positions, although they now have no official rank; in contrast, former Premier Khrushchev, in a classless society (actually no society) presumably has no authority now that he has been divested of the power associated with his former rank. In Marxian theory, classlessness results from the withering away of the state; history has shown that it is actually produced by the systematic suppression of society.

Aristocracy and Voluntary Associations

Family and class, then, are of the essence of society. Both are weakened in democratic ages. But, as Tocqueville so clearly saw, the societal principle, and the protection of freedom against an all-inclusive state, came to reside in the course of the late eighteenth and nineteenth centuries in the *voluntary association*, especially in America where family and class were weak to begin with. Freedom and the continuing strength of society in America have largely been due to our genius for forming associations, which range from political parties and clubs, charitable organizations and foundations, and scientific and cultural societies to the National Association for the Advancement of the Colored People and the American Civil Liberties Union. Rightly understood, we are an associational rather than an individualistic or familistic republic; in this sense, religion is not merely a private affair; freedom of religion, sociologically, means right of religious association and not freedom of thought.

As with society as a whole, the aristocratic principle, in both England and America especially, has in the course of the nineteenth and twentieth centuries become increasingly associational rather than familistic. This is reflected primarily in the form of the private educational associations and the private clubs. Thus, during the period of transition to democracy in England, club, school, and college were added to, if they did not entirely replace, the family as aristocratic status-ascribing institutions. It was during the period of the Reform Bill, for instance, that the Whig aristocrats joined and soon dominated the newly formed Reform Club, while their Tory opponents founded the Carleton. Club and party government replaced the familistic and factional ("connections") contests of the more aristocratic eighteenth century. At the same time, the public schools (privately run and supported), originally charitable institutions, became class institutions. Whigs went to Harrow and Tories to Eton, while both Cambridge, which was Whig and nonconformist, and Oxford, which was Tory and Church of England, became secular and societal institutions for acculturating the sons of the newly rich into a ruling class rather than educating a priesthood.

America went through the same process at the end of the nineteenth century. After the Civil War the upper-class status-ascribing function, especially in the older cities along the eastern seaboard, gradually devolved upon the private schools, especially the New England boarding schools, upon prestige institutions like Harvard, Yale, and Princeton—all founded to educate a priesthood—and upon a whole new network of private clubs, both downtown and suburban, which boomed among the upper classes at the turn of the century. In the generation of President Eliot of Harvard, proper Boston families were content to send their sons to the Boston Latin School; it was in the next generation that the private school became popular. And it was during Eliot's era that the boys from private schools, rather than from good families alone, began to dominate the Gold Coast. In other words, by the 1920s, except for such famous consanguine families as the Adamses, Roosevelts, or Rockefellers, the individual was marked in urban America, if not yet in the small town, by his achievable-ascribed status of Groton '03 or Harvard '07, rather than by his ascribed family status. And these associationally ascribed statuses inevitably paved the way to proper club membership, entrée into the best Wall or State Street banks or law firms, or into appointive positions in Washington, especially in the State Department or the Treasury. These schools and colleges, of course, served the function of surrogate families; a sizeable proportion of each entering class consisted of sons or grandsons of alumni. Thus was the aristocratic and societal principle carried down into the twentieth century. (It would be interesting to speculate on the consequences of Harvard, for instance, becoming a pure meritocracy: thus hypothetically, if 90 percent of Harvard students were sons of alumni or originated in upper-class families, an achievable-ascribed upper-class status would tend to rub off on the remaining 10 percent of the students; if, on the other hand, 90 percent of the Harvard student body were to be recruited on merit alone, and only 10 percent were of upper-class origin, Harvard would no longer, in this particular sense, be a surrogate family for aristocratic ascription; this is a possibility today but not as yet an actuality.)

In closing, it should be emphasized again that the aristocratic principle thrives when the family, society, and the hereditary principle are strong. At the same time, in all advanced and industrial societies, which perhaps must inevitably be highly centralized and collectivized, with the state or public property encroaching on private property, the status ascribing function must be increasingly associational and partly achievable rather than familistic and entirely ascribed from birth. This is why freedom is now threatened as never before in that part of the world which is going through the painful transition from rural familism to a centralized urban society. All the traditional societal forms of clan, family, or tribe must be ruthlessly obliterated; as these traditional societies have had no experience with associationalism, society becomes atomized and drawn within the all-inclusive state machine.

There is hope, nevertheless, that in the third or fourth generation, the societal and aristocratic principles, grounded in association as well as family, will gradually reassert themselves as they have in the past. As the British historian of the Soviet Union, E.H. Carr, has written, "a school was started in the Kremlin in Moscow for children of high party and Soviet officials. Nobody supposes that its function was to enable these children to start equal with other Russian children." Nor will society fail to be eventually strengthened by the laws encouraging a stronger family, which were passed in the Soviet Union in 1936 and in 1944. The priests of the Soviet theocracy may surely have descendants who will be compromising trimmers, as the principle of aristocracy reasserts itself in the third and fourth generations.

11

The Search for Community in Modern America

History's lessons but record
One death-grapple in the darkness
'Twixt old systems and the Word.
—James Russell Lowell

None of us is primarily interested in abstractions; we become so only because they often help us to understand unique and concrete events and issues. After teaching a wide variety of students at a large urban university for some years, one has the impression that majors in the social sciences are too often burdened with abstract concepts (or analytical points of view) without much knowledge of past or present events; history majors, on the other hand, do know some history but often lack a conceptual point of view with which to organize their knowledge in some meaningful way. In this brief essay, therefore, an attempt has been made to deal rather concretely with various aspects of a central theoretical issue—the nature of community cohesion.

Coming home from a night job in the early hours of a March morning in 1964, a young lady, Catherine Genovese, was stabbed repeatedly and over an extended period of time. Thirty-eight fellow residents of Kew Gardens, a respectable New York City neighborhood, admitted to have witnessed at least part of the attack. None of them, however, went to her aid, nor did anyone call the police until after she was dead. The crime, or rather the lack of community response to it, produced a sense of indignation and frustration which spread across the nation. Senator Richard Russell of Georgia read the *New York Times* account of it into the *Congressional Record*, and the Law School of the University of Chicago eventually sponsored a "Conference on the Good Samaritan and the Bad—The Law and Morality of Volunteering in Situations of Peril, or of Failing to Do So." The "Genovese case," and especially the wide and overly emotional discussions of it in the mass media, served to dramatize the problem of community cohesion in modern society.

The concept of community is often used, but less often defined. Perhaps the following definition will be helpful; it was set forth by Robert A. Nisbet in an exhaustive treatment of the classic sociological discussions of the problem:

> By community [he wrote], I mean something that goes far beyond mere local community. The word as we find it in much nineteenth- and twentieth-century thought encompasses all forms of relationships which are characterized by a high degree of personal intimacy, emotional depth, moral commitment, social cohesion, and continuity in time. Community is founded on man conceived in his wholeness rather than in one or another of the roles, taken separately, that he may hold in the social order. It draws its psychological strength from levels of motivation deeper than those of mere volition or interest, and it achieves its fulfillment in a submergence of individual will that is not possible in unions of mere convenience or rational assent. Community is a fusion of feeling and thought, of tradition and commitment, of membership and volition. It may be found in, or given symbolic expression by, locality, religion, nation, race, occupation, or crusade.

The gradual erosion, in modern society, of the traditional community ties which Professor Nisbet describes is both the cause and the results of extensive social mobility, individuation, anonymity, and the consequent prevalence of purely monetary social relationships. In one of the classic community studies, *Middletown* by Robert and Helen Lynd, a leading citizen of the town explained to the authors the local custom of "placing" newcomers to Middletown by where they live, the size of their house, the kind of car they drive, and similar monetary externals: "It's perfectly natural," he said. "You see, they know money, and they don't know you." And of course the rational and anonymous social relations which one finds in so much of metropolitan New York made the Genovese case possible, if not inevitable or excusable. It should be pointed out, however, that since anonymity and mobility lie at the very roots of our kind of society, they must be understood rather than denounced, as has too often been characteristic of a great deal of social criticism, to say nothing of the denunciations of the thirty-eight Kew Gardens residents by the mass media at the time of the Genovese case.

An understanding of the need for anonymity in modern society has nowhere been discussed more wisely than in a recent book, The Secular City by Harvey Cox. After carefully describing what social theorists like Professor Nisbet mean by primary (intimate, emotional, continuous, and communal) as against secondary (rational, impersonal, segmental, and functional) social relationships, Cox goes on, in a simple and matter-of-fact style, to illustrate the differences:

> Having lived both as a villager and as an urbanite I know just what these terms mean. During my boyhood, my parents never referred to "the milkman," "the insurance agent," "the junk collector." These people were, respectively, Paul Weaver, Joe Villanova, and Roxy Barazano. All of our family's market transactions took place within a web of wider and more inclusive friendship and kinship ties with the same people. They were never anonymous. In fact, the occasional salesman or repairman whom we did not know was always viewed with dark suspicion until we could make sure where he came from, who his parents were, and whether his family was "any good." Trips to the grocery store, gasoline station, or post office were invariably social visits, never merely functional contacts.

There was little mobility or anonymity in the small Pennsylvania community in which Professor Cox grew up. Status seeking and the compulsion to conform were unthought-of in a world where everyone had his place in an intricate web of primary relationships. Nor would anything quite like the Genovese case have been possible. On the other hand, Professor Cox sees the inevitability of anonymity in our present urban environment. He writes:

> Now, as an urbanite, my transactions are of a very different sort. If I need to have the transmission on my car repaired, buy a television antenna, or

> cash a check, I find myself in functional relationships with mechanics, salesmen, and bank clerks whom I never see in any other capacity. These "contacts" are in no sense "mean, nasty or brutish," though they do tend to be short, at least not any longer than the time required to make the transactions and to exchange a brief pleasantry. Some of these human contacts occur with considerable frequency, so that I come to know the mannerisms and maybe even the names of some of the people. But the relationships are unifaceted and "segmental." I meet these people in no other context. . . . The important point here is that my relationships with bank clerks and garagemen are no less human or authentic merely because we both prefer to keep them anonymous. . . . Urban anonymity need not be heartless. Village sociability can mask a murderous hostility.

All too many of us are more or less nostalgic about the good old days of spatial cohesion in the small, local community. But modern urban man must guard his privacy precisely because he needs to have many many more social relationships than in the past; consequently, he must of necessity keep most of them on the secondary level in order to reserve time for the few, more meaningful, primary relationships which we all need. Moreover, rather than being rooted in vicinage, kinship, and place, urban man's primary relationships are more likely to be based on free choice and common interests. Professor Cox illustrates this point by referring to a survey of attitudes among high-rise-apartment dwellers by some Protestant clergymen; they were horrified to find that many of the residents simply did not want to know their neighbors socially, but preferred to choose their friends elsewhere in the city. Inevitably, there is a certain amount of loneliness in any large city and perhaps especially among apartment dwellers. But it is not just these people who have firm friends on a transcommunal basis, gained along with professional, cultural, and recreational interests, who are the very ones who do not have time for extensive neighborhood sociability? What is needed is not condemnation but a realization that urban man has, as it were, come of age (all childhood social relationships, both now and in the past, have been based on kinship and propinquity), and is seeking new kinds of transcommunal friendships and voluntary associational loyalties.

For the student of history (which is essentially a record of the ever-changing nature of social relationships), it is important to ask the right questions about the present, rather than to seek pat answers in some idealized past. For perhaps the problem of neighborliness is as old as recorded history. In this connection, it might be helpful to recall that the Judeo-Christian ethic grew out of the experiences of a mobile people who replaced the idolatries of place (Baal), which characterized the religions of more settled peoples, with the universal God (Yahweh) of history and eternal time. But in spite of the fact that now *all* men were supposed to be brothers under the fatherhood of *one* God, neighborly responsibility was still a problem, as the Good Samaritan parable in the New Testament suggests. Thus, the man who fell among thieves and was left half dead on the road from Jerusalem to Jericho was no more a next-door neighbor of the Samaritan than of the priest or the Levite, both of whom passed by on the other side of the road. Yet the Samaritan helped this stranger in an efficient and unsentimental way by bandaging his wounds, taking him to a nearby inn, and paying the innkeeper to look after him. In this parable, Jesus was not engaged in decrying the decline of community cohesion but in showing us what a moral man would do in an impersonal situation.

Rather than lament the loss of traditional community ties in the Kew Gardens of America, then, it would be wiser to try to understand what neighborliness means in a large-scale and urban society. First of all, modern man can never return to the communal mores of Main Street, with its attendant tyrannies of gossip and overheard conversations on the party line. His moral duty is no longer reinforced by the social sanctions of his next-door neighbors.

This means that urban society places far more emphasis on individual morality and personal ethics than is the case under simpler social structures. Is this too much to expect of men? Do we perhaps need laws to replace the older communal sanctions? Our Anglo-Saxon traditions, in contrast to those of continental Europe, for instance, do not legally require us to come to the aid of a person in danger. Yet the reader should ask himself whether or not he prefers our kind of voluntary society, which still emphasizes privacy and the minding of one's own business, to the more communal and cohesive, but perhaps more restrictive, societies of the Continent, where legal Samaritanism, or enforced neighborliness, is now found on the statute books of fifteen out of sixteen nations. The Russians have had such legal sanctions since 1917, for example, and the Germans ever since the Nazis instituted such laws in 1935. It is this kind of question—that is to say, how can old and perennial problems be handled in ways more suitable to new situations—which is raised by the Genovese case. At any rate, it might be well to outline briefly, by way of a few historical facts, how and why urban America came to be the way it is today.

By and large, it may be said that, until the Civil War, or perhaps through the 1870s, most Americans grew up and lived most of their lives in more or less small communities where social relationships were predominantly of the communal type defined by Professor Nisbet and illustrated by Professor Cox's picture of his boyhood. Not only were the majority of social relationships within the various class levels close and diffuse rather than impersonal and segmental, but also, and perhaps of more importance, community leaders were usually bred locally and were accustomed to making decisions on the basis of firsthand knowledge of, and primary relations with, members of the other class levels, especially their constituents or employees.

Thus, Richard Hofstadter, in the following passage in his *Age of Reform*, shows how the "old gentry" once ruled America:

> Up to about 1870, the United States was a nation with a rather broad diffusion of wealth, status, and power, in which men of moderate means, especially in the many small communities, could command much deference and exert much influence. The small merchant or manufacturer, the distinguished lawyer, editor, or preacher, was a person of local eminence in an age when local eminence mattered a great deal.

All this is not to deny, of course, that local paternalism did not produce its share of cruelty and injustices as between social and economic classes.

In many ways, the decade of the 1880s marked a turning point in our history and the birth of the urban, centralized, and highly organized society which characterizes our twentieth-century world. At our first census in 1790, for instance, 95 percent of the American people were living on farms and engaged in agriculture; in the 1880s, for the first time, less than half the population was engaged in agriculture. At the same time, while no city in the United States had as many as 50,000 inhabitants in 1790, and only two exceeded 25,000, it was in the 1880s that our first city, New York, reached a million in population (today we have five cities with more than a million inhabitants and more than a hundred between 100,000 and a million in size). In fact, today we are virtually an urban nation, that is, some three-fifths of our population now resides in 168 metropolitan areas.

Urbanization was, of course, the product of industrialization and the resulting increase in the production of wealth. Between 1870 and 1900 the national wealth quadrupled, then doubled again by 1914. And this new wealth became increasingly centralized in the hands of a few. In 1891, *Forum* magazine published an article, "The Coming Billionaire," which estimated that there were 120 men in the nation worth over $10 million. The next year, the *New York Times* published a list of 4,047 millionaires, and the U.S. Census Bureau estimated that 9 percent of the nation's families owned 71 percent of the wealth.

This new inequality of wealth was accompanied by an increasing centralization of business power. President Eliot of Harvard, in a speech before the Phi Beta Kappa Society in 1888, noted this new corporate dominance when he pointed out that, while in that year the Pennsylvania Railroad had gross receipts of $115 million and employed more than 100,000 men, the Commonwealth of Massachusetts had gross receipts of only $17 million and employed no more than 6,000 persons. And this corporate economy was further centralized financially on Wall Street. The capital required to launch the United States Steel Corporation, for example, would at that time have covered the costs of all functions of the federal government for almost two years. The centralization of entrepreneurial and family capitalism in larger and larger corporate structures preceded, and indeed anticipated, the eventual growth of the state and the federal bureaucracy. J. P. Morgan and his associates, who put together the steel empire, were in almost unregulated control of a national corporate system.

These newly rich captains of industry and their families gradually formed a new, urban, and national upper class, increasingly divorced from any local community roots or organic ties with the rest of society. As rootless and parvenu aristocrats, they engaged in all sorts of conspicuous consumption and irresponsible behavior, which, in turn, was minutely chronicled in the national press. It was no wonder that the laboring classes lost faith in these new absentee owners, who now made decisions on Wall Street, decisions reflecting financial rather than human concern, and which affected the lives of thousands of anonymous workers and their families in countless mining and manufacturing towns throughout the nation. And some of the bloodiest civil disorders in our history, such as the Haymarket Square riot and the Homestead Steel and Pullman strikes, were parallelled by passionate criticism of anonymous capitalism, which ranged from the writings of Edward Bellamy, Henry George, and Thorstein Veblen to the slogans and creeds of such protest movements as anarchism and socialism, the Populists, Grangers, Knights of Labor, and so forth. The irresponsible and crude behavior of the members of this new, national elite led to a mistrust which arose throughout the rest of society. Here, it is enough to stress that it was *the search for community* which lay behind the various protest writings and movements in the Age of Reform, beginning in the late nineteenth century and continuing through the New Deal. The tone and style of the Marxian criticism of classical capitalism, for instance, are suggested in the following famous lines from the *Communist Manifesto*:

> The bourgeoisie, wherever it has got the upper hand, has put an end to all feudal, patriarchal, idyllic relations. It has pitilessly torn asunder the motley feudal ties that bound man to his "natural superior," and has left remaining no other nexus between man and man than naked self-interest, than callous "cash payment." It has drowned the most heavenly ecstacies of religious fervor, of chivalrous enthusiasm, of philistine sentimentalism, in the icy waters of egotistical calculation. It has resolved personal worth into exchange value

The Christian Socialists in England took seriously Marx's diagnosis of the ills of laissez-faire capitalism; at the same time, they sought different solutions to the problems of community distintegration, among them the founding of Toynbee Hall in

London's East End in 1884. Thus began the settlement house movement, which almost immediately spread to America.

Members of the "old gentry" referred to by Hofstadter, and especially their college-educated sons and daughters, not only suffered from the status revolution which was pushing them out of power in the new corporate America. Many of them, gradually realizing that the callous cash nexus was creating increasing affluence at the top of society, along with increasing poverty at the bottom, eventually became absorbed in the social gospel and settlement house movements, which, in turn, fed into the Progressive movement led by Theodore Roosevelt, Wilson's New Freedom, and Franklin D. Roosevelt's New Deal. One of the most inspiring leaders of the settlement house movement in this country was Jane Addams. Her father, a pious Quaker and successful business entrepreneur, had been one of the "old gentry" in a small town in Illinois. Upon completing college and receiving a legacy from her recently deceased father, Jane Addams traveled abroad in the 1880s. She was so horrified at the conditions in London's East End, and so impressed with the valuable work being done at Toynbee Hall, that she returned to America and, with Ellen G. Starr, founded Hull House in Chicago in 1889. In the meantime, settlement houses were being founded in most major cities along the eastern seaboard. In many ways, the settlement house movement was an attempt at institutionalizing a new kind of neighborliness, as the following passage from an early history of the movement suggests:

> A settlement is a colony of members of the upper classes, formed in a poor neighborhood, with the double purpose of getting to know local conditions of life from personal observation, and of helping where help is needed. The settler gives up the comfort of a West End home, and becomes a friend of the poor. He sacrifices to them his hours of leisure, and fills his imagination with pictures of misery and crime, instead of with the impressions of beauty and happiness. For a shorter or longer time the slum becomes his home. . . . The settler comes to the poor as man to man, in the conviction that it means a misfortune for all parties and a danger for the nation, if the different classes live in complete isolation of thought and environment. He comes to bridge the gulf between the classes.

The ugliness, political corruption, and the various lower-class pathologies which social scientists and settlement house workers were trying to do something about, at the same time produced the flight to the suburbs which began first among the rich during the last part of the nineteenth century. Thus the wealthy citizens of Boston, according to Justice Brandeis, told their sons: "Boston holds nothing for you except heavy taxes and political misrule. When you marry, pick out a suburb to build your house in, join the country club, and make your life center about your club, your home and your children." The country club, first of its kind in America, was founded in a Boston suburb in 1882. And suburban America remained largely an upper-class preserve until after World War I. During the prosperous twenties, the more affluent members of the middle classes moved in droves to new developments typified by "Floral Heights," built by George F. Babbitt, whose life and values were immortalized in Sinclair Lewis's novel, *Babbitt.* But the real flood began after World War II, when more and more members of the lower-middle class, and of the white working class as well, fled from what were becoming the urban Negro ghettos in the postwar suburban development boom symbolized by the Levittowns of Long Island, New Jersey, and Pennsylvania. The bulldozer, the moving van, and the traffic jam became major symbols of our postwar affluence; country clubs spread across the land and the new democratization of status seeking was now symbolized by millions of lost golf balls.

While, according to the 1960 census, two-thirds of the American people resided within 168 standard metropolitan areas, most of them were living in the white suburban fringe; the Negroes and other poor minority groups were crowded into the central cores of the great cities. Between 1950 and 1960, for instance, the population of the nation as a whole increased by 18 percent, that of the center, or "inner," cities by only 11 percent, and of the suburbs by over 50 percent. During this same period, New York City lost 1.5 percent of its population while the surrounding suburbs gained by 75 percent.

The suburban trend, of course, reflects a tremendous increase in social mobility. According to the U.S. Department of Commerce, one-half of the American people changed houses or apartments between 1955 and 1960; in Florida and California, the most rapidly growing states in the Union, 65 percent of the population moved during this period. The city of Los Angeles, sometimes referred to as "six suburbs in search of a city," is situated in one of the most mobile areas of the nation. While the Boston-to-Washington urban complex increased by some 15 percent between 1950 and 1960, for example, the San Francisco-to-San Diego complex increased by over 50 percent. One-tenth of the automobiles in the nation are now registered in California.

There is every indication that excessive social mobility and the resulting rootlessness breed insecurity and various forms of extremism. It is perhaps no accident that Henry Wallace, representing the extreme Left, did remarkably well in southern California in the presidential campaign of 1948; similarly, Barry Goldwater, representing the extreme Right in the 1964 campaign, was very popular in southern California, but be lost some of the more cohesive suburbs in the East to the Democrats for the first time in the twentieth century. Also, various fringe sects, cults, and crusades, such as the John Birch Society and the Jehovah's Witnesses, which Professor Nisbet sees as substitute communities that arise when normal social relationships prove inadequate, have attracted a multitude of followers in and around the Los Angeles area.

Whereas at the turn of the century the nation's press and members of the intellectual community were largely concerned with the growing irresponsibility and selfishness of America's business and financial leaders and with the consequent unrest of the working class, during the past few years in America the mass media and concerned intellectuals have focused their attention on the unrest on the nation's campuses. Given the fact of the more general insecurity, mistrust, and alienation which seem to be characteristic of California's adult population today, it would seem quite natural that this national (and international) concern should have come to a head in the fall of 1964, when the Free Speech Movement (FSM) led a revolt on the Berkeley campus of the University of California.

The causes of today's unrest on the campuses of the nation are, of course, highly complex and vary from institution to institution. It is due as much, however, to the decline in community as between the leadership and their student followers. Much like their business predecessors in the Gilded Age, members of the academic community have only recently achieved a position of relative affluence and prestige. And, quite like the businessmen and financiers whose decisions were based on their own financial self-interest rather than on the human needs of their employees, the more highly mobile members of the present academic community, especially at high- (yet new) prestige institutions such as Berkeley, have lost human contact with the mass of anonymous students, both undergraduate and graduate. History sometimes seems to repeat itself in strange ways. In 1864, George Mortimer Pullman built his first sleeping car. In 1894, the inhabitants of his model company town, Pullman, Illinois, started a devastating strike because they had lost faith in their superiors, who had felt it necessary to cut back their wages. In 1964, many of the students on the idyllic Berkeley campuses were moved by a similar feeling.

This essay has had to do with one central problem: How can a society institutionalize new social and legal relationships which will best promote a mature and responsible neighborliness appropriate to an urban, bureaucratized, and rational (rather than local and patriarchal) social order?

This question and others like it will be disturbing, and may require discouraging answers. Yet just as the rhythms of nature demand that the budding rebirths of springtime be preceded by the dying fall and dormant winter, so the forces of rebirth and renewal in human society, so often unnoticed, or misunderstood and therefore feared and resisted, are always preceded, or paralleled, by apparently destructive social forces and the dying out of ancient traditions, so noticeable primarily because so vigorously defended. In this connection, it is well to recall that within a year of the Genovese case, we Americans were witnessing one of the greatest outpourings of mass Samaritanism in our history. Thus the Selma-Montgomery march, supported by many clergymen-heirs of the Social Gospel movement of the last century and understandably feared by many other sincere people, was a witness to our continuing concern for reform, and the never-ending quest for a more moral community in America.

12

To Be a Phoenix: Reflections on Two Noisy Ages of Prose

Heroic ages of poetry are often followed by hesitant ages of prose, literary creativity by literary criticism, and the doing of sociology by the sociology of sociology. At least as I see it, the central thrust of this volume of the *American Journal of Sociology* (vol. 78, no. 1, July 1972), largely concerned as it is with the sociology of sociology, nicely reflects our hesitant age of prose. The poetic core of sociology, I like to think on the other hand, lies in the doing tradition of the great problematic monographs like *Le suicide, L'ancien regime, The Protestant Ethic, The Polish Peasant, The Gang, Yankee City, Deep South*, and *Middletown, White Collar, The Lonely Crowd, Black Bourgeoisie*, *Union Democracy, Asylums*, and so forth. Merton's *Science, Technology and Society in Seventeenth-Century England* is very much a part of this poetic tradition. Its review by Benjamin Nelson, more than three decades after its original publication, may well be the most symbolically important thing about this volume.

All civilizations, at one unfortunate time or another, have been pushed to the polar, *lawless* extremes of autocracy or anarchy. If autocracy is the anarchy of lawless, lonely tyrants, anarchy is the tyranny of lawless, lonely crowds. It is interesting that such a timeless and poetic work as Solzhenitsyn's *First Circle* was produced in autocratic Moscow, while the timely prose of Mailer's *Advertisements for Myself* seems such a telling symptom of anarchic New York. Perhaps the silence of autocracy is less of an obstacle to real poetic genius than the infernal noise of anarchy. In our own discipline, for example, the major monographs of Erving Goffman, poetic doer par excellence, were all done before the noise began. On the other hand, it is probably inevitable that sociologists, at the end of the noisiest decade in modern history, should be preoccupied with the sociology of sociology (see the recent books by Friedrichs, *A Sociology of Sociology* (1970); Gouldner, *The Coming Crisis of Western Sociology* (1970); and Tiryakian, *The Phenomenon of Sociology* (1971). Thus the relevant problem today, so they say, is *not* the doing of sociology but rather *how* it should be done, for *whom* (adults or children, boozers or potheads), and by persons of *what* theoretical, political, sexual, racial, class, or sartorial persuasions. But surely, as even Becker and Horowitz admit, it is "good sociology" which will last, regardless of what contemporaries think of the theoretical, political, or social positions of the doers. When the doing of political sociology, as for example Lipset's *Political Man*, gives way to the concentration on the politics of sociological theorists (as shown in Lipset and Ladd, "The Politics of American Sociologists"), the discipline is betraying its best and most fruitful traditions. When my own graduate students, so often the less secure and talented among them, are noisily engaged in arguing the pros and cons of the Tumin criticisms of the "iniquitous" Davis and Moore thesis, I urge them instead to take some problem, preferably dear to their own hearts or personal experiences, and to go to work in the hopes of adding something, however great or small, to the great doing tradition, from Durkheim to Goffman.

When asked by the editor for my "reactions" to these articles,[1] I hesitated to interrupt my own work on the problem of the rise of Quakerism in Puritan England. I accepted the invitation, however, because I was convinced that an understanding of this crucial period in English history had something to tell us about our own age. During the anarchical and violent years of the Puritan Revolution, for example, John Milton shelved his poetic genius and produced a series of polemical and relevant pamphlets, including his famous defense of freedom of the press and a less famous justification of regicide;[2] he survived the Restoration of 1660, though he was arrested as an Enemy of the State and two of his pamphlets were burned by the public hangman, only because of his friends at court; and he did not publish *Paradise Lost* until 1667, a year before his sixtieth birthday. Milton witnessed the rise and agonizing death of Puritanism, which a modern historian, Alan Simpson, has briefly outlined as follows: "The origins of English Puritanism are to be found among the Protestant reformers of the mid-sixteenth century; it takes shape in the reign of Elizabeth; produces thrust after thrust of energy in the seventeenth century, until the final thrust throws up the Quakers; and then ebbs away."

Alvin Gouldner's brilliant book, *The Coming Crisis of Western Sociology*, which is the subject of two of the essays in this collection, as well as the articles by Janowitz, Merton, and Becker and Horowitz, are all very much a product of our anarchic age and the consequent "balcanization of social science," as Merton puts it. In other words, as I see it, they are a reflection of sociology's attempt to cope with and understand the agonizing death of liberalism, about which some future, intellectual historian may write as follows: "The origins of Western liberalism are to be found among the utilitarian reformers of the mid-nineteenth century; it takes shape in the Victorian age; produces thrust after thrust in America during the Progressive, New Freedom, New Deal, and New Frontier years of the twentieth century, until the final thrust throws up the New Left and a host of other secular-sectarian movements; and then, like the Puritans of another day, ebbs away."

Now the content and the ideas of seventeenth-century Puritanism were hardly similar to those of twentieth-century liberalism; for one thing the rhetoric of one was religious, the other secular. But seventeenth-century Puritans and modern liberals, on the other hand, played functionally equivalent roles, as reformers and advocates of change, in their respective societies. As Weber, Tawney, Merton, and others have shown, Puritans took the lead in science, law, medicine, manufacturing, and in military tactics. Their political leaders were largely members of the country gentry whose power lay in the House of Commons. These gentlemen reformers, allied with city merchants and lawyers, were seeking to enlarge their power and authority as against the establishment of Church, Lords, and Monarchy. Oliver Cromwell, for example, was a prominent member of this gentry class. He was born in the last years of Elizabeth's reign, in 1599, to the poorer branch of a wealthy and prominent family in the county of Huntington, near the Puritan stronghold of Cambridge. Before going to Parliament in 1628, he had spent a year at Sidney Sussex, a Puritan college at Cambridge, and then settled down as a gentleman farmer and leader in local county affairs. In social background and in politics, then, he was not unlike the gentlemen reformers who followed the leadership of Theodore and Franklin Roosevelt, both of whom challenged the established power and authority of big business in twentieth-century America. And this seventeenth-century English gentleman would have been quite at home among the Roosevelts at Oyster Bay or Hyde Park. Just as the two Roosevelts were essentially Victorians in education, background, and temperament, so the leading men of the great Puritan generation were essentially Elizabethans and men of order, who nevertheless believed in change, the continual reform of the inevitable abuses of authority, and the steady equalizing of opportunity. They *never*, however, advocated the abolition of authority or the possibility, or desirability, of complete equality of conditions; they were reformers but not radicals, equalizers but certainly not egalitarians.

For approximately a century, Puritan and liberal reformers were successful in backing more or less orderly and evolutionary change in their respective eras. Then suddenly and in times of seeming victory, reform turned upon itself and died in a period of radicalism and anarchy. Among other things, there was a generation problem. Thus John Winthrop, who brought Puritanism to New England, was born in the Armada year of 1588, while William Penn, founder of Quaker Pennsylvania, was born the year of the great parliamentary victory at Marston Moor (1644). Winthrop was born the same year as Hobbes, while Penn was a friend of Locke. To put it another way, Winthrop and Penn were born as far apart in time and societal values as Franklin Roosevelt was from the younger generation of the 1960s.

At any rate, in England both the reformers and the radicals

eventually lost out at the Restoration of 1660. What will happen here nobody knows. Marx, following Hegel, saw historical patterns repeating themselves at least twice, first as tragedy and second as farce. There is a haunting similarity between the pattern of anarchy which followed the execution of England's king, in January 1649, and the years in America since the assassination of our president in November 1963.[3] In the interest of avoiding farce, I should like to take a look at the first tragedy. Though I must be brief, I shall try to include enough concrete detail to make the historical parallels meaningful and more than mere abstractions.

The 1630s in England were much like the Eisenhower years in America. Society went through a period of confident calm under the benevolent authority of Charles I. As a contemporary poet wrote, with smugness and pride:

> Tourneys, masques, theatres better become
> Our Halcyon days; what though German drums
> Bellow for Freedom and revenge, the noise
> Concerns us not, nor should divert our joys.

But the placid thirties were followed by the revolutionary forties and anarchical fifties, when Englishmen, for the first and last time in their history, fought each other to the bloody and bitter end, abolishing bishops and lords, beheading their king, and eventually setting up a kind of military dictatorship in the face of increasing anarchy.

This is no place to go into the causes of the Civil War. But it is safe to say, I think, that war broke out in 1642, not because the leaders on either side wanted it, but rather because, as with our own involvement in Vietnam today, they failed to see the collective and cumulative consequences of their individual actions.

The vast majority of leaders of both parties, for instance, believed in a monarchical form of government and an established church. When the members of the Long Parliament passed the Grand Remonstrance, a mild-mannered listing of the abuses of monarchical and Episcopal authority, they included the following statement of their belief in religious uniformity and authority: "We do here declare that it is far from our purpose or desire to let loose the golden reigns of discipline and government in the Church, to leave private persons of particular congregations to take up what form of divine service they please, for we hold it requisite that there should be through-out the whole realm a conformity to that order which the laws enjoin according to the word of God." The parliamentary army, moreover, was raised "for the safety of the King's person, defence of both Houses of Parliament, the preservation of the true religion, the laws, liberty and peace of the kingdom." The commissions of its officers, moreover, ran "in the name of King and Parliament."

The Long Parliament was certainly no revolutionary body. Its members were essentially a conservative cousinhood of knights, squires, and gentlemen from the counties, along with some city lawyers and wealthy merchants. When young Cromwell first went to Parliament in 1628, for instance, he found nine cousins there; at the opening of the Long Parliament, he sat with eleven cousins, including John Hampden, then the richest man in England; six more cousins and three other relatives joined him there later on. In addition to the gentry-merchant cousinage, no less than forty-eight members were sons of peers. That the extremely mild Grand Remonstrance was passed by a slim majority of only 11 votes out of 307 members present attested to the conservative and conciliatory mood as of December 1641. Unfortunately, Charles rejected the mild criticism and impeached six members for treason (including Hampden, one of the most widely respected men of his day). It was the slender straw that broke the camel's back, and war broke out at the Battle of Edgehill. The Parliamentary party eventually won a military victory due, among other things, to the efficiency and leadership of the New Model Army.

The New Model was something new in English history. In the Puritan tradition of the calling, Cromwell had a great sense of professional pride. In striking contrast to the aristocratic ideal, he organized the New Model on the basis of merit rather than status: "The officers," wrote his more conservative contemporary, Clarendon, "are of no better family than the common soldiers." The New Model not only provided for careers open to talents; it was also an ideological army made up of voluntary, true believers in the righteousness of the Holy Crusade. Unfortunately it was this Cromwellian tradition, transplanted to America, which has produced such moral disillusionment after each of our own military crusades in the twentieth century, from the days of Wilson and Roosevelt through Kennedy and Johnson. All this was, of course, quite in contrast to the aristocratic ideal of warfare as a sport, with rules protecting priests, women, and children, and fought for limited interests rather than ideological abstractions.

As was to be expected with this new ideological army, there soon developed, from colonel to common soldier, a belief in the right of self-expression, or a kind of participatory democracy. We often forget the revolutionary potential of all standing armies, of which the New Model was the first in English history. Down to 1640, for example, most Englishmen were extremely provincial. Even after years of Tudor and Stuart attempts at centralization, there was little sense of nationhood; one's *country* meant one's county, where everyone was bound together by local loyalties of family, lord and manor, vicar and village, all reinforcing the established customs of degree, priority, and place. Now, for the first time, large numbers of Englishmen were away from home and easily influenced by the sway of opinion so characteristic of the all-male and atomized life in the ranks.

And the men of the New Model were exposed to all kinds of new enthusiasms. According to George Sabine, the great political scientist and biographer of the "Digger" leader, Gerrard Winstanley, the debates and heated discussions which took place around the army campfires marked the first appearance of public opinion as a factor in British politics. These debates, mirroring and reinforcing those of revolutionary society as a whole, were part of the greatest outpouring of pamphleteering in British history (a fine collection of the pamphlets in the British Museum includes some 20,000 titles, obviously only part of the whole). In order to organize and regulate the expression of opinion, there was set up a Council of the Army, representing the officers, and a Council of Agitators, representing the ranks. As Clarendon, the first great historian of the Rebellion and a contemporary witness, wrote, the army had "set itself up as a rival parliament with the agitators as the house of commons and the officers as peers."

The most famous of the army debates took place in the little village church at Putney, in the autumn of 1647, after military victory in the Civil War had been won. Although the Leveller leader, John Lilburne, was imprisoned in the Tower at the time, the debates centered around his draft constitution, called Agreement of the People which was concerned mainly with the franchise. This was the first time in English history that the possibility of manhood suffrage was taken seriously: in the now-famous words of Colonel Rainsborough (kin by marriage to John Winthrop of New England), "The poorest he that is in England has a life to live as the greatest he, and therefore . . . every man that is to live under a government ought first by his own consent to put himself under that government." The Putney debates dragged on through October, many of the generals and colonels being horrified at the extreme views of the agitators with all their leveling ideas. Finally in November, Cromwell terminated the debates and ordered the men back to their regiments, shooting one agitator on the spot for insubordination.

Events now moved steadily to the left, toward the logical conclusion of the revolution: execution of the king. During the course of the next year (1648), the generals revived their alliance with the Levellers and proceeded to occupy London. In December, Colonel Pride forcefully expelled ninety-six conservative Presbyterians from Parliament. This left only some sixty more radical members, called the Rump, who abolished the House of Lords and brought Charles before the High Court of Justice, which sent him to the scaffold on January 30, 1649. "All is quiet," wrote John Winthrop's son, Stephen, from London, in the hush which followed the execution of the king: "All is quiet, but I know not how long it will last. . . . New England seems the only safe place."

Stephen Winthrop's premonitions of strife were justified. With the final abolition of all traditional authorities, only anarchy or the sword remained. Even the perpetual opponent of authority, John Lilburne, was horrified. He denied the lawfulness of both

Pride's purge and the king's trial: "To have the name of Commonwealth imposed upon us by the Sword," he told Cromwell at the time, "wherein we are and shall be more slaves than ever we were under kingship. . . . and therefore I had rather be under a King reasonable bound than under you, and your new Sword Tyranny called Common-wealth."

As long as history had recorded, authority in England had been symbolized in the now-abolished orders of Kings, lords, and bishops. The regicide had so uniquely shocked the people that, according to a contemporary witness, "Women miscarried, men fell into melancholy, some with consternation expired." The great physician, William Harvey, told a bishop at the time that he met with "more diseases generated by the mind than from any other cause." All, indeed, was now in doubt, all coherence gone, and a host of "seekers" began to populate the melancholy land of England, very much in the style of the lonely and lost souls of our own day who once gathered at Woodstock and are now joining the Jesus cults. Clarendon was horrified at the decline in traditional authority: "All relations," he wrote, "were confounded by the several Sects in Religion, which discountenanced all Forms of Reverence and Respect. . . . Parents had no Manner of Authority over their Children, nor Children any Obedience or Submission to their Parents; but everyone did that which was good in their own Eyes." Quite naturally, Clarendon saw the extreme egalitarianism abroad in the land as a reversion to primitivism: "In all well instituted governments," he wrote, "the heirs and descendants from worthy and eminent parents, if they do not degenerate from their virtue, have always been allowed a preference and kind of title to employments and offices of honour and trust. . . . Whatever is of Civility and good Manners, all that is Art and Beauty, or of real and solid Wealth in the World, is the . . . child of beloved propriety; and they who would strangle this Issue, desire to demolish all Buildings, eradicate all Plantations, to make the Earth barren, and Mankind to live again in Tents, and nourish his Cattle where the grass grows. Nothing but the joy in Propriety reduced us from barbarity; and nothing but security in the same, can preserve us from returning into it again."

Clarendon's view of the barbaric consequences of the proposed "greening" of his England would also apply to the proposals of our academic seekers for the "Greening of America."

All revolts against the inevitable hypocrisies of established authority have called for the return to the simplicities of naked and nonliterate primitivisms. Thus many of the early founders of Quakerism went naked through marketplaces, and even into churches, as a witness of their martyrdom to the "naked truth." Even as late as 1672, the one and only great Quaker theologian, Robert Barkley, went "naked as a sign through the chilly streets of Aberdeen." George Fox and other leaders of the Quaker movement preached the futility of "mere book knowledge," which only tended to pervert the purity of the untainted prompting of the "inner light." Gerrard Winstanley, in his relevant pamphlet *The New Law of Righteousness* (1649), wrote that "the Universities are the standing ponds of stinking waters." Even Emanuel College, at Cambridge, once the seat of Puritan intellectualism and the founding seed of Harvard College, went through a period of extreme mysticism during this period. It is no wonder that at both Oxford and Cambridge there was the smashing of stained-glass windows and the decimation of altar decorations, all in the name of Puritan and sectarian relevance.

Among a host of other parallels of our own noisy years, there was, finally, the digging up and replanting of the Common land on St. George's Hill, in Surrey, by the followers of Winstanley, a once-religious mystic turned utopian "communist." The Diggers, in appealing their arrest to the House of Commons, demanded, much in the manner of their modern imitators, "whether the common people shall have the quiet enjoyment of the Commons, or Waste Land, or whether they shall be under the will of the Lords of the Manor." In that anarchical regicide year, similar diggings took place in Buckinghamshire, Middlesex, Hertfordshire, and Berkshire—altogether in some thirty-four towns. The following lines, attributed to Winstanley, would have appealed to the modern "Diggers" of the People's Park at Berkeley:

> The gentrye are all round, on each side they are found,
> Theire wisdom's so profound, to cheat us of our
> ground . . .

The clergy they come in, and say it is a sin
That we should now begin, our freedom for to win.

Stand up now, Diggers all.
To conquer them by love . . .
To conquer them by love, as it does you behove,
For he is King above; no power is like to love:
Glory here, Diggers all.

Viable civilizations, are, almost literally, *clothed* in authority; and when the emperor's clothes are removed his only recourse is the exercise of *naked* power. The Diggers dug up St. George's Hill in April, and in May mutinies broke out in the army which soon turned into a full-scale Leveller revolt. Parliament immediately declared mutiny in the army to be treason, and Cromwell led a lightning night attack on the rebels at Buford; three leaders were shot on the spot and a fourth was caught and shot three days later. Cromwell and Fairfax now returned to Oxford, Royalist stronghold in Charles's last days, where they were feasted by the conservative city fathers. After Buford, the Revolution turned conservative.

As part of the reactionary trend, John Lilburne was brought to trial for sedition in October. If Cromwell was respected, admired, and feared, Lilburne was undoubtedly the most popular man in England at this time. When hc was finally acquitted by a jury of his peers, the people shouted with joy. A cheering mob followed him all the way from the Guild Hall to the Tower, where, in spite of his recent acquittal, and another in 1652, he was to remain until the end of his life. In the meantime, Lilburne lost all hope of secular solutions and became a Quaker, "renouncing all weapons except the Sword of the Spirit." When he died in 1657, his funeral was held at the Bull and Mouth Meeting House, in London; some 4,000 Quakers accompanied his body to the burial grounds.

Lilburne, who had spent almost two-thirds of his life in jail and was in perpetual revolt against authority, whether monarchical, Episcopal, Presbyterian, or Cromwellian, was an ideal spiritual ancestor of a sect of martyrs. The great Quaker preacher and historian, Rufus Jones, considered him, along with Winstanley, a noble ancestor of both modern democracy and Quakerism. Thus it was that "the Quakers passed on the Leveller torch to the New World."

When formalism declines, fanaticism comes to the fore, and the church is replaced by a host of sects. Just as we are witnessing the spread of fanatical sectarianism in America today, so the Puritan Interregnum was faced with the rise of the Ethringtonians, Grindlestonians, Mugglestonians, Fifth Monarchy Men, Family of Love, Ranters, and a veritable swarm of other seeking sectarians. It is always the ex-radicals who hate and hunt the newer radicals. Thus the Reverend Thomas Edwards, who back in 1628 had been dismissed from his post as University Preacher at Cambridge for his violent attacks on the establishment of bishops, now turned around and attacked, in even more fanatical terms, the fanaticisms and heresies of the 199 sects which he now found abroad in the land. Many of the new sectarians and seekers joined the Quaker movement, which was unquestionably was most interesting and important of them all.

In striking contrast to the university-educated, and theologically sophisticated, builders of Puritanism, the founder of Quakerism, George Fox, was not unlike that "rough beast slouching towards Bethlehem" which Yeats saw as the only possible savior of our own seeking and anarchic generation. Born the son of a humble weaver in a small village in the North Country—the most backward, feudal, royalist, and Catholic part of England—Fox was almost entirely self-educated and a charismatic mystic whom many have called the only religious genius of the English Reformation. A year after the outbreak of the Civil War, young Fox, at the age of nineteen, left home like so many of today's soul-hungry seekers of the counterculture, and wandered through the countryside, dressed in leather breeches, sleeping in haystacks, under hedges, and even, as legend has it, in the trunks of hollow trees. He was desperately seeking for some new vision of life outside the establishment of hated "steeplehouses" and their hypocritical "professors." After four years of lonely seeking, five years of preaching to other seekers (and two periods in prison), he came to Pendle Hill, famous in local folklore as the haunt of witches and warlocks, where he had a vision of "a great people to be gathered." Modern Quakers have always dated the founding of their sect with this vision on Pendle Hill, in the spring of 1652.

Just as the hated Anabaptists rose to haunt the reformers and Lutherans during the fifteenth-century Reformation on the Continent, so the Quakers marked the extreme left wing of the English Reformation. "The Society of Friends," wrote Ernst Troeltsch, "represents the final expression in its purest form of the Anabaptist Movement." After a century of reform, religious authority in England—once lodged in the pope and the priestly control of the seven sacraments, then in the Anglican bishops and the priestly control of two sacraments, and finally in local preachers interpreting the Bible—was suddenly transformed by the radically individualistic and subjective doctrine of the "inner-light." The hierarchical yet reforming ethic of the Puritans now gave way to the radical egalitarianism of the Quakers: "When the Lord sent me into the world," so Fox says in one of the key passages of his *Journal*, "He forbade me to put off my hat to any, high or low: and I was required to 'thee' and 'thou' all men and women, without any respect to rich or poor, great or small." While the Puritans were closer to Hobbes, the Quakers anticipated the tradition of Rousseau.

This is no time to go into a detailed discussion of the differences between the Puritan and Quaker ethics. The following skeleton list (table 12.1) of the differences (in emphasis, of course) should, however, show how similar they were to our present conflicts between culture and counterculture.

"Anyone who knows anything about history," Marx once wrote to a friend, "knows that great social changes are impossible without the feminine ferment." It is happening today as it did in the seventeenth century, as a voguish ditty of that day put it:

We will not be wives
And tie up our lives
To villainous slavery.

As might be expected, women played a major role in the Quaker movement. In fact, Clarendon thought the Quakers were a female sect, as well he might have: Fox's first convert was Elizabeth

TABLE 12.1
Differences Between Puritan and Quaker Ethics

Puritan Ethic	Quaker Ethic
God transcendent (man anxious to prove himself)	God imminent (peace of mind)
Old Testament (Decalogue)	New Testament (Sermon on Mount)
Head (learning)	Heart (feeling)
Law	Love
Danger: legalism and rationalism	Danger: anarchy and mysticism
Elitism (elect of Saints)	Egalitarianism (that of God in every man)
Institution building	Anti-institutional (spontaneity)
Aristocratic (antimonarchical)	Democratic (anti–all hierarchy)
Representative democracy (majority 51% rule)	Direct democracy (sense of meeting, like "general will" of Rousseau)
Calling (great professional pride in ministry and magistry)	Calling (more like Thomism: to God rather than profession; exaltation of laymen and amateurs
Ideal man: magistrate	Ideal person: martyr
Evil: in sinful man	Evil: in corrupt institutions
Major vice: arrogance	Major vice: self-righteousness

Hooton, of whom more later; his most important early convert, later his wife and mother of the movement, was Margaret Fell, mistress of Swarthmoor Hall, which became the movement's headquarters; the first Quaker "publishers of truth" in London, in the universities, and in Dublin, were women; Mary Fisher, a young Yorkshire house servant, was the first Quaker in America; even today, more women than men are registered as ministers in England.

The Quakers of the first generation were a hardy, fanatical, and apocalyptical band of martyrs who were hated, hunted down, and hung, imprisoned, and tortured for their convictions. Puritan England was no permissive age. That the female "Friends of Truth" had a particular affinity for fanaticism and martyrdom was illustrated in the career of Fox's first convert, Elizabeth Hooton.

A woman of good position, forty-seven years old and the mother of seven children when she first met Fox in 1646, Elizabeth took up the active ministry in 1650 and almost immediately went to prison, first at Derby then at York Castle (sixteen months). After continuing her ministry in England, where she was imprisoned six months in 1654 and three months in 1655, she set sail for America in 1657, but was soon shipped back by the Boston authorities (after they had nearly starved her in the wilderness). At the age of sixty-five, she went back to New England where, according to her *Journal*, she suffered fantastic hardships, including four days in prison without bread or water and being whipped "for a wandering vagabond Quaker at three towns, ten stripes at whipping post in Cambridge, and ten at Watertown and ten stripes at Dedham at the cart's tail with a three cord whip three knots at the end, and a handful of willow rods at Watertown on a cold frosty morning. Then they put me on a horse and carried me into the wilderness many miles, where was many wild beasts both bears and wolves . . . but the Lord delivered me." Before leaving New England, she was sent to prison for attending, and probably preaching at, the funeral of Governor Endicott, the great opponent of the Quakers who had previously ordered the hanging of Mary Dyer on Boston Commons, where her statue now stands. Elizabeth Hooton's last service to the cause was when she went with George Fox, as one of his "twelve" companions, on her third trip to America, where she died in Jamaica at the age of seventy-three.

Like Elizabeth Hooton, hundreds of Quakers in the first generation were martyrs for their cause. In England, some 3,000 were sent to prison under Cromwell (20 died there) and over 15,000 during the Restoration (300 deaths). Almost every leader, from George Fox and Margeret Fell to Robert Barclay and William Penn, went to prison, usually more than once. But of course the martyr thrives on, and often seeks out punishment and persecution, and the movement spread rapidly throughout England, Ireland, and Wales, and thence to the New World. By 1700 there were over 40,000 Quakers in the American and Caribbean colonies and 50,000 at home in Britain. The evangelical zeal of the first generation eventually spent itself, and the movement became a very solid, bourgeois sect, which reached its numerical peak in the middle of the eighteenth century. The miracle of the Quakers is that they have survived both persecution and prosperity.

C. Wright Mills once wrote that we sociologists must "try to understand men and women as historical and social actors." My reaction to this volume of the *AJS* is to place it within some historical context. The two excellent articles by Coser and Dibble, for instance, might have appeared in this *Journal* a decade or two ago. On the other hand, as I have said above, the Gouldner book and the comments on it here, as well as Merton's concept of the "Insider," are all infinitely relevant to the Oz-like world which Becker and Horowitz describe in the following lines at the beginning of their article:

> Greater sensitivity to the undemocratic character of ordinary institutions and relationships (ironically fostered by social scientists themselves) has revealed how research frequently represents the interests of adults and teachers instead of those of children and students; of men instead of women; of the white middle class instead of the lower class, blacks, Chicanos, and other minorities; of the conventional straight world instead of freaks; of boozers instead of potheads. . . . Younger men have debated whether it was moral to be affiliated with the sociological enterprise. Older sociologists have searched their work and their consciences to see if, far from being the political liberals they imagined themselves, they were in fact lackeys of capitalist repression.
>
> In the midst of these reconsiderations, positions hardened. The language of scholarly journals became increasingly polemical. Meetings thought to be scientific were disrupted by political protest and discussion. Presidential addresses at national and regional meetings were interrupted. . . . Some teachers found themselves unable to bear the discourtesies of their radical students. Some professors saw attempts to change the hierarchical relations of a department as an attack on the very idea of scholarship. They assumed that a student who called their ideas "bullshit" was attacking rational thought.

Once again the "Church" has disintegrated and a host of self-righteous sectarians are loosed upon the world. In this climate of opinion, it is understandable that the anti-institutional, egalitarian, perfectionist, and mystical ideals of the Quakers are now more popular in America, especially among intellectuals and academics, than at any other time in our history. Since the close of the Second World War, for example, there has been both a reversal of the downward trend in numbers and a very real renaissance within the Society, such as the winning of the Nobel Peace Prize by the American Friends Service Committee.

The Quaker ranks have been swelled by all sorts of refugees from the institutional "Church" of their ancestors. In a recent, excellent study of the American Friends Service Committee by a *New Yorker* writer, for instance, it was interesting to observe that a majority of the leaders of various projects he mentioned were "convinced" rather than "birthright" Friends. As the rabbi put it: "Some of my best Jews are Friends."

Most of the new Quaker meetings which have sprung up around the country since the war have been formed, often by academics, in and around college or university communities. Today, for instance, the largest meeting in Massachusetts is located in Cambridge, right off fashionable Brattle Street. Only a few years ago, moreover, several departments in the humanities and the social sciences (including Parson's own department) had chairmen who were "convinced" Friends and members of the Cambridge Meeting. As the Cambridge meetings are unstructured, permissive, and antiauthoritarian in the extreme, the sober and square families, in recent years, apparently avoid the freaks from the Yard by attending the earlier of the First Day meetings.

It is indeed part of the irony of this age of the absurd that the quiet Quakers have really come into their own once again in America during the 1960s, the decade of noise. But when martyrs of all kinds are abroad in the land, it is quite appropriate that the Quakers, by now having institutionalized their perfectionist and pacifist ideals, should be drawn into the very heart of the various protests and antiwar movements.[4] Three centuries after George Fox personally appealed to Cromwell to lay down his "carnal weapons," his spiritual descendants were "visiting" with leaders in Hanoi and Washington, "treating" with them to do the same.

It was indeed a fitting forecast of the shape of things to come that, when he died in March 1962, the great disestablishmentarian guru, C. Wright Mills, the John Lilburne of modern social science, was buried after a Quaker memorial service. He, unlike Lilburne, died "unconvinced" and an atheist, or as Mills himself would have more dramatically put it, a Pagan. It is fitting, too, that virtually before the ink was dry on Mills's death certificate, to put it figuratively, Professor Horowitz should have published a collection of Mills's essays, in the introduction to which he called Mills the "singular intellectual 'hero' of our age." And Horowitz went on to say that Mills, in the good tradition of George Fox, "was singularly unimpressed with titles, honors, degrees, positions and the entire world of inherited feudal values [?] that have been mysteriously grafted on to present-day status-conscious America." Now I should have thought that men and women have been "status conscious" ever since they put on clothes after their emergence forever (except in the minds of perfectionist sectarians) from the Garden of Eden. In point of historical fact, men in feudal times were far more interested in the state of their souls than in their secular status, which, being fixed by fate, produced little of the status anxiety which so marks our own age. But it must be said that in my day at Columbia, when ambitious graduate students still looked to Brooks Brothers rather than the local Army and Navy Store for their sartorial standards, Professor Mills was a prophet in life-styles, as well as in sociology, as he roared up to Fayerweather Hall on a motorcycle, clothed more often than not in the style now cultivated, as a badge of baptism, by the followers of Professor Gouldner.

Gouldner, like Mills, is very much in the anti-institutional and egalitarian tradition of the seventeenth-century sectarians. Thus a great deal of space in his prophetic book is devoted to denouncing the sociological establishment, now dominated, so he says, by a priestly caste of Parsonian functionalists. Its prophetic tone can be summed up, I think, in his antinomian concept of "authenticity," which he wants to substitute for the priestly concept of "legitimacy." In the seventeenth century, John Donne, great metaphysical poet and famous preacher at St. Paul's Cathedral, put it this way:

> The new philosophy calls all in doubt;
> 'Tis all in pieces, all coherence gone;
> All just supply and all relation.
> Prince, subject, father, son, are things forgot,
> For every man alone thinks he has got
> To be a Phoenix, and that he can be
> None of that kind of which he is but he.

A society of Phoenixes would surely be a sociological monstrosity, though a few "authentic" geniuses are always needed, in every generation, to change the meaning of "legitimacy." What the egalitarian perfectionists will not face is the moral ambiguity of all institutional life; "authenticities" in one generation forever become legitimacies in the next. As the late Reinhold Niebuhr once wrote: "But the fact is that not only property, but the two institutions of property and social stratification are in the same position of moral ambiguity. Both are necessary instruments of justice and order, and yet both are fruitful of injustice. Both have, no less than government, grown up organically in traditional civilizations in the sense that they are unconscious adaptations to the needs of justice and order. The revolts against both of them by both the radical Christians and the radical secular idealists of the seventeenth and eighteenth centuries tended to be indiscriminate."

This is what I think Gouldner means in his description of the functionalists: "Functionalism postulates that, even if a society might be reformed in some ways, there are other profound ways in which it cannot be reformed and which men must accept." In spite of the poetic license taken by Edward Hicks in *The Peaceable Kingdom*, the most famous and popular painting ever done by a Quaker, the lion will probably never lie down with the lamb.

Ages are known by the questions they raise; not by the answers they may seem to give. By definition, important questions are never answered. Thus the debate between Gouldner and the Parsonian functionalists is, in many fundamental ways, a continuation of the Quaker-Puritan debate of the 1650s, which Hugh Barbour, in his book on *The Quakers in Puritan England*, summarizes as follows: "The Quaker preacher and the Puritan pastor worked in opposite directions and never understood each other. . . . The Puritan leaders were men who had known life in all its complexity. They knew the ambiguous mixture of sin and grace in their own best actions and in the motives they least admired. They had discovered new levels of sin and evil in the moment of seeming victory, when Cromwell and the forces of Parliament broke apart in the struggle to remake England. Inevitably they regarded the Quakers as self-righteous and unrealistic. . . . While Baxter was daily praying to receive God's Spirit, Friends insisted that they had it."

Noisy and ideological ages raise questions which sober ages somehow have to solve, preferably in compromise. Who knows what solutions lie ahead for tragically troubled America? Here again, I think, we have something to learn from seventeenth-century England. For there is something in the English character which tells them that, in the long run, order and civility are only possible in sober societies where left and right extremists, though always necessary as critics of the status quo and stimulants to change, are *never* allowed to *win*. In both the French and Russian Revolutions, for example, the revolutionaries *won out*, but, at the same time, the French and Russian people *lost out* to the one-party and autocratic regimes of Napoleon and Stalin. In the English Revolution, on the other hand, both the revolutionary Puritans and the radical sectarians *lost out* when the traditional authorities of throne and altar were finally restored.

Though cruel and vindictive at first, the Restoration Settlement eventually produced a vigorous two-party system which lasted down through the Victorian age; Cavalier squires, supporters of throne and altar, became Tories; and Roundhead, gentry-merchants, supporters of parliamentary authority, became dissenters and Whigs. After a period of bitter party battles, including a series of plots and counterplots, the more moderate leaders of both parties were finally united, as G. M. Trevelyan once put it, by "the wit and wisdom of George Savile, Marquis of Halifax, 'the Trimmer,' the Philosopher Statesman, whose dislike of extremes always caused him to 'trim' away from whichever party was at the moment enjoying and abusing power." Trimmer politics of Halifax, which incidentally became a Whig tradition in England, led the way to the bloodless, Glorious Revolution of 1688 and the Toleration Act of 1689, thereby securing parliamentary authority and religious toleration. This final settlement of the Reformation in England was, as usual, quite in contrast to the extreme positions taken on the Continent. While the reactionary princes of Germany, for instance, abolished all sectarian dissent after the bloody Peasant Wars and settled for Caesaropapism (the religion of the prince is the religion of all his subjects), and Louis XIV, in 1685, exiled the valuable and prosprous Huguenots from France, the English Toleration Act allowed dissenters or nonconformists to act as a continuing and liberating balance to the conserving, Anglican Establishment. Power warmly clothed in authority can always afford to be tolerant, naked power never. Thus it was the tolerating of this dissenting-nonconformist tradition which produced the reforming approach to social change, so often led by the Quakers, which characterized nineteenth-century England; the lack of a dissenting religious tradition in France and Germany, on the other hand, allowed for the growth of a stronger socialist-Marxist approach to social change, with its endless cycles of revolution and reaction. If history and sociology are any guide, we in America are surely in for a conservative reaction of one sort or another. Let us hope that it is not too late to follow in the English, rather than the Continental, tradition.

Finally, does the spirit of the Restoration compromise and the Trimmer-inspired Glorious Revolution have anything to tell us about the possible future course of sociology? In the first place, I should like to argue that we are all functionalists. If sociology is a cumulative science rather than a mildly disguised ideology—a moot assumption at best—then social theory is primarily a *point of departure*, a conceptual guide in the endless adventure of doing research, and never an end in itself or a final answer. To be brief, and unavoidably to simplify, there are two functionalist points of departure: (1) *the order-hierarchical* and (2) *the conflict-egalitarian*. Take, for instance, the following statement by Karl Marx: "The more a ruling class is able to assimilate the most prominent men of the dominated classes, the more stable and *dangerous* its rule." This is a functionalist generalization, and a valid one, of course, from the *conflict-egalitarian* point of departure. Change the word "dangerous" to "desirable," on the other hand, and one has an equally valid generalization from the *order-hierarchical* point of view. To say, however, that the use of the word "dangerous" derives from a more or less valid social theory than the use of the word "desirable" is, or so it seems to me, to confuse ideology with social theory. Or take another generalization about human behavior, which I find this morning, as I write these lines, in the *Wall Street Journal*. Thus the *Journal*'s diplomatic correspondent, in sociological rather than ideological style, contrasts the *order* with the *conflict* theories of international relations: "The U.S. contends that tensions in international relations are abnormal: smoothing things over is the prime reason for having diplomats. The Soviets, on the other hand, find such tensions an inevitable result of conflicting social systems; their diplomats strive for competitive advantage while hoping to stave off disasters. Compromise and self-restraint for their own sake have little appeal; they are often considered weaknesses."

The quotation above, as it stands, is a perfectly valid outline of two approaches to international tension. And the *Journal*'s correspondent does not, like all too many sociologists today, go on to say that one is more valid than the other.

In the Trimmer spirit of the last lines of Merton's article, then, I would urge that Order and Conflict functionalists unite: "We have nothing to loose but our claims. We have a world of understanding to win." Let us all, above all, get away from the ideological, from the sociology of sociology, and get down to the doing of it, as best we can, in the grand tradition of Durkheim and Weber. And if we have some sort of restoration of authority in this country, instead of a blind reaction into some kind of violent anti-intellectualism, we may yet experience a flowering of social science much like that which England experienced in its seventeenth century of genius in the natural and biological sciences. One more backward glance should serve as a guide to hope.

The foundations of science in England were laid in the great Elizabethan age of poetry. It first flourished, as might have been expected, outside the conservative and church-controlled universities. Many of the early followers of the New Philosophy, as the scientific attitude was then called, congregated at Gresham College, a kind of adult-education center in the heart of London, founded in 1575 by one of Elizabeth's first councillors and son of the Lord Mayor of London, Thomas Gresham. Despite pleas from Cambridge, his alma mater, that he leave his money to them, Gresham amply endowed his college and made sure that it would remain in control of merchants like himself rather than the clerical guardians of the old tradition. The theoretician of the New Philosophy was Francis Bacon, twice related to Gresham, and attorney general under James I. His famous *Novum Organum* was published in 1620. The popularity of the New Philosophy may be measured by the fact that Bacon's *Essays* went through seventeen editions in the years before the outbreak of the Revolution. Another pioneer, William Harvey, discovered the circulation of the blood in 1617 and published his findings in 1628. Harvey was appointed physician extraordinary by James I and was on the Royalist side during the Revolution. The two ideological decades of anarchy witnessed a definite decline in the doing of science, which finally flowered after the Restoration. In the single year of 1662, for instance, the Royal Society was founded (four of the twelve founding members had been teachers at Gresham College), Robert Boyle published his famous law on the behavior of gases, and William Petty, in his *Treatises of Taxes and Contributions*, founded the science of vital statistics. Three years later, Thomas Sydenham, often called the "English Hippocrates," published his first book, which brought him fame throughout Europe. In the doing tradition, Sydenham insisted on the importance of clinical observation rather than theory. Finally, the *summa* of mechanistic science was given to the world in the year preceding the Glorious Revolution, in 1687, when Edmond Halley, discoverer of the comet named in his honor, brought out Newton's

TABLE 12.2
Number of Important Discoveries and Inventions (5) England, 1601–1700

Years	Number	Years	Number
1601–1610	10	1651–1660	13
1611–1620	13	1661–1670	44
1621–1630	7	1671–1680	29
1631–1640	12	1681–1690	32
1641–1650	3	1691–1700	17

Source: Robert K. Merton, *Science, Technology and Society in Seventeenth-Century England* (New York: Harper Torchbooks, 1970), p. 40. Originally published in *Osiris: Studies on the History and Philosophy of Science, and on the History of Learning and Culture* (Bruges: St. Catherine Press, 1938).

classic, *Principia*. Halley not only constantly encouraged Newton to finish and publish his *Principia*; he also published his good friend's work at his own expense. I have, of course, only mentioned the few outstanding leaders of this great age of English science. For more quantitative evidence of how the doing of science declined during the two ideological decades and then flowered under the Restoration compromise, I should like to refer to a table in Merton's early book on England (table 12.2):

Notes

1. Baltzell wrote this article as an epilogue to a special *AJS* issue on "Varieties of Political Expression in Sociology" (ed.).
2. According to the Oxford Dictionary, the term "anarchism" came into the English language in 1642, the year the English Revolution broke out ("antinomianism," the theological counterpart of our own sociological jargon-term, "anomie," was introduced in 1645).
3. There are, according to Webster, at least two meanings of the term anarchy: (1) a state of political disorder and (2) a state of confusion or disorder. In the British, French, and Russian revolutions, the states were overthrown, creating political as well as societal disorder (1 and 2). The twentieth-century welfare state, on the other hand, is highly centralized and strong: thus the anarchy of the 1960s in America was largely societal confusion and normlessness (2) rather than political anarchy (1). Anarchy, chaos, and lawlessness, according to Webster, are synonyms: anarchy implies absence or suspension of government; chaos, the utter negation of law and order; lawlessness, a prevalent or habitual disregard for law and order. I use the term *anarchy* here more in the sense of chaos or lawlessness than in simple political anarchy. In many ways, the theological term *antinomian* and the sociological term *anomie* might better serve my purpose than *anarchy*.
4. Even Quaker ideals do not operate in a vacuum. Thus during the First World War, Haverford College let one of its spirited young faculty members go when he allowed as how perhaps the German people were not all representatives of Satan. He went on to Harvard, where he eventually became Hollis Professor of Divinity and a great New Testament scholar. Hollis was a wealthy English Baptist, which did not prevent Cotton Mather from putting his loyalty to Harvard above ideology in influencing Hollis to endow this oldest chair in America.

13

Cultural Pluralism in Modern America and William Penn's Colony of Pennsylvania

In his definitive study of the religious history of the American people, Sydney E. Ahlstrom wrote that "Pennsylvania flourished as a model state where people of diverse ethnic and racial backgrounds could live together under equitable laws in a single commonwealth" and thus was "more nearly a paradigm of latter-day American democracy than any other colony."[1] In this paper, I shall take a look at the classic theories of assimilation and their relevance to American history, especially emphasizing the consequences of the leveling theories of cultural pluralism which came to dominate American thinking after World War II, and especially during the 1960s and since. I shall then go back to see how William Penn's theories of cultural pluralism influenced the history of the colony and the state of Pennsylvania (contrasting that history, where relevant, with that of Boston and Massachusetts, which until very recent times was dominated by the theory of Anglo-conformity).

Theories of Assimilation

In the course of American history, according to Milton M. Gordon's classic study of *Assimilation in American Life*, there have been three main theories of the assimilation process: "Anglo-conformity," "the melting pot," and, more recently, "cultural pluralism."[2] On the whole, the theory of Anglo-conformity postulates the complete renunciation of the immigrant's ancestral culture in favor of the behavior and cultural values of the Anglo-Saxon majority. Thus, John Quincy Adams wrote in 1818 that immigrants "must cast off their European skin, never to resume it. They must look forward to posterity rather than backward to their ancestors; they must be sure that whatever their own feelings may be, those of their children will cling to the prejudices of this country."[3] And Theodore Roosevelt echoed Adams when he wrote that "we have no room for any people who do not act and vote simply as Americans and as nothing else . . . where immigrants, or the sons of immigrants, do not heartily and in good faith throw in their lot with us, but cling to the speech, the customs, the ways of life, and the habits of thought of the Old World which they have left, they thereby do harm both to themselves and us."[4] And Woodrow Wilson told a group of newly naturalized citizens in Philadelphia in 1915: "America does not consist of groups. A man who thinks of himself as belonging to a particular national group in America has not yet become an American."[5]

The theory of Anglo-conformity dominated leadership opinion in America throughout the nineteenth century and down to the Second World War, or at least until the stock market crash in 1929 and the coming of the New Deal in the 1930s. At the same time, the attitudes of the dominant Anglo-Saxon majority toward the immigrants and their children—especially in the decades between the end of the Napoleonic wars and the First World War when many millions of immigrants came to these shores—were at best ambivalent and often downright antagonistic. The anti-Catholicism which marked the Native American and Know-Nothing movements was a reaction to the great Irish immigration in the decades before the Civil War; the rise of anti-Semitism in the 1880s and 1890s was a reaction to the large number of East European Jews who came here from Czarist Russia. The Immigration Restriction League, founded by three Boston Brahmins in 1894, soon had a large elite membership, including most of the leading social scientists of that day; needless to say, it was far more popular among Bostonians than among Philadelphians. That even the educated classes in Boston were still ambivalent, however, was indicated by the fact that while Henry Cabot Lodge and Abbott Lawrence Lowell were strong supporters of the League, William James and Charles W. Eliot were opposed.[6] In any case, the excessive xenophobia which marked the First World War and the Big Red Scare of 1919 finally led the Congress to pass a series of laws between 1924 and 1929 restricting immigration.

The theory of the melting pot, less harsh and more generous than that of Anglo-conformity, is an old one and has also been supported by many American leaders from Abraham Lincoln to Franklin D. Roosevelt. When Roosevelt asked his fellow Americans to "Remember, remember always that all of us, and you and I especially, are descended from immigrants and revolutionists," he was implying his faith in the melting pot.[7]

The theory was given its name by an Englishman, Israel Zangwell, whose play, *The Melting Pot*, was first produced in New York in 1908. The play's hero, David Quixano, a Russian Jewish immigrant to America, falls in love with a beautiful gentile girl and delivers an impassioned speech which included the following sentiments: "America is God's crucible, the great Melting Pot where all races of Europe are melting and reforming. . . . A fig for your feuds and vendettas! Germans and Frenchmen, Irishmen and Englishmen, Jews and Russians—into the crucible with you all! God is making the American."[8] When the play was first published in America, it was dedicated to Theodore Roosevelt.

Although Zangwell gave the theory its name, the idea of the melting pot goes back at least to an immigrant French farmer, J. Hector St. John Crevecoeur, who in 1782, in a small volume entitled *Letters from an American Farmer*, found the American to be a "new man" forged of a "promiscuous breed" of English, Scotch, Irish, French, Dutch, German, and Swedish stock. Emerson, in 1845, followed Crevecoeur in his now-famous theory of the melting pot:

> I hate the narrowness of the Native American party. . . . Man is the most composite of all creatures. . . . As in the old burning of the Temple at Corinth, by the melting and intermixture of silver and gold and other metals a new compound more precious than any, called Corinthian brass, was formed; so in this continent—asylum of all nations—the energy of Irish, Germans, Swedes, Poles, and Cossacks, and all the European tribes—of the Africans and the Polynesians—will construct a new race, a new state, a new religion,

> a new literature, which will be as vigorous as the new Europe which came out of the smelting-pot of the Dark ages, or that which earlier emerged from the Pelasgic and Etruscan barbarism. *La Nature aime les croisements.*[9]

Perhaps the most influential advocate of the melting-pot theory was Frederick Jackson Turner, whose paper on "The Significance of the Frontier in American History," delivered at the annual meeting of the American Historical Association in Chicago in 1893, proved to be one of the most famous essays in American historical scholarship. His extreme environmentalism is nicely revealed in the following lines: "The frontier promoted the formation of a composite nationality for the American people. . . . In the crucible of the frontier the immigrants were Americanized, liberated, and fused into a mixed race, English in neither nationality or characteristics."[10]

While Turner's optimistic environmentalism may well have been valid for the frontier melting pot made up primarily of the old immigration from northern and western Europe, it was far less relevant for a melting pot filled with the immigrants from southern and eastern Europe who came to our major cities after 1880. At the very least, the theory of the single melting pot has to be modified in the direction of what came to be called the "triple melting pot," as outlined in Ruby Jo Reeves Kennedy's well-known article, "Single or Triple Melting Pot? Intermarriage Trends in New Haven 1870–1940," published in the *American Journal of Sociology* in 1944, and later elaborated in Will Herberg's important interpretation of post-World War II America, *Protestant-Catholic-Jew* (1955).[11]

Both the theories of Anglo-conformity and the melting pot envisioned the disappearance of the immigrant culture and social organization, at least in the second and third generations. But while conventional wisdom in America clung to these ideals of *cultural assimilation*, the stubborn reality of *structural exclusion* on the part of the dominant majority and the persistence of ethnic associations such as churches, schools, newspapers, mutual aid and benefit societies, and even hospitals, made for a de facto structural pluralism—long before the theory of cultural pluralism was first articulated in the writings of a young instructor in the

Harvard philosophy department, Horace Kallen, whose article "Democracy *versus* the Melting Pot" appeared in the *Nation* on February 18 and 25, 1915. Actually, Kallen worked out his theory over several decades, first using the term "cultural pluralism" in the 1920s. For our purposes here, Kallen's view of twentieth-century America is best summed up in the following statement of his theory of cultural pluralism in an essay, "Americanism and Its Makers," published in 1944:

> The American way is the way of orchestration. As in an orchestra, the different instruments, each with its own characteristic timbre and theme, contribute distinct and recognizable parts to the composition, so in the life and culture of a nation, the different regional, ethnic, occupational, religious, and other communities compound their different activities to make up the national spirit. The national spirit is constituted by this union of the different. . . . In all directions there obtains . . . a mutual give and take in equal liberty on equal terms. The result is a strength and a richness in the arts and sciences which nations of a more homogeneous strain and an imposed culture . . . do not attain.[12]

The Hegemony of Cultural Pluralism

Kallen's analogy between the symphony orchestra and our pluralistic democracy was, contrary to his optimistic intentions, surely unfortunate but prophetic; for as everyone knows, modern symphony orchestras are highly hierarchical and disciplined autocracies, the best of them led by charismatic and authoritarian conductors. Just as an egalitarian and democratically organized symphony orchestra would be, like un-wet water, a contradiction in terms, so we are coming to see that the extreme cultural pluralism of our contemporary democracy—no longer held together by any common class, religious, or hierarchical ideal—is tending more and more toward anarchy and moral relativism on the one hand and an increasingly authoritarian state on the other. No wonder Alistair Cook, in a recent address to the Philadelphia Bar Association on the occasion of the city's 300th anniversary, should say that the twin disasters of our time were a radical cultural pluralism combined with the New Federalism. To put it another way, *e pluribus unum* is rapidly being replaced in modern America by *ex uno plures*.

It was also symbolically important that Kallen should have summed up his work on cultural pluralism in a book published just as the Second World War was coming to an end; for at this very same time, the ideal of Anglo-conformity was coming to an end, too. Thus, in an excellent analysis of *The Decline of the WASP* (1971), Peter Schrag wrote as follows: "Given the WASP ideal, World War II was the Moment Supreme. It was the last great ritual, the last time that we believed—really believed—in the possibilities of the America that we learned about in the textbook . . . it was the last great cause, the last unequivocal act of self-celebration . . . the last time we were together.[13] And in the final paragraph of his book, the author writes that "America is not on the verge of becoming two separate societies, one rich and white, the other poor and black. It is becoming, in all its dreams and anxieties, a nation of outsiders for whom no single style or ethic remains possible.[14]

Today, more than a decade after Schrag wrote of a "nation of outsiders," the process of cultural pluralism has gone so far that larger and larger segments of the Anglo-Saxon-Protestant majority now see themselves as resentful outsiders, trying to capture the authoritarian state which successfully disestablished their historic hegemony in the years since World War II. On elite campuses where invidious sniping at blacks, women, lesbians, gays, Jews, or Hispanics is no longer tolerated, abusive remarks against the Moral Majority are not only tolerated but encouraged; antifundamentalism is now the anti-Semitism of the cultivated and campus classes in America. (The latest pariahs on my own campus are what the present arbitors of prejudice call "heterosexists.")

At this point, it should be emphasized that these three theories of assimilation are merely abstract conceptualizations of concrete social forces which have been constantly and simultaneously operating throughout twentieth-century American society, varying in intensity, of course, by class, decade, and region. Anglo-conformity, for instance, was surely the dominant social force in the older eastern seaboard cities at the turn of the century. Today, in Los Angeles, on the other hand, where the students at Hollywood High School speak thirty-eight different languages in their homes, the forces of cultural pluralism are overwhelming. In between these two extremes, there has been and still is a great deal of melting, Anglo-conforming, and preserving (as well as active returning to) a plurality of cultural heritages. Though it is not possible to analyze all these processes here, we shall concentrate on the major break in the assimilation process which occurred in the 1960s and witnessed, for the first time, a precipitous decline in the authority of the Protestant establishment at the elite levels of society and a consequent increase in all forms of extreme pluralism. A host of new words such as life-style, dress code, people power, black power, gay power, sexism, racism, and generation gap entered the language in this New Age when personal, psychological, moral, and religious problems were suddenly translated into sociological, legal, and political power struggles between groups. At the same time, more and more, intimate social relations were replaced by legal action.

Throughout the first half of the twentieth century, as one moved up the social structure, the authority of Anglo-conformity increased; at the top elite levels of society, the norms, values, and life-styles of the Protestant establishment predominated. At the same time, in the course of the 1950s, for the first time (the term "Ivy League" was coined in this decade), the prestige colleges became the major carriers of elite norms; performance on SAT tests replaced "character" as a criterion for admission to the best institutions, and deans of admissions replaced parents and debutante rituals as the major upper-class marriage brokers in America. As Peter Schrag noted in *The Decline of the WASP*: "Growing up in Queens in the forties, I regarded myself simply as a New York Jew: thereafter, going to Amherst College, I tried (with less success than I imagined at the time) to become a WASP.[15] And very soon everyone gave up trying, as the Brooks Brothers dress code was replaced by the blue-jean-and-backpack campus culture of the 1960s. In an article entitled "Prodigal Fathers and Existential Sons," published in *Dissent* in the May-June issue of 1966, Professor Reginald E. Zelnick at the University of California,

Berkeley, wrote of the decline of the WASP establishment and the rise of generational mistrust ("When the chips are down the professors cannot be trusted") as follows:

> When I was an undergraduate at Princeton some ten years ago, things were just the opposite. Then the university subtly demanded of its students that they be like *it*, fashioning themselves in its image. The style of Princeton and many of its professors drew the students like a magnet. The "multiversity" of the 1960's, on the other hand, finds it impossible to play this kind of role. To be a mediator among the conflicting interests of the community is no goal for idealistic youth, and the arguments that such a role is essential for the functioning of the university within the body politic are unpersuasive.[16]

The forces of cultural pluralism and moral relativism have increased at all levels of American society in the course of the twentieth century; but, until the revolt on the elite campuses in the country in the 1960s, these divisive and anarchistic forces had always been balanced by the authority of the Protestant establishment. Sydney E. Ahlstrom summed up the impact of unfettered cultural pluralism this way:

> Between 1954 and 1963 the Supreme Court removed crucial legal supports for the power of the Protestant Establishment. The legal and political basis of equality, liberty, civil rights, censorship, and freedom from arbitrary arrest were greatly strengthened. Most important by far, Black America first in the context of the civil rights movement and then after 1966 under the banner of Black Power began to seek rectification of the historic inequalities that had featured its situation. For the first time in American history, in other words, the traumatic implications of true pluralism began to be realized. As a result of these traumas, radical discontent, militancy, and violence became as never before common features of American life. John Kennedy, Martin Luther King, Jr., and Robert Kennedy—all of them men on whom vast multitudes pinned their hopes for a better world—were assassinated.[17]

Perhaps the insane tend to absorb, and carry to irrational extremes, the conventional wisdom of their age; in an age of ideological equality, the insane will use the great equalizer (as the gangster's "gat" was called in the 1920s) to cut down to size their exceptional contemporaries. If, in other words, cultural values condition both the sane and the insane, one would expect a greater proportion of equalizing assassinations in our own defiant democracy than the deference democracies of Canada and England.

"The traumatic implications of true pluralism" noted by Sydney Ahlstrom have not been, even today, fully understood. One might have thought, for example, that now that there is no secure class of WASPs dominating the most important elite positions in society (the presidency, the Supreme Court, college presidencies, deanships, and so forth), alienation and frustration would have declined and self-respect throughout society, especially among minority leaders, would have increased. Instead, however, there are endless indications of a general loss of confidence in America: "Americans," wrote Ahlstrom of the 1960s, "whether conservative, liberal, or radical, found it increasingly difficult to believe that the United States was still a beacon and blessing to the world.[18] In fact, more and more educated Americans are finding the enemy here at home to be in Washington, and around the world in the CIA (actually the last gasp of WASP hegemony in post-World War II American society). How many of us, regardless of background, have the optimism felt by a leader of the oppressed Irish at the beginning of this century, when a WASP upper class and establishment was firmly in the saddle? Thus Archbishop John Ireland of St. Paul, Minnesota, gave a speech in 1905 from which I quote a few lines:

> In the course of history, Providence selects now one nation, now another, to be the guide and exemplar of humanity's progress. . . . Of this nation it is the mission to give forth a new humanity. She embodies in her life and her institutions the hopes, the ambitions, the dreamings of humanity's priests and prophets. . . . The nation of the future! Need I name it? Your hearts quiver loving it.[19]

No wonder one of our greatest living historians, C. Vann Woodward, should have dwelt on the decline of the American myth of innocent optimism and the rise of a new and virulent myth of guilty pessimism. For historiography and historians are actually at the heart of the barometers of a nation's definition of itself. Thus Terry Eastland, writing in a recent issue of *Commentary* magazine, contrasts the moral relativism of our modern pluralistic and rabidly secular educational system with an earlier era when the influence of William Holmes McGuffey (1800–1873), a Presbyterian educator and philosopher, was dominant: "His *Eclectic*

Readers were published in 1836, and from that year until 1920 his books sold more than 120 million copies, a total that put them in a class with only the Bible and Webster's Dictionary. McGuffey's Readers stressed, as the Northwest Ordinance did, 'religion, morality, and knowledge,' in that order."[20]

But far more than just religion and morality is now at issue in our school system. American history itself has become problematic. Before the 1960s, for example, the writing of American history was more or less an elitist and successful story of the doings of Anglo-Saxon heterosexual males; now that we know that the country has long been filled with blacks, ethnics, Indians, Asians, women, and even gays and lesbians, history must be rewritten from a new point of view—or perhaps from many new points of view. As Frances Fitzgerald in her brilliant little book *America Revised* put it: "The message of the texts would be that Americans have no common history, no common culture, and no common values, and that membership in a racial or cultural group constitutes the most fundamental experience of each individual. The message would be that the center cannot, and *should not* hold."[21]

Fitzgerald nicely contrasts the present anarchic situation, where no textbook is widely popular for any length of time, with David Saville Muzzey's famous book, *American History*, which, like the McGuffey Readers, was standard fare for high school students for well over half a century after its first edition came out in 1911. Muzzey was born in Massachusetts of pre-Revolutionary stock, was educated at Harvard and Union Theological Seminary, and was a professor at Columbia for many years. He was frankly elitist and saw history as being made by great men. Throughout most of his career, he was an Anglo-conformist and (in what little he wrote about minorities) saw Americanization as the solution to "our" immigrant problem. It was not until the 1955 edition that he even mentioned the melting pot, which had become popular in other texts by the 1940s. He was finally spared the necessity of writing history in terms of abstractions, which of necessity is what happens when masses or groups, rather than elite individuals, become the units of historical analysis.

There is, I think, no better way to highlight the contrast between our present values of cultural pluralism and radical egalitarianism and the hierarchical values of an earlier age, which was still dominated by an old-stock WASP establishment, than to quote from Fitzgerald's speculations as to why Muzzey was so popular for so long:

> Just why Muzzey's textbook—and this very particular world of a New England gentleman—should have been so attractive to Americans for fifty years, is an interesting question to speculate upon. The book was, after all, read by people of all ethnic backgrounds, and its popularity endured through three major ideological shifts in the country. A part of the attraction may have been Muzzey's tone of self-assurance, his assumption of his own legitimacy in the American tradition. For Westerners and people of less ancient American ancestry than he, Muzzey may have seemed to be the voice of the real America—the America they wanted to, or felt they should, belong to.[22]

Or as Shakespeare wrote in another age of change:

> Oh, when degree is shaked
> Which is the ladder to all high designs,
> The enterprise is sick.
> Take but degree away, untune that string,
> And hark, what discord follows. Each thing meets
> In mere opugnosity.

The sensitive black author, James Baldwin, was well aware of the "mere opugnosity" loosed upon a world in which class and hierarchy have disintegrated; and he wrote of other Americans, when there were still classes whose values all men could aspire to:

> I suppose it can be said that there was a time in this country when an entity existed which could be called a majority, let us say a class, for the lack of a better word, which created the standards to which the country aspired. I am refering or have in mind, perhaps somewhat arbitrarily, the aristocracies of Virginia and New England. These were mainly of Anglo-Saxon stock and they created what Henry James was to refer to, not very much later, as our Anglo-American heritage, or Anglo-American connections. Now at no time did these men ever form anything resembling a popular majority. Their importance was that they kept alive and they bore witness to two elements of a man's life which are not greatly respected among us now: (1) the social forms, called manners, which prevent us from rubbing too abrasively against one another and (2) the interior life, or the life of the mind. These things are important; these things were realities for them and no matter how roughhewn or dark the country was then, it is important to remember that this was also the time when people sat up in log cabins studying very hard by lamplight or candlelight.[23]

Or, as a black colleague of mine has put it more recently: "It was as though," Houston A. Baker, Jr., writes in *The Journey Back*, "Blacks, after a long pilgrimage, had arrived at the Western city only to find it stricken with plague, or caught in the lurid flames of its destruction."[24]

Never at any time since our Constitution replaced the Articles of Confederation have these once-confident and united states of America been so like the "house divided against itself," which Abraham Lincoln so dreaded in his own age. Now that we have no common culture, no common values, and no common history, it may eventually come to pass that we shall have no common schools in which to shape our future citizens; for the antinomian forces of cultural pluralism and moral relativism have surely sown the seeds for the present decline of our public school system itself and the rise of an infinite variety of private schools, each one teaching its own values and its own version of history. On this crucial point, we can learn something from history. For it was no accident that the state of Massachusetts, where the ideal of Anglo-conformity was dominant until very recent times, led our nation in establishing the principle of community schools, and also was the first state in the nation to pass a compulsory school attendance law in 1852. At the same time, Pennsylvania, plagued with sectarian cultural pluralism from the beginning, had no common school system in the early days and did not pass a compulsory school attendance law until 1895, the twenty-eighth and last eastern seaboard state above the Mason-Dixon line to do so.[25] In Boston today, the public Latin School is the oldest school in the city, while the oldest secondary schools in Philadelphia, such as the William Penn Charter School (1689) and the Protestant Episcopal Academy (1760), are private.

The Antinomian Cultural Pluralism of William Penn

The Puritans (Calvinists of the English Reformation) came to Massachusetts Bay in the 1630s and produced a class of tenured clergymen who, according to Richard Hofstadter, "came as close to being an intellectual ruling class—or, more properly, a class of intellectuals intimately associated with the ruling power—as America has ever had."[26] Massachusetts, and its cultural capital in Boston, remained a homogeneous, Bible-centered, and clerically led commonwealth for two hundred years, until the decline of Federalism and the coming of the Irish in the decades before the Civil War. More important, however, is the fact that the hierarchical and opportunitarian ideals of Puritanism dominated the American value system as a whole, at least until the First World War. The great German sociologist of religion, Ernst Troeltsch, for instance, wrote in 1911 that "Calvinism . . . may be described as 'Americanism.'"[27] On the other hand, it is my thesis that our modern loss of confidence in ourselves and our increasing inability to act as a nation (along with the increasing anarchy and radicalism of the left, right, *and* center characteristic of our society today are best understood by looking back at the history of the commonwealth of Pennsylvania, which was founded by the antinomian ideals of Quakerism, and its leader in the second generation, William Penn. Just as Quakerism was born in the anarchy and chaos of the English Revolution of the seventeenth century, so Quakers have come into their own in America during the anarchic 1960s. Thus I wrote at the conclusion of my study of Puritan Boston and Quaker Philadelphia:

> There is a haunting similarity between the pattern of anarchy that followed the execution of England's king in January 1649 and the assassination of President Kennedy in November 1963. Once again, the established church has disintegrated and a host of self-righteous seekers are loose upon the land. In this climate of opinion, it is understandable that the ideas and ideals of Quakerism are now more popular in America, especially among intellectuals and academics, than at any other time in our history. Since the close of the Second World War, for example, there has been both a reversal of the downward trend in numbers and a very real renaissance within the Society, as symbolized by the award of the Nobel Peace Prize to the American Friends Service Committee. The Quaker ranks have been swelled by all sorts of refugees from the institutional churches and synagogues. . . . Most of the Quaker meetings founded since the war have been formed, often by academics, in and around college or university communities. In the 1960s, for instance, the largest meeting in Massachusetts was located in Cambridge, right off fashionable Brattle Street. And the chairmen of several departments in the humanities and the social sciences at Harvard were convinced Friends and members of the Cambridge meeting, as were three faculty members of the divinity school.[28]

To celebrate the 300th anniversary of Penn's landing in America, the *Pennsylvania Magazine of History and Biography* has dedicated a recent volume to William Penn. From our point of view here, the most interesting article is one by Melvin B. Endy, Jr., in which he discusses Penn's contributions to theology and their relevance to our religiously plural world. We have just seen how American secular history has recently been called into question; so Endy shows how the traditional history of Christianity is similarly in trouble today because of its roots in the salvation-event of Jesus Christ's crucifixion on the Cross at Calvary: "Beyond evangelical-fundamentalist circles," Endy writes, "it is difficult to find a Christian theologian who makes the atoning death of Christ the central event of salvation-history in the manner of . . . theories that have reigned supreme since the early Middle Ages."[29]

The point to be made and stressed is that Quakerism has always been infinitely ahistorical, stressing the "eternal Christ in Every Man" as against the historical Jesus of Nazareth; Quakers have never felt the need for seeing the historic Christ-event as the major causal agent in Christian history. In this extremely important sense, then, Quakerism did anticipate many of the theological problems of the pluralistic global village which is our modern world. And no wonder that the conventional wisdom of modern theology—among liberal Protestants as well as liberal Catholics, both the World Council of Churches and Vatican II, if not Pope Paul and neoconservative Protestantism—has been radically Quakerized, as it were, within a decade or two. After all, it was English Quakers who, soon after World War II, took the lead in repudiating the intolerant Christian position on the sinfulness of homosexual behavior, and of course women have always been held in the highest esteem in essentially matriarchal Quaker circles. (As a witness to the modern mood, the statues of two famous antinomian women, Anne Hutchinson and Mary Dyer, now stand in front of the State House on Boston's Beacon Hill, which for most of our history stood as a symbol of patriarchal authority.)

Quakers have always prided themselves on their pragmatism and ardent antipathy to all forms of abstract theorizing, so I would heartily agree with Penn's contemporaries who, according to Endy, "found his intellectual acumen less clear than his passionate commitment to human rights and to a new social order." Thus William Penn, the privileged son of a highly successful, self-made man, dropped out of the Puritan ruling class circles of his birth and joined the pariah sect of Quakers in Ireland, where he had been sent to look after his father's landed interests. He was promptly thrown in jail, and his whole generation of Quaker leaders (many of them sons of Puritan autocrats) spent many, many months in the jails of both Commonwealth and Restoration England. Quakers were a pariah people in Puritan England, and it was a quite natural and pragmatic response to their outcast status that their faith should have elevated tolerance to the very top of their hierarchy (sic) of virtues.

At any rate, after Admiral Penn's death, King James granted young William an almost feudal barony in the New World, which he insisted be called Pennsylvania in memory of his friend, Admiral Penn. Quakerism was a fairly small sect, so Penn and his close associates traveled all over the continent of Europe advertising the advantages of settling in the religiously tolerant colony of Pennsylvania. By 1740 Pennsylvania was the most ethnically and religiously heterogeneous colony in English North America—about one-third British, one-third German, and another third Scotch-Irish from Northern Ireland. Though wealthy Quakers dominated the city of Philadelphia in the early years, by 1700 there were some 200 Anglican communicants at Christ Church, three congregations of English and Welsh Baptists, and a Presbyterian congregation organized by immigrants from Barbados. The first Catholic church was organized in 1732, and by 1750 there were eleven Catholic congregations, second only in the colonies to Maryland (fifteen congregations).

Finally, and of great symbolic importance because attitudes toward Jews have been a kind of sociological barometer of ethnic and religious prejudices in modern times, Philadelphia had one of the first Jewish communities in the colonies. Founded in 1740, the city's Jewish community became the leader in American Jewry between 1840 and 1940, when the Second World War came and leadership passed to New York in the postwar world. Here, also, we see the most striking difference between Puritan Boston and

Quaker Philadelphia. Thus the Old Testament and philo-Hebraic Puritans permitted no Jewish community to develop in Boston for over two centuries after settlement. As I have shown elsewhere, moreover, Boston Jewish leadership was from its beginning (1840s) philo-Brahmin and favorable to assimilation (Anglo-conformity), quite in contrast to Philadelphia's conservatism and retention of Jewish identity (cultural pluralism). I shall return to the Jewish question in a moment.

Most modern religious historians and theologians have lauded the Pennsylvania experiment in religious liberty and cultural pluralism, while few have praised the intolerance and establishment policies of Puritan New England (outside antinomian and Quaker Rhode Island—which, incidentally, was in such a chaotic state by the end of the colonial period that it was the only colony to send no representatives to the Continental Congress or to the Constitutional Convention in Philadelphia).[30] We have seen how Professor Endy found Penn's colony to be "the most forward-looking of all the utopian ventures."[31] Also reflecting the best modern conventional wisdom, Sydney Ahlstrom wrote of Pennsylvania as follows:

> Yet William Penn's Holy Experiment, the last great flowering of Puritan political innovation, with the City of Brotherly Love at its heart, was truly to become the "Keystone State" of American religious history. Facing Europe through Philadelphia's teeming harbor, with Pittsburgh at the gateway to the Ohio Valley and the great West, and astride the valleys leading into the southern back country, Pennsylvania was to become a crossroads of the nation. It would remain a world center of Quaker influence. The country's first presbytery would be organized in Philadelphia, and a later influx of Scotch-Irish would keep the state a Presbyterian stronghold. For more than a century after its founding in 1707, the Philadelphia Association was a dominant force in the organization and expansion of the Baptists, and the national headquarters of the American Baptist Convention is still located there. The Protestant Episcopal church in the United States would be constituted in Philadelphia, with that city's Bishop White playing a major role. Its toleration would allow the Roman Catholic church to lay deep foundations on which later immigration would build. For similar reasons the Pennsylvania Ministerium would become a key force in American Lutheranism. The German Reformed church also had its chief strength in this state, and its theologians at Mercersburg Seminary would write a brilliant chapter in the church's intellectual history. Moravians, Mennonites, Amish, Schwenkfelders, Dunkers, and other German groups, including Rosicrucians, would flourish there. During the early decades of the nineteenth century followers of Otterbein,

> Albright, and Winebrenner would first be marshaled in Pennsylvania; and from its western edge the Restorationist movement of Thomas and Alexander Campbell would be launched. In Philadelphia, too, the African Methodist Episcopal church—the first independent Negro denomination—had its origins. As the chief residence of Benjamin Franklin, the seat of the American Philosophical Society, and the birthplace of both the Declaration of Independence and the Constitution, Philadelphia also served as a symbol of the Enlightenment's vast contribution to American religion. Finally, it was in this province that all of these groups experienced the difficulties and discovered the possibilities for fruitful coexistence that American democracy was to offer. Within the borders of no other state was so much American church history anticipated or enacted.[32]

Let me make several points about Penn's theology or his theories of cultural pluralism:

In the first place, as already suggested, William Penn and the Quakers in both England and America were definitely not theologians and came to their antinomian and pluralistic views of church and state largely as a pragmatic reaction to their pariah status in England; and they brought their antiauthoritarian habits of mind to Pennsylvania, where they were still guided by them even after they had become wealthy merchants at the heart of Philadelphia's commercial establishment. As a leading Quaker historian of early Pennsylvania has written: "There was a greater disrespect for law and order in Pennsylvania than might have been expected from a Quaker colony dedicated to a 'holy experiment.'"[33]

Having no theory of authority, Penn fell back, by default rather than design, on a purely plutocratic hierarchy and counted on a few wealthy immigrants, to whom he sold almost half the land in his colony, to take the lead. He even referred to these big purchasers as his "barons" on occasion. But money men have notoriously been far more concerned with their own prosperity than with any such thing as whole-community responsibility; in sum, they have tended to be tolerant but irresponsible.

Just as with Penn's theories of authority, or lack of them, so with his theories of cultural pluralism. In this connection, I should like to suggest an analogy between eighteenth-century Pennsylvania and America as a whole in the twentieth century. William Penn in the late seventeenth century, and the Pennsylvania coal and iron barons at the end of the nineteenth, both sowed the seeds of cultural pluralism by encouraging immigration, not due to any theories of democracy but rather because of their dreams of economic success. As Penn wrote in 1681, "Though I desire to extend religious freedom, yet I want some recompense for my trouble."[34] It was the masters of the steel mills and coal mines who were the "liberals" supporting a free immigration policy in the early twentieth century and the intellectuals, social scientists, and reformers who took a stand against unlimited immigration. They were intolerant partly because they had some theories about the threat to democracy, which cultural pluralism posed; perhaps they seemed intolerant (on hindsight), but they were surely not irresponsible.

At any rate, Pennsylvania was the most economically successful of all the British colonies in North America. But from the very beginning, governmental chaos was the rule. Even Professor Garry Nash, a Marxist egalitarian, was obliged to write of early Pennsylvania, "Utopian propaganda, frail institutions, and the anti-authoritarian instincts of the Quakers, all contributed to the breakdown of the sense of community in early Pennsylvania."[35] And if we recall my earlier comments on Horace Kallen's likening a culturally pluralistic society to a symphony orchestra, it is interesting that Professor Nash saw that charismatic, one-man rule was the only solution in Pennsylvania. "Penn," he writes, "who alone possessed the charisma to stabilize the Quaker community, if it could be unified at all, was absent for all but a few years during the first three decades of the colony's existence."[36] To make a very long, but tragically consistent, story short, the colony was only led out of chaos by political bossism in the persons of two Welsh kinsmen, Thomas and David Lloyd; and one-man charismatic leadership (or amiable anarchy) has been characteristic of Pennsylvania's political history, from the Lloyds to Benjamin Franklin, down to the famous series of nineteenth-century political bosses, including Simon Cameron, Matthew Quay (Quaism entered the language as a synonym for cynical bossism), and Boies Penrose.

In contrast to boss-ridden Pennsylvania, Massachusetts from the very beginning was a class-dominated, deference democracy. It was a colony and state led by the "top layers of society," as the historian Samuel Morison wrote, "accepted by the community, not imposed on it, I say; for men of education were the chosen leaders of the Puritan immigration. . . . They were the shepherds to whom the people looked for guidance and inspiration, on whose spoken word they hung, and whose written word they perused eagerly."[37] (While there were over 130 graduates of Oxford or Cambridge in Massachusetts Bay in the first decade, there were not even a handful of educated men in Pennsylvania.)

What Morison was referring to is what I would like to call deference democracy, in the style of Bagehot's discussion of the British constitution. If Massachusetts was governed by the ideals of cultural assimilation, class authority, and deference democracy, Pennsylvania has tended toward the opposite pole of cultural pluralism, the absence of class authority, and what I would call defiant democracy. My book on Puritan Boston and Quaker Philadelphia was devoted to documenting the different leadership characteristics of these two contrasting social and political structures; here I should like to illustrate these differences, with a look at the governors of the two states. In the first place, Massachusetts produced a greater continuity and higher quality of leadership on Beacon Hill (the cultural capital of the state), than did Pennsylvania at Harrisburg (a cultural and social backwater).

The greater continuity and the trust between leader and led in Massachusetts is evident by the fact that the original constitution of the state (1780) is still in force today. Pennsylvania, on the other hand, has had five different constitutions, written in 1776, 1790, 1838, 1873, and 1967. Trust in Massachusetts was also indicated by the constitution's providing for annual elections, combined with allowing governors to succeed themselves as often as the voters wished: of the fifty-eight annually elected governors between 1780 and 1965 (due to cost, the term was lengthened to two years), forty-four were elected more than once (Governors John Hancock and Caleb Strong, eleven times each; Levi Lincoln, Jr., nine times; and Leverett Saltonstall, three times). In contrast, the defiant democracy of Pennsylvania removed the governor from immediate voter control by providing for a longer term in office (three, and then four, years), and then restricting the terms in office, and finally abolishing consecutive reelection altogether (it should be noted here that the first radical constitution of 1776 called for a group executive rather than a single governor). Of the sixteen Pennsylvania governors between 1790 and 1873, during which period they were allowed to succeed themselves, none were elected more than once (and eight served only one term). All governors between 1873 and 1967 entered office as lame ducks (only two, Robert E. Patterson, a Mugwump reformer, and Gifford Pinchot, were elected twice, but not in succession).

Not only was continuity and trust lacking in Pennsylvania; the quality was mediocre throughout. Let us compare the fifty-eight governors of Massachusetts who served between 1790 and the close of Endicott Peabody's term in 1965, with the thirty-eight governors of Pennsylvania who served between 1790 and 1967, when Governor Scranton's term came to an end.

1. Only 4 to 8 percent of the Pennsylvania governors were born at the cultural heart of the state, or the Philadelphia area, as contrasted to 44 percent of the Massachusetts governors born in Boston or its suburbs.
2. While 72 percent of the Massachusetts governors were college graduates (30 percent Harvard), only 43 percent of the Pennsylvania governors graduated from college (only two from Penn—after Thomas Mifflin, the first governor, no Penn alumnus held the governor's office until George Leader went there in 1955).
3. While 57 percent of the Massachusetts governors went on to national office, only 33 percent of the Pennsylvanians did so: eight from Massachusetts became U.S. senators, two from Pennsylvania; Calvin Coolidge became president and Elbridge Gerry, a vice-president, but no president or vice-president from Pennsylvania; seven from Massachusetts served in Washington at the cabinet level (Eustis, Everett, Boutwell, Long, Tobin, Herter, and Volpe), none from Pennsylvania.
4. In sum, while most of the Massachusetts governors were college graduates and many of them Harvard men, most of the Pennsylvania governors were self-made men—predominantly salesmen and ex-generals. Needless to say, Philadelphia gentlemen avoided Harrisburg (of the fifty families which made up the class core of my Puritan Boston and Quaker Philadelphia book, six of the Boston group supplied governors but only one from the Philadelphia sample).[38]

No one has summed up the contrasting spirits of Puritanism and Quakerism better than the distinguished journalist, Mark

Sullivan, in an article called "The Ills of Pennsylvania," published in the *Atlantic Monthly* in 1901, and from which I quote the following lines:

> It is one of the anomalies of history that when the Puritan hanged the Quaker, both were happy—the one to hang a man for his belief, the other to die for his belief. This brings out strongly the distinction between them. The Puritans were a church militant. The Puritans went to church with a Bible in one hand and in the other a musket for hostile Indians. The Quaker settled his difficulties with the Indians by reading tracts to them. When the Quaker came to the Puritan commonwealth to spread a doctrine which the Puritan didn't like, the Puritan beat him and drove him out; and when the Quaker came meekly back to turn the other cheek, the Puritan hanged him. The point is this: the Puritan insisted in governing his commonwealth in his own way. He founded his commonwealth to carry out a certain set of ideas, and he never let his eye wander from that purpose. What the Puritan resolved upon was to be done: he would have no objector, be he Roger Williams, Anne Hutchinson, or Quaker. The Puritan formed the dominating habit, and to this day Puritan ideas dominate the essentially non-Puritan population of Massachusetts. Among the Quakers, on the other hand, meekness was the cardinal virtue. Their creed forbids them to bear arms. It does not, in so many words, forbid them to take part in politics, but certainly the rough and tumble of actual party contest is hostile to the ideal which the Quaker seeks to follow. The early Quakers, instead of strangling doctrines not in agreement with their own, instead of casting out the apostles of strange creeds welcomed them, tolerated them. They soon came to the point where they were tolerating intolerance. Put in a minority by the unrestricted immigration of less worthy people, and lacking the strenuous, dominating spirit of the Puritans, the early Quakers soon let the control of the colony pass into the hands of the less desirable elements; and there it has always remained."[39]

Perhaps every society gets the quality of leadership it deserves. I have only barely suggested the abysmal quality of Pennsylvania's leadership from its founding days to the twentieth century. Surely the quality of leadership in Pennsylvania throughout its history, as well as in America as a whole today, suggests that any culturally plural society will foster a moral relativism which will, in turn, produce an almost unworkable political system.

In closing, I should like to quote Nathan Glazer, who has done as much as anyone in exploring the consequences of our changing attitudes toward assimilation, and especially the consequences of our modern preference for various extreme forms of cultural pluralism; thus he closed a recent article in *Commentary* magazine as follows:

> The "melting pot" is now attacked not only on the ground that it never really melted that much or that fast, which is quite true, but on the ground that it should not have been allowed to melt in the first place. "Americanization" has thus become a dirty word. . . . Today the most strongly supported goals seem to be, first, that every group must match every other group in economic resources, occupational status, and political representation; and second, that every group should be maintained in its distinctiveness, insofar as it is in the public power to do so, through an educational system that supports its language and its culture. That is a sure recipe for conflict. Perhaps the much-maligned goal of assimilation still has a good deal to teach us about managing our multi-ethnic society.[40]

Notes

1. Sydney E. Ahlstrom, *A Religious History of the American People* (New Haven: Yale University Press, 1972), 112.
2. Milton M. Gordon, *Assimilation in American Life* (New York: Oxford University Press, 1964).
3. Ibid., 94.
4. Quoted in Peter Schrag, *The Decline of the WASP* (New York: Simon & Schuster, 1971), 20.
5. Gordon, *Assimilation*, 101.
6. For an excellent analysis of the Immigrant Restriction League, See Barbara Miller Solomon, *Ancestors and Immigrants* (Cambridge: Harvard University Press, 1956).
7. Quoted in E. Digby Baltzell, *The Protestant Establishment* (New York: Vintage, 1966), 226.
8. Gordon, *Assimilation*, 120.
9. Ibid., 117.
10. Frederick Jackson Turner, *The Frontier in American History* (New York: Henry Holt, 19), 22–23.
11. Ruby Jo Reeves Kennedy, "Single or Triple Melting Pot? Intermarriage Trends in New Haven, 1870–1940," *American Journal of Sociology* 58, no. 1 (July 1952): 56–59; Will Herberg, *Protestant-Catholic-Jew* (New York: Doubleday, 1955).
12. Quoted in Gordon, *Assimilation*, 147–48.
13. Shrag, *Decline of WASP*, 51.
14. Ibid., 255.
15. Ibid., 9.
16. Reginald E. Zelnick, "Prodigal Fathers and Existential Sons," *Dissent*, May/June 1966,
17. Ahlstrom, *Religious History*, 1091–92.
18. Ibid., 1093.
19. Quoted in Werner Stark, *The Sociology of Religion: A Study of Christendom*, Vol. 3 (New York: Fordham University Press, 1967), 247.
20. Terry Eastland, "In Defense of Religious America," *Commentary*, June 1981, 40.

21. Francis Fitzgerald, *America Revised: History Schoolbooks in the Twentieth Century* (New York: Vintage, 1980), 104.
22. Ibid., 68.
23. James Baldwin, *Nobody Knows My Name* (New York: Delta, 1962), 129.
24. Houston A. Baker, Jr., *The Journey Back* (Chicago: University of Chicago Press, 1980), 81.
25. E. Digby Baltzell, *Puritan Boston and Quaker Philadelphia* (New York: The Free Press, 1979), 268–69.
26. Richard Hofstadter, *Anti-Intellectualism in American Life* (New York: Alfred A. Knopf, 1963), 59.
27. Ernst Troeltsch, *The Social Teaching of the Christian Churches*, Vol. 2 (New York: Harper Torchbooks, 1960), 577.
28. Baltzell, *Puritan Boston*, 455.
29. Melvin B. Endy, Jr., "Theology in a Religiously Plural World: Some Contributions of William Penn," *Pennsylvania Magazine of History and Biography* 105, no. 4 (October 1981): 463.
30. See Howard G. Schneiderman, *The Antinomian Founding of Rhode Island and the Spirit of Factionalism*. Ph.D. diss., University of Pennsylvania, 1978.
31. Endy, "Theology in a Religiously Plural World," 453.
32. Ahlstrom, *Religious History*, 212–13.
33. Edwin B. Bronner, *William Penn's "Holy Experiment": The Founding of Pennsylvania 1681–1701* (Philadelphia: Temple University Publications, 1962), 252.
34. Hannah Benner Roach, "The Planting of Philadelphia: A Seventeenth-Century Real Estate Development," *Pennsylvania Magazine of History and Biography* 112, no. 1, 9.
35. Gary B. Nash, *Quakers and Politics: Pennsylvania 1681–1726* (Princeton, N.J.: Princeton University Press, 1968), 175.
36. Ibid.
37. Samuel Eliot Morison, *The Intellectual Life of Colonial New England* (Ithaca, N.Y.: Cornell University Press, 1963), 18.
38. For a discussion of the contrasting political structures of these two states, see Baltzell, *Puritan Boston*, 369–414.
39. Mark Sullivan, "The Ills of Pennsylvania," *Atlantic Monthly*, October 1901, 559.
40. Nathan Glazer "North, South, West," *Commentary*, May 1982, 78.

14

Social Class in the Oval Office

With Howard G. Schneiderman

In this election year, with a race between the son of immigrants and an upper-class candidate of some wealth, the question of class, even when not openly discussed, is certainly in the backs of many minds. Governor Dukakis has made repeated references to his social origins; and the "log cabin" myth, which has been around for over a hundred years, is having its latest incarnation. In spite of this, our own examinations of historical records and polls of American historians have led us to an unpopular conclusion, one that goes against the conventional wisdom: presidents from high social-class backgrounds have performed better in office and been ranked as more effective than presidents from lower-class origins. Our point is not that upper-class candidates should be preferred, but that their privileged social origins should not automatically be used as a basis for dismissal of their ability to govern a nation of many economic and social levels.

Franklin D. Roosevelt once described the presidency of the United States as "preeminently a place of moral leadership." During the Watergate affair, Arthur M. Schlesinger, Jr., paraphrasing Clark Clifford, a distinguished presidential adviser, wrote that the government of the United States "was like a chameleon, taking its colors from the character and personality of the President." At about the same time, the *London Spectator* noted that two centuries of American history had come full circle "from George Washington, who could not tell a lie, to Richard Nixon, who cannot tell the truth." In January 1988, the *Washington Post* summed up 1987, the year in which we celebrated the 200th anniversary of the writing of our Constitution, as "The Year of Lying Dangerously," and then went on to note that "66 percent of Americans believe that Ronald Reagan is an honest man—at the same time 65 percent of Americans believe he was lying about the Iran-Contra affair." Perhaps James Bryce was right just a century ago, in 1888, when he wrote in the famous chapter "Why Great Men Are Not Chosen Presidents" in his classic book, *The American Commonwealth*, that the best men in America do not go into public life nor do they seek the presidency, at least not since the aristocratic generation which made a revolution, wrote the Constitution, and founded the new nation.

Forty years ago, in 1948, when we were the most powerful and respected nation in the world and American authority reigned supreme, Professor Arthur M. Schlesinger, Sr., of Harvard, took issue with Bryce and asked a group of leading American historians to rank our presidents from Washington through Franklin Roosevelt in terms of their performances in office. The twenty-nine presidents (W.H. Harrison and James Garfield were left out since they had spent less than a year in office) were ranked by the fifty-five men who responded as follows:

> Great: (1) Lincoln, (2) Washington, (3) Franklin Roosevelt, (4) Wilson, (5) Jefferson, (6) Jackson; Near Great: (7) Theodore Roosevelt, (8) Cleveland, (9) John Adams, (10) Polk; Average: (11) J.Q. Adams, (12) Monroe, (13) Hayes, (14) Madison, (15) Van Buren, (16) Taft, (17) Arthur, (18) McKinley, (19) A. Johnson, (20) Hoover, (21) Benjamin Harrison; Below Average: (22) Tyler, (23) Coolidge, (24) Fillmore, (25) Taylor, (26) Buchanan, (27) Pierce; Failure: (28) Grant, (29) Harding.

In the 156 years between Washington's inauguration and Franklin Roosevelt's death in office, moreover, the ten presidents of great and near-great ranking were in office for seventy-two years, or 45 percent of the time. Professor Schlesinger considered this "a creditable showing for any system of government." And he was backed by the British expert on the American Presidency,

Harold Laski, who wrote in *Parliamentary Affairs* (Winter 1949), that the seven leading British prime ministers between the American Revolution and the New Deal—Pitt, Peel, Palmerston, Disraeli, Gladstone, Lloyd George, and Churchill—were easily matched in distinction by Washington, Jefferson, Jackson, Lincoln, Theodore Roosevelt, Wilson, and Franklin Roosevelt.

Schlesinger's 1948 article had great popular appeal when it was published in *Life* magazine. In 1962, during the optimistic Kennedy presidency, he published a second article on presidential ranking in the *New York Times Magazine*, which was not too different from the first: the top five presidents ranked great remained in the same order; Jackson was moved down to near great among other minor changes; and Truman (near great) and Eisenhower (average) were added.

Since the Kennedy assassination, the American presidency has passed through increasingly debilitating times of trouble. Lyndon Johnson, after a brilliant period of social reform, was finally defeated by the Vietnam War and almost revolutionary unrest at home. Richard Nixon was utterly disgraced by Watergate when he was forced to resign, as was his vice-president before him. Jimmy Carter floundered and finally failed to free the American hostages in Iran. And, after the most successful and popular first term since Franklin Roosevelt's, Ronald Reagan lost much of his authority in the Iran-Contra affair. The authority of the presidency has surely reached one of its lowest points in our history.

All the while, scholarly research on the presidency has steadily increased; books and articles have not only continued to rank the presidents but also have employed all sorts of scientific methods in attempting to fathom the causes of presidential greatness in order to better predict performance in office. As an index of this new interest, a learned journal, *Presidential Studies Quarterly*, was founded in 1970 and is still thriving.

The latest scientific attempt to rank the presidents was undertaken in 1981 by Robert K. Murray, senior research fellow at Pennsylvania State University, and his graduate student, Tim H. Blessing. While Professor Schlesinger had been rather informal and elitist in methodology (his two panels included Felix Frankfurter of the U.S. Supreme Court, five past presidents of the

American Historical Association, and a dozen Pulitzer Prize winners), Murray and Blessing, in keeping with our more egalitarian and quantitative age, were far more systematic and scientific. In November 1981, they sent out 1,997 nineteen-page questionnaires to all Ph.D-holding American historians who were teaching full-time at the assistant professor level and above. "By March 1982," they wrote in their article published in the December 1983 issue of the *Journal of American History*, "846 completed questionnaires were in hand and coding of the information for the computer was begun. While the coding was being undertaken, 107 additional completed questionnaires were received. . . . The reply rate of 48.6 percent, representing almost one-half of the total mailed, was a response beyond our rosiest expectations."

The presidents ranked by the Murray-Blessing respondents were as follows:

> Great: (1) Lincoln, (2) Franklin Roosevelt, (3) Washington, (4) Jefferson; Near Great: (5) Theodore Roosevelt, (6) Wilson, (7) Jackson, (8) Truman; Above Average: (9) John Adams, (10) Lyndon Johnson, (11) Eisenhower, (12) Polk, (13) Kennedy, (14) Madison (15) Monroe, (16) J.Q. Adams, (17) Cleveland; Average: (18) McKinley, (19) Taft, (20) Van Buren, (21) Hoover, (22) Hayes, (23) Arthur, (24) Ford, (25) Carter, (26) Benjamin Harrison; Below Average: (27) Taylor, (28) Tyler, (29) Fillmore, (30) Coolidge, (31) Pierce; Failures: (32) A. Johnson, (33) Buchanan, (34) Nixon, (35) Grant, (36) Harding.

The rankings of the Murray-Blessing respondents did not vary greatly from those of the two Schlesinger panels. They added Kennedy, L.B. Johnson, Nixon, Ford, and Carter (and left out W.H. Harrison and Garfield as did Schlesinger). Among the important changes in ranking were the movement of Franklin Roosevelt to second place, ahead of George Washington, placing Theodore Roosevelt ahead of both Wilson and Jackson, and, most interestingly, moving Eisenhower from the low average rank of twenty-second to a high above-average rank of eleventh. Finally, A. Johnson, just below Eisenhower in 1962, was moved down to the top of the list of failures.

While Schlesinger listed the seventy-five distinguished participants in his 1962 poll by name and function at the end of his article in the *New York Times Magazine*, Murray and Blessing made an exhaustive quantitative analysis of their anonymous respondents by age, sex, birthplace, field of specialization, where they had obtained their Ph.D's, and so forth. A large part of the article was devoted to a fascinating discussion of how the different categories of respondents ranked the presidents. Two examples seem to nicely reveal the changing climate of opinion in America since the 1962 Schlesinger poll.

First, the authors separated out the seventy-five most distinguished historians on the panel and compared their ranking with the rest. This elite group happened to be predominantly male and over forty-five years of age, yet their rankings, interestingly enough, were quite similar to the rest, except for their more traditional placing of Washington, rather than Franklin Roosevelt, in second place. On the other hand, the fifty-nine women on the panel, on the whole much harsher on presidential performance than their male colleagues, were particularly severe in their treatment of Washington, ranking him almost a half-category lower than the males did. As might be expected, Jimmy Carter, surely the least sexist and most egalitarian of recent presidents (in style at least), was ranked "significantly" higher by females than by males. In this connection, the fifteen women's history specialists rated Washington "lower by as much as two-thirds of a category than any of the others." They also downgraded Teddy Roosevelt, the Rough Rider, while the respondents as a whole elevated him above Woodrow Wilson and Andrew Jackson. At the moment, the Murray-Blessing study is widely recognized as state of the art in presidential ranking research.

In addition to ranking, there is another problem of equal importance: What biographical factors are the best predictors of success or greatness in office? A large literature has been produced in this field since Schlesinger's day. Political psychologists, historians, sociologists, and others have analyzed the presidents in terms of birth order, family size, education, age at time of election, occupation, political career before entering office, and such slippery psychological factors as the need for power, the need for achievement, the need for social approval. None have proved highly significant as predictive variables. Dean Keith Simonton, a psychologist at the University of California, Davis, has published profusely in this field. In his latest book, *Why Presidents Succeed* (1987), he writes that "it must be acknowledged that there really may not be many direct biographical predictors."

Evidence of this difficulty is the hardly useful fact that one of the best predictors of greatness in office has proved to be the ascriptive factor of height: of the four great presidents, Lincoln was 6'4" and Franklin Roosevelt, Washington, and Jefferson were 6'2" or more. Strangely enough, having had a college education, which we Americans so value in our day, seems not to have been a very good predictor at all. The ten presidents rated below average or as failures were more likely to have graduated from college than the eight men of great and near-great stature: college graduates among the great numbered 50 percent, near great 50 percent, above average 78 percent, below average 60 percent, and failures 60 percent.

Although not remarked on by any studies we have seen, by far the best (100 percent) predictor of high performance in office has been the possession of a Harvard University undergraduate degree. The two Roosevelts, the two Adamses, and John Fitzgerald Kennedy were all rated above average as presidents. Up until Kennedy's time at least, Harvard was known as a snobbish college where the sons of the rich and well-born had always set the tone; and the Harvard Yard had always been a long distance socially from the mythical log cabin on the ever-moving American frontier.

Curiously, in all the thousands of tedious hours devoted to analyzing the biographical factors which most contribute to success in the Oval Office, nobody has ever considered the ascribed social class origins of our presidents as significant for explaining their performance in office. Soon after the publication of the Murray-Blessing article, however, this problem was first attached systematically by Edward Pessen, in *The Log Cabin Myth: The Social Backgrounds of the Presidents*.

Pessen is a prolific writer on a wide variety of subjects in American history. Among other things, he is thoroughly familiar with the sociological literature on social stratification. Knowing that American society has always been relatively fluid and classes have been difficult to define or identify, Pessen, nevertheless, followed the lead of an influential school of American sociologists and divided the social structure into six basic class levels: upper upper, lower upper, upper middle, lower middle, upper lower, and lower lower. Even though he devotes a whole chapter to defining just what he means by these six levels, Pessen is well aware that all classifications or categories in the social sciences are ultimately arbitrary. They are useful and necessary tools of analysis at best.

At any rate, Pessen, rightly arguing that the family of origin is the basis of social-class position, ranked the families of all the presidents from Washington through Reagan in the following hierarchy: in the upper-upper class he placed the families of Washington, Jefferson, Madison, John Quincy Adams, William Henry Harrison, Tyler, Taylor, Benjamin Harrison, Theodore Roosevelt, Taft, and Franklin Roosevelt; running into his first difficulty with his model, he ranked Polk and Kennedy in a category "straddling the upper upper and lower upper classes"; he ranked the families of John Adams, Monroe, and Wilson in the lower-upper class; "on a plateau between the lower upper and the upper middle class" he placed the families of Pierce, Hayes, Cleveland, Harding, Coolidge, and Truman; the upper-middle class families included those of Jackson, Van Buren, Buchanan, Grant, Arthur, McKinley, Hoover, Lyndon Johnson, Ford, and Carter; "in the 'true' middle or between the upper and lower middle classes" he placed the families of Lincoln, Eisenhower, and Reagan; in the lower middle class, the families of Fillmore, Garfield, and Nixon; and alone in the lower class, upper lower at that, was the family of Andrew Johnson. To summarize Pessen's ranking of the families of the thirty-nine presidents: the top sixteen (41 percent) include eleven upper upper, two middle upper, and three lower upper; the next sixteen (41 percent) include six lower upper to upper middle and ten upper middle; the lowest seven (18 percent) include three true middle, three lower middle, and one upper lower.

Pessen was surprised to find that only seven of our presidents were born to middle-class status or below, and that the vast majority (82 percent) were born into families of privileged upper-middle-class status or better. Those who place their faith in the log cabin myth have a hard time facing those facts. But Pessen had to agree with an economic historian who wrote that self-made men "have always been more conspicuous in American history books than in American history."

The very essence of the log cabin myth is to be found in the legendary life of Abraham Lincoln: "Everybody in this world knows," Lincoln's son, Tad, once said, "that Pa used to split rails." Honest Abe carefully fostered and dramatized the self-made myth throughout his political career. "I am a living witness that any one of your children may look to come here as my father's child has," he once told some members of an Ohio regiment who were visiting the White House. "I presume you all know who I am," he said at another time, "I am humble Abraham Lincoln." And so it always went; no wonder his enemies resented this Uriah Heep style.

In reality, Lincoln's grandfather was an officer in the Revolution and the owner of a two-hundred-acre farm in Virginia before he brought his family West. His father, Thomas Lincoln, "at the time of his great son's birth," to quote Pessen, "owned two farms of six hundred acres, several town lots, livestock, and horses, property that was quite close to the total owned by the wealthiest man in the area. Five years later he belonged to the richest fifteen percent of taxpaying property owners in his community." But the truth also is that it was a long way socially from Abraham Lincoln's birthplace in a small town in Hardin County, Kentucky, to the White House.

The log cabin myth was born in the cynical campaign of 1840. The power-starved Whigs, led by Daniel Webster and the Eastern money men, chose the old hero of Tippecanoe, General William Henry Harrison, as their candidate. Picturing Martin Van Buren as a champagne-drinking aristocrat, they manipulatively portrayed Harrison as a hard cider-drinking man of the people whose simple tastes nicely fitted the midwestern, log cabin stereotype. Although his campaign featured log cabin songs, log cabin clubs, and log cabin badges, Old Tippecanoe was the son of Benjamin Harrison, acme of Virginia's patrician-planter class, signer of the Declaration of Independence, and one-time governor of his state (the first Harrison was elected to the Virginia House of Burgesses in 1642, and the family, like the Adamses and Roosevelts, produced two presidents).

Throughout history, great men have tended both to have had mothers who were socially, morally, or intellectually superior to their husbands and also to have chosen as wives women who were above them in one way or another. Pessen became well aware of this pattern in his study of the presidents' origins.

Abraham Lincoln's marriage was, of course, the classic example of a man-on-the-make marrying well. Such marriages were not always happy ones, and Mary Todd spent a miserable married life looking down socially on her great husband. Even ambitious young men of higher-class origins have done the same. Thus George Washington's grandfather, like other Washingtons after him, married "above himself" into what Pessen called "the crème de la crème of Virginia society." When George Washington married Martha Dandridge Custis, he moved into "another economic sphere." Similarly with John Adams of Massachusetts, whose marriage to Abigail Smith brought a "strain of aristocracy . . . into the Adams line."Actually, the second president not only married above himself but his father before him had done the same: the president's mother was born Susanna Boylston, a member of one of the leading families of the entire commonwealth of Massachusetts. To round out the founding trio of presidents, Jefferson, at the age of twenty-five, was one of the five richest men in Virginia and also the best educated. His father had married Jane Randolph, whose distinguished family was both wealthy and socially at the top of the First Families of Virginia hierarchy at the time. Two years after Jefferson married, his new wife inherited 135 slaves and some 11,000 acres of farmland.

Of recent presidents, one great difference between Dwight Eisenhower and his vice-president, Richard Nixon, was that the former married way above himself while the latter did not. Right after graduation from West Point, young Ike married Mamie Dowd, whose ancestors were evidently part of the British aristocracy when they came to Guilford, Connecticut, in 1639. Both sides of the family had prospered and her father made a fortune. "Small wonder," writes Pessen, "that her parents pointed out that 'a second lieutenant's pay could not support her in the style to which she was accustomed.'" Of all the thirty-nine presidents, only Nixon, Ford, and Carter, according to Pessen, married beneath themselves.

This is not the place to go into the details of Pessen's rating of each president's social origins; although perhaps differing in some respects, most historians or sociologists would go along with the usefulness and accuracy of his overall model. It is our own view that he has leaned over backwards to be fair in his treatment of the log cabin myth, by tending to rank a number of presidents lower then we would. Hayes and Cleveland, to take two examples, might very well have been placed in at least the lower-upper class. Hayes's grandfather was known as Rutherford Hayes, Esquire, before he moved from a small Vermont town to Delaware, Ohio, where he built the first brick house in town. Because his father died just before he was born, Hayes was brought up by his mother's brother who, even after the panic of 1830, was "independently wealthy for life," having accumulated a fortune in merchandising and land speculation. Hayes's uncle (whom he called "father") was also reputed to enjoy "one of the widest circles of influential acquaintances in Ohio." Cleveland, though spending his happy early life as the son of a poor clergyman who held pulpits in various small towns in New Jersey and New York state, came not from "poor and commonplace stock," as most superficial biographers have had it but, according to Allan Nevins, "from the truest aristocracy that America can boast . . . men who made themselves community leaders." And most of these leaders were Puritan clergymen, from his great-great-grandfather, Aaron Cleveland, a graduate of Harvard in 1735 and friend of Franklin, down to his father, who graduated from Yale with honors and also trained at the Princeton Theological Seminary. After his father's death when he was but sixteen, young Grover went to live with his uncle, one of the wealthiest and most eminent men in the thriving young city of Buffalo. Thus he began the way to eminence at the Buffalo bar with the best social and business connections, not only in Buffalo but in the whole northern part of the state. This brief look at Hayes and Cleveland should emphasize that Pessen did not overestimate the number of presidents born to upper-class status.

Pessen is certainly not pleased with the fact that a majority of our presidents have been born to privilege. Although no Marxist himself, and in disagreement with "three well-known non-Marxist social scientists who could actually write that 'a person thinks, politically, as he is socially. Social characteristics determine political preference,'" Pessen ends his book with the following sentence: "A decent respect to the opinion and needs of mankind requires that we seek in the future, as we have not sought in the past, to select candidates of *commanding intelligence, learning*, and above all patience, wisdom and humanity—all traits that are *not* necessarily revealed by high social standing and the *ideological preferences* that *typically accompany such standing*" (italics ours). That is indeed a curious ending to this study. A reader would find that on an earlier page, Pessen picked out the six most brilliant presidents—John Adams, Jefferson, Madison, J.Q. Adams, Taft, and Wilson—all of whom were bred to the highest levels of privilege; later on he noted, moreover, that the only four presidents who were political philosophers of any stature—"John Adams, Jefferson, Madison, and perhaps Wilson"—were of upper-class origins; and finally, one does not get the impression that Pessen prefers the "ideological preferences" of Dwight Eisenhower, Richard Nixon, or Ronald Reagan over those of Woodrow Wilson, Franklin Roosevelt, or John Kennedy.

Pessen also comes to another interesting conclusion about his book: "Although I have challenged James Bryce's observations that most presidents were men of humble or ordinary beginnings who rose to the nation's highest office primarily because of their own 'merits,'" he writes, "I have no quarrel with his equally famous dictum that few great men have been elected president." About this, we make two observations. First, all of the thirty-nine men who have reached the White House have gotten there by "their own merits"; no man ever got to the White House entirely because of his class origins, and many have gotten there in spite of their class origins, high or low as the case may be. Second, we disagree sharply with both Bryce and Pessen in their judgments as to the quality of our presidents. It is revealing that nowhere in Professor Pessen's book does he mention the Schlesinger rankings or any of the other systematic efforts to rank presidential performance in office. But, of course, that was not what he set out to do.

All of which suggests that it should be fruitful to systematically compare the Pessen rankings of our presidents by social origins with the Schlesinger and Murray-Blessing rankings of them by accomplishments in office. In the long run, facts and theories in themselves are far less important then the relationship between them (see table 14.1).

For convenience of analysis, thirty-six presidents (W. H. Harrison, Garfield, and Reagan were not included, as of 1981, for lack of evidence of performance) may be divided into the fifteen men of upper-class origins and the twenty-one men born of less privileged families. That there is a positive correlation between high accomplishment and high social origins is clearly shown in a four-fold table (table 14.2):

There has been, then, not only a high correlation between high social origins and getting to the presidency, as Pessen clearly has shown, but once elected to office, men of privileged origins have performed far better than those of lower social status. This has been especially the case with the great presidents: of the eight great and near-great presidents, five were born of highly privileged families. On the other hand, men of low social origin have tended to be the least successful presidents. While Lincoln has

TABLE 14.1
Relationship Between Accomplishments and Social Origins

Accomplishments in Office	**Social-Class Origins**	
	Upper Class	Below Upper Class
Above Average	11–73%	6–29%
Average and Below	4–27%	15–71%

TABLE 14.2
Murray-Blessing's Ranking of Presidential Performance Related to Pessen's Ranking of Social-Class Origins

	Upper Class	Upper Middle Class	Middle and Lower Class
GREAT			
1. Lincoln			Middle
2. F. Roosevelt	Upper Upper		
3. Washington	Upper Upper		
4. Jefferson	Upper Upper		
NEAR GREAT			
5. T. Roosevelt	Upper Upper		
6. Wilson	Lower Upper		
7. Jackson		Upper Middle	
8. Truman		L. Upper/U. Middle	
ABOVE AVERAGE			
9. J. Adams	Lower Upper		
10. L. Johnson		Upper Middle	
11. Eisenhower			Middle
12. Polk	Middle Upper		
13. Kennedy	Middle Upper		
14. Madison	Upper Upper		
15. Monroe	Lower Upper		
16. J.Q. Adams	Upper Upper		
17. Cleveland		L. Upper/U. Middle	
AVERAGE			
18. McKinley		Upper Middle	
19. Taft	Upper Upper		
20. Van Buren		Upper Middle	
21. Hoover		Upper Middle	
22. Hayes		L. Upper/U. Middle	
23. Arthur		Upper Middle	
24. Ford		Upper Middle	
25. Carter		Upper Middle	
26. B. Harrison	Upper Upper		
BELOW AVERAGE			
27. Taylor	Upper Upper		
28. Tyler	Upper Upper		
29. Fillmore			Lower Middle
30. Coolidge		L. Upper/U. Middle	
31. Pierce		L. Upper/U. Middle	

TABLE 14.2
(Continued)

	Upper Class	Upper Middle Class	Middle and Lower Class
FAILURE			
32. A. Johnson			Upper Lower
33. Buchanan		Upper Middle	
34. Nixon			Lower Middle
35. Grant		Upper Middle	
36. Harding		L. Upper/U. Middle	

Note: W.H. Harrison and Garfield are not included because both served less than one year in office.

been ranked number one in all the studies of accomplishment in office which we have seen, three of the other four men born of simple origins—Fillmore, A. Johnson, and Nixon—were ranked as below average or as failures by the Murray-Blessing respondents. Fillmore was actually the only president to have been born in a log cabin. His father was a Vermont farmer who went west to Cayuga County, New York, where Millard was born, as he later wrote, "in a log house in the middle of a forest, having no neighbors nearer than four miles." Millard's mother, true to form, "was brought up in comfortable surroundings in Pittsfield, Massachusetts, where her father was a doctor." Although Fillmore had only a fitful formal education in his youth, he married a widely read school teacher who later built the first library in the White House. Bitter about his grim youth on his father's farm, Millard began to read law at the age of nineteen under a judge in a small town near Buffalo, where he later moved and made a fortune at the bar. Pessen seems hardly to have admired this man of the soil, whose "adult lifestyle consisted of formal dinners, dances, recitals, and hobnobbing with celebrities," and whose political career was devoted "largely to pursuit of the main chance." Fillmore reached the presidency after Zachary Taylor's death at midterm. Both the Schlesinger and Murray-Blessing respondents agreed on ranking him as below average in performance.

We have as much, or more, to learn from failure as from success. In this sense, the careers of Andrew Johnson and Richard

Nixon, both ranked as failures by the Murray-Blessing respondents, are of great interest. Both came of lowly origins and spent parts of their youths in bitter struggles with poverty; both married orphans of equally plebeian origins (Johnson, who had no schooling, was taught by his wife to write). In contrast to Lincoln and Eisenhower, who rose to become insiders, on the surface in Lincoln's case, through judicious marriages and flexible political and personal styles, both Johnson and Nixon resented their early struggles and remained outsiders and loners throughout their political careers, always mistrusting the establishment even after they became relatively affluent and moved in establishment circles.

Although similar in so many ways, both men were rated failures for almost opposite reasons. Thus Richard Nixon, the first president to be driven from office, was finally defeated because of his inability to tell the truth in the Watergate affair. Johnson, a man of absolute honesty and great courage, was impeached by the Senate, although acquitted by one vote, because, following Lincoln, he fervently believed in the Union (he was the only southern senator to remain loyal during the Civil War) and stood for sectional reconciliation and constitutional rights as against the vindictive radical Republicans and predatory northern business interests bent on consolidating their power and wartime gains. His tactless honesty almost caused his downfall. This is the view of those who followed the classic interpretation of Reconstruction and saw it as a "tragic era." Thus Clinton Rossiter in *The American Presidency* (1956) gave Johnson a near-great ranking, finding him to be a man of "much courage, whose protests against the ravages of the Radicals and Congress were a high rather than a low point in the progress of the presidency." Both the Schlesinger polls ranked him as average. The failure ranking given him by the Murray-Blessing respondents reflects a revisionist view of Reconstruction, which came to the fore in the 1960s, and stressed the civil rights aspect of Reconstruction more than their predecessors had done. As Kenneth Stampp, a leading revisionist historian wrote in 1969: "What was crucial in the failure of Andrew Johnson was his refusal to demand even minimal civil rights for Negroes and a crystallization of Republican sentiment over this fundamental question." But perhaps it is understandable that Johnson, who rose from red-neck to slaveholder status in the years before the war, found it hard to change.

In 1949 Arthur Schlesinger, Sr., published an essay in which he outlined how American history had moved in cycles of alternating liberal and conservative periods. His son, in *The Cycles of American History*, following his father's theme, has conceptualized these cycles in terms of alternating emphases on "private interests" and "public purposes." Our view that the ebb and flow of upper-class hegemony in the White House has followed a pattern not entirely unlike the Schlesinger cycles. This may be seen by breaking down the social class and accomplishment rankings of the same thirty-six presidents into four periods: (1) The Age of Aristocracy 1789–1850; (2) Middle-Class Ascendency 1851–1901; (3) WASP Hegemony 1901–1953; and (4) Ethnic Democracy 1953–1981.

During the first sixty years of the American presidency, men of patrician or aristocratic background held office for all but twelve years. The stereotypical exception, Andrew Jackson, who held office for eight of those twelve years, was actually a frontier aristocrat who inherited land and a substantial sum of money at an early age, was educated at a local Latin academy, and read the Declaration of Independence to thirty or forty adult neighbors when he was only eleven years of age. Martin Van Buren, Jackson's handpicked successor in the White House, had a long-established and upper-middle-class standing in Kinderhook, New York. In short, leaving Jackson and Van Buren as Pessen ranked them, 83 percent of the presidents in this aristocratic period originated in the upper classes and 73 percent were rated above average by the Murray-Blessing respondents.

The period of aristocratic presidential leadership came to an end with the death of Zachary Taylor in 1850. For the next half-century, from Fillmore through McKinley, only Abraham Lincoln and Grover Cleveland were above average in performance; Fillmore and Pierce were below average, and Buchanan was a failure. After the Lincoln presidency, Johnson and Grant were failures, while Hayes, Arthur, Harrison, and McKinley were only average. This period was not only the lowest of the four in performance, but also the lowest in social origins: only Harrison was a born aristocrat, and four men, including Lincoln, were born to middle- or lower-class families. Except for Lincoln's wartime presidency, moreover, in Arthur Schlesinger, Jr.'s, terms, "private interests" predominated over "public purpose," these private interests being the selfish slave-holding interests during the 1850s and the selfish business interests from the times of Grant through McKinley. Small wonder Bryce held a low view of the presidency when he wrote *The American Commonwealth* during the 1880s.

After McKinley's assassination, Theodore Roosevelt came to power, beginning the third cycle of leadership, the period of WASP hegemony. A Harvard man of impeccable patrician background, Roosevelt was extremely proud of, and self-conscious about, his class position and was determined to justify it by attaining leadership not only in government but also in molding the attitudes and values of the country as a whole; probably no president before or since has so dominated the imagination of the nation.

Following Roosevelt, Taft, who graduated second in his class at Yale, was a great and brilliant man from one of America's finest families whose members have been leaders in education, religion, law, and politics for several generations. Taft was only an average president; he was far more at home on the United States Supreme Court.

The next president during this period, Woodrow Wilson, a keen student of political science and history, was surely one of the best-prepared men for the office; and he was one of our greatest presidents, even though the Murray-Blessing respondents demoted him to near-great status.

If the first two decades of our presidency, under Washington, Adams, and Jefferson, were the greatest in our history, the two decades after 1901, when Roosevelt, Taft, and Wilson were in office, were surely the second greatest. After the "private interest" twenties, when Harding (failure), Coolidge (below average), and Hoover (average) were in office, the presidency went through a third great twenty-year period under Franklin Roosevelt and Harry Truman. And "public purpose" surely dominated over "private interest" under the patrician leadership of the two Roosevelts and Taft, as well as under Wilson and Truman, both from only slightly less-privileged backgrounds. Perhaps this high quality of performance and emphasis on public service has been partly due to the fact that our best aristocratic traditions have stressed *doing* a better job rather than the prevalent, middle-class ideology which has always stressed *getting* a better job.

The period since Truman's presidency, characterized by ethnic democracy, has come full circle since the 1850s. Just as the issues of slavery and the civil rights of Negroes greatly influenced politics in the thirty years after 1850, so the issue of civil rights for blacks became a major political issue during this fourth period, especially after May 1954 when the Supreme Court unanimously decided (in *Brown v. Board of Education*) that public schools must be desegregated. While the presidents after 1953 have been of higher caliber than their predecessors following 1850, their performances in office have been above average but flawed by unmanageable obstacles in the end, especially since Kennedy's assassination.

In social origins the presidents during these two periods were much alike: Kennedy matched Harrison in privileged origin if not in lineage; Lincoln, though certainly superior to all presidents, was much like Eisenhower in origin and success in office; and of course Nixon and Andrew Johnson were much alike in both origin and achievement. Most important of all, this last period is the only one of the four in which no great president occupied the Oval Office. Since Kennedy's tragic assassination, this may be due partly to the anti-elitist ideology which was born in the mid-1960s and still dominates conventional wisdom today.

In 1938, for example, when we were a poor but proud and hopeful country under the leadership of Franklin Roosevelt, Mrs. Robert Alonzo Taft made a statement to the mineworkers of Ohio, which the political pundits branded as political suicide. "My husband is not a simple man," she said during the senatorial race that year. "He did not start from humble beginnings. My husband is a very brilliant man. He had a fine education at Yale. He has been well trained for his job. Isn't that what you prefer when you pick leaders to work for you?" Taft won.

Today the television pundits would brand such a statement as suicidal nonsense with far more venom than their professional antecedents of New Deal days. But let us not forget that in that hopeful era, the administration was dominated by such "preppies," as they would be derisively called today, as Franklin D. Roosevelt, John G. Winant, who was chairman of the first Social Security Board, William C. Bullitt, our first ambassador to the Soviet Union, Attorney General Francis Biddle, and many others like them. In every age, the "truth" has a hard time when it runs counter to conventional wisdom.

Our findings would suggest that the anti-elitist, conventional wisdom of our day may run counter to the traditional wisdom of our ancestors who repeatedly, although not unerringly, sought out the best men for the presidency, regardless of their social origins. We shall continue to build on our best democratic traditions by choosing the most talented available men and women to represent us in high positions of moral and political leadership, regardless of their class, religious, ethnic, or racial origins.

Some among these (like Louis Brandeis, John F. Kennedy, and Martin Luther King, Jr., before them) may be born into families which have already achieved high social standing, if not nationally, then at least in their own local, ethnic, or minority communities. Such privileged backgrounds of high social standing should not stand in the way of our choosing them as leaders if they are among our "best and brightest" citizens.

Index